Filming the Gods

Filming the Gods examines the role and depiction of religion in Indian cinema, showing that the relationship between the modern and the traditional in contemporary India is not exotic, but part of everyday life. Concentrating mainly on the Hindi cinema of Mumbai, Bollywood, it also discusses India's other cinemas.

Rachel Dwyer's lively discussion encompasses the mythological genre which continues India's long tradition of retelling Hindu myths and legends, and draws on sources such as the national epics of the *Mahabharata* and the *Ramayana*; the devotional genre, which flourished at the height of the nationalist movement in the 1930s and 1940s; and the films made in Bombay that depict India's Islamicate culture, including the historical, the courtesan film and the 'Muslim social' genre. *Filming the Gods* also examines the presence of the religious across other genres and how cinema represents religious communities and their beliefs and practices. It draws on interviews with film stars, directors and producers, as well as popular fiction, fan magazines and the films themselves. As a result, *Filming the Gods* is both a guide to the study of film in religious culture as well as a historical overview of Indian religious film.

Rachel Dwyer is a Reader in Indian Studies and Cinema at the School of Oriental and African Studies (SOAS), University of London. Her books include: *100 Bollywood Films* (2005); *Cinema India: The Visual Culture of Hindi Film* (2002) (with Diria Patel); *Yash Chopra* (BFI World Directors Series, 2002); *Pleasure and the Nation: The History, Politics and Consumption of Popular Culture in India* (2000); and *All You Want is Money, All You Need is Love: Sexuality and Romance in Modern India* (2000).

Filming the Gods

Religion and Indian cinema

Rachel Dwyer

Routledge
Taylor & Francis Group

LONDON AND NEW YORK

First published 2006
by Routledge
2 Park Square, Milton Park, Abingdon, Oxon OX14 4RN

Simultaneously published in the USA and Canada
by Routledge
270 Madison Avenue, New York, NY 10016

Routledge is an imprint of the Taylor & Francis Group

Typeset in Gill Sans and Sabon by
Florence Production Ltd, Stoodleigh, Devon
Printed and bound in Great Britain by
MPG Books Ltd, Bodmin

British Library Cataloguing in Publication Data
A catalogue record for this book is available from the British Library
Library of Congress Cataloging-in-Publication Data
Dwyer, Rachel.
  Filming the gods: religion and Indian cinema / Rachel Dwyer.
    p. cm.
  Includes bibliographical references and index.
  1. Motion pictures–India–History. 2. Motion pictures–Religious
aspects. I. Title.
  PN1993.5.I4D88 2006   791.43'68294–dc22

ISBN 10: 0–415–31424–0 (hbk)
ISBN 10: 0–415–31425–9 (pbk)
ISBN 10: 0–203–08865–4 (ebk)

ISBN 13: 978–0–415–31424–4 (hbk)
ISBN 13: 978–0–415–31425–1 (pbk)
ISBN 13: 978–0–203–08865–4 (ebk)

To Michael
saepe stylum vertas

'Chaitanya'

sweet as grapes
are the stones of jejuri
said chaitanya

he popped a stone
in his mouth
and spat out gods

Arun Kolatkar
Jejuri

Fifth edition, Pras Prakashan, Mumbai
Printed with the kind permission of Mrs Soonoo Kolatkar

Contents

Figures

Illustrations 1.1–1.7, 2.1–2.5, 3.2–3.5, 4.1 are reproduced courtesy of the National Film Archive of India
Illustration 3.1 is reproduced courtesy of Shaukat Khan, Mehboob Productions
Illustration 4.2 is reproduced courtesy of Yash Chopra, Yash Raj Films Ltd
Illustration 4.3 is reproduced courtesy of K.K. Barjatya, Rajshri Productions
Illustration 4.4 is reproduced courtesy of Karan Johar, Dharma Productions

Acknowledgements

I should like to thank Birgit Meyer and Annelies Moors for inviting me to speak at a conference in Amsterdam (Meyer and Moores 2005), where the idea of this book first came to me. David Morgan, who was at the conference, encouraged me to go ahead with its writing.

Sohini Dasgupta and Atreyee Sen spent several months (funded by the Leverhulme Trust) as my research assistants and their contribution to this book is seen mostly in Chapter 1 (Sohini) and Chapter 2 (Atreyee).

I have had substantial funding for different parts of this study from the Society for South Asian Studies, the British Academy, the Arts and Humanities Research Council and the Leverhulme Trust.

I have been invited to speak on the whole and the parts of this book by Anna King at the Spalding Symposium, Ali Asani at Harvard University, Dipesh Chakrabarty at the University of Chicago, David Smith at the University of Lancaster, Daniel Rycroft at the University of Sussex, Rahul Srivastava at PUKAR, Nick Dirks at Columbia University, and Jim Masselos at the Asian Studies Association of Australia.

Part of Chapter 3 draws on my earlier paper, Dwyer (2004a) 'Representing the Muslim: the "courtesan film" in Indian popular cinema.'

Mr Shashidharan and the staff at the National Film Archive in Pune, including Dilip Rajput, Mrs Joshi, Arti Kharkanis and Lakshmi Iyer provided an ideal working environment, and their endless helpfulness, politeness and patience were always appreciated.

I have held discussions on the project which have informed my thinking about it, in particular with Shyam Benegal, Govind Nihalani, Karan Johar, Titu Ahluwalia, Subhash Ghai, Rajni Bakshi and Ashis Nandy.

Two friends and advisors must be thanked for their patience with my endless demands. Jerry Pinto, my Mumbai manager, is likely to be considered for canonisation for supplying me with DVDs, VCDs, books, knowledge, friendship, phonecards, food and constant telephone and email support. I also thank him for reading through an earlier form of the manuscript. Faisal Devji, whether in London, Bombay or New York, has given me daily encouragement and criticism and has kept me supplied with products.

My readers gave me invaluable advice which I have tried to incorporate into the manuscript: Faisal Devji, Christopher Pinney, Jolyon Mitchell, Francesca Orsini and Bhaskar Mukhopadhyay.

Kaushik Bhaumik and Ron Inden have helped shape my views on Indian cinema.

The warmth and support of my friends in Bombay make this city feel more like home to me than my own. Imtiaz Dharker and Vinci Wadia found me ideal work environments, while Pamela Chopra helped me with travel logistics, in particular with the help of Shakir. I should also like to thank Pamela and Yash Chopra and all the family, Maithili Rao, Subhashini Ali, Shaad Ali Sehgal, Imtiaz Dharker, Ayesha Dharker (and Sunanda Bai), Shobhaa Dé, Reima and Owais Husain, Meera and Saumil Mehta, Adil Jussawala, Jordyn Steig, Richard Delacy, Abhay Deol, Gautam Pemmaraju, Christophe Carvalho, Udita Jhunjhunwala, Apurva Asrani, Pravesh Kumar, Nargis and Vinci Wadia, the late Riyad Wadia, Anurag Chaturvedi, Deepa Gahlot, Naresh Fernandes, Rajeev Masand, Sameer Sharma, Jehangir Modi, Paul Smith, the late Iqbal Masud, Ramdas Bhatkal, Harsha and Smita Bhatkal, and Angad Chowdhry.

In Pune I received hospitality and advice from: Gayatri Chatterjee, Somnath Zutschi, Suresh and Priya Chabria, Mohan Agashe, Arshia Sattar, Laurie Patton, Mr Fattelal and Mrs Damle. In Delhi: Ashis and Uma Nandy, Ravi Vasudevan, Radhika Singha, Pankaj Pachauri, Pramila Phatarphekar, Julian Parr, Rohit Khattar, Madhu Jain, Rukmini Bhaya Nair, Indu and Chandru Chandrashekhar, and Narayani Gupta.

I should like to thank my former and present students from whom I have learnt so much: especially Anna Morcom, Urvi Mukhopadhyay, Meenu Gaur and Kush Varia.

Thanks are due to my colleagues at SOAS, in particular those who supported me with the formalities of grant applications: Peter Robb, Michael Hutt, Rupert Snell, Jacqui Arrol-Barker, Maureen Gaskin and Caroline Redahan.

Finally, I thank my family and friends who put up with silences and absences and other strange behaviour. Thanks in particular to the Aldridges for taking me away on holiday.

Introduction

> While the life of Christ was rolling fast before my eyes I was mentally visualizing the gods Shri Krishna, Shri Ramachandra, their Gokul and Ayodhya ... Could we, the sons of India, ever be able to see Indian images on the screen? [1]

Inspired by this 'Biblical' movie,[2] D.G. 'Dadasaheb' Phalke, 'the father of Indian cinema', made the first entirely Indian film (*Raja Harischandra*, 1913), in which he achieved these aims as he established India's first filmic genre, the 'mythological', creating an immediate connection between religion and cinema in India which persists to this day. *Filming the Gods* contextualises India's first film before examining other religious genres and then questioning notions of the secular over almost a century of cultural production in Indian cinema. These are topics that have been largely ignored by scholars in spite of their profound implications for the study of cinema and religion and beyond into other ideological areas. *Filming the Gods* examines the relationship between film and religion not so much as a history of religious cinema but more as a way of examining the religious imagination in India, as it has been manifested in this major form of public culture.

Indian cinema, more than any other media, whether newspapers or the novel (the print media which Benedict Anderson (1991) argues are one of the major prerequisites for imagining a national community), has mediated the imagination of the Indian nation through its extensive reach across the nation and the diaspora, and its consumption beyond the cinematic moment in other media, notably recorded music, radio, television, magazines and so on.

While the sheer size of the Indian film industry is remarkable in itself, here I am interested in its creation of a public culture for the 'common people', which shows everyday, Indian cultural values, and examines qualities of 'Indian-ness'. Through its combination of tradition and the familiar with the modern and the national, Indian cinema presents what Ashish Rajadhyaksha (1987) calls 'neo-traditionalism'.

Yet before these new media existed, traditional media (drama, poetry, music, dance and painting) were used for Indian religious practices. They continue to be deployed with complex interactions between these various media as they share and mediate symbols and practices in different forms. All these media affect religion itself, and their study is important to show how religion is represented (mediated) in various myths, rituals and symbols in the media themselves.

These media keep religion very much in the public eye, and are often privately controlled (such as cinema in India) rather than state-owned. Although the media are monitored by the state (censorship), it is increasingly difficult for the state to control the new media in an electronic age, and thus they may pose a threat to state politics of culture and identity. Religion is not confined to a separate religious sphere but is moving into the public sphere rather than out of it, as it is part of politics, a constituent of other arenas.

My aim here is not to give a detailed analysis of religion in the media as this has been done elsewhere.[3] Instead I examine the ways in which the media actually mediate religious practice and have transformed it in the context of Indian cinema.[4]

Religion and cinema

Indian cinema studies have mostly been overdetermined by the study of nationalism. The idea of the nation has not always been central in Indian cinema, as has often been suggested by the examination of certain key films, but has been found in specific films at given times, notably the 1950s, which is often regarded as the 'golden age' of Indian cinema. Nationalism has been important in certain genres, such as the social film, which dominates the post-independence cinema that is the focus of much of Indian cinema studies. Nationalism has also been explored in the older genres of Indian cinema including the historical (Mukhopadhyay 2004), and has a complex history in the religious genres. Since its beginnings, Indian nationalism has been closely entwined with religion (van der Veer 1994), and while its religious nationalisms have been studied in other media such as literature (Dalmia 1997, Kaviraj 1995) and chromolithography (Pinney 2004), they have hardly been studied in cinema. *Filming the Gods* is not a political history of Indian cinema and religious nationalisms or the formation of religious communities, but the significance of cinema in the construction of these identities is discussed throughout the book.

The study of religion in Indian film studies is long overdue as it has been ever present as the dominant worldview of Indian cinema, not just represented directly by divine presences or by religious communities, but also manifested in ways of creating an ideal world through the individual, the family and society. The films do not just show literal representations of religions (Hinduism, Islam), religious communities and beliefs, but also are grounded in wider concerns of customs and society that can be said to be religious, however loosely. These concerns cross the boundaries of regional and religious communities and so may be said to form pan-Indian views and beliefs which then reach beyond the artificial boundaries and limited imagination of the nation to the diaspora and to people of non-Indian origin in other countries from Pakistan to Africa, Asia and parts of Europe.

The nation state's influence over the media has declined sharply of late as new transnational links between people are formed and as technology allows for new arenas of debate between communities that transcend political boundaries (Appadurai 1997). This is particularly true of religion as one sees the global rise of religious movements who use new media (Roy 2004), such as Islamist websites or US evangelical television channels, despite secularists' attempts to keep religion out of the state-controlled media.

This transnational religioscape, as it has been labelled by Appadurai, is always separate from other ideologies, notably that of nationalism, but the scholarly neglect of this area of core beliefs and attitudes, except among the more art historical approaches (Kapur 2000 and Rajadhyaksha 1993), is a major lacuna in any understanding of wider ideologies, whether of nationalism itself or, indeed, of other forms of identity and belief.

This study also has at its heart a re-examination of religiosity and secularism in India, which have been debated hitherto almost exclusively in terms of politics rather than as possible cultural imaginaries.[5] Interrogating the study of the cinema is one of the few ways of gaining access to wider imaginaries in contemporary debates about religion and secularism to allow the term to be questioned in meaningful ways. If we want to study various imaginaries in the Indian context, the best place to start is with film, as it presents us not only with images and symbols of the public and the popular but also with their consumption by the audience. Of course, not everyone watches films, but they are an important way of measuring not only how the nation sees itself but also how communities see themselves and others. The Indian film industry itself has always had a mixture of communities, from different regions and religions, whether as directors, writers and stars, and the production of these representations has not been determined by any one community, although different communities could be said to dominate the industry at different times.

Religion and modernity

I am not proposing here to define what I mean by the religious as there is no all-embracing definition[6] and Hinduism is a notoriously difficult term,[7] but a working definition could be that of Clifford Geertz (1973), who takes it to be a combination of myths, values and rituals. I include in its popular meanings, visual representations (often efficacious), narratives, beliefs and emotions; the way the world should be and the way that we as the audience would like it to be.

Although the divine has been much discussed in other areas of Indian culture, notably art and chromolithography, the silence about religion in cinema is no doubt due to its status as an emblem of the modern: cinema has been India's great experiment to fashion an Indian modernity. Ashis Nandy has long argued that there are many modernities in India and elsewhere, a claim that is supported by research on Islamic modernity which shows that the decline of religion as a feature of modernity may well be true only of western modernity, and perhaps is not true of American modernity either.[8] Eickelman and Anderson (1999) argue that modernity sees the creation of a new Muslim public sphere where religious, political and social worlds meet and religion reappears alongside global capitalism, while Birgit Meyer (2003) has shown how Ghanaians, disillusioned with modernity's unfulfilled promises, now seek economic gain and consumerist opportunities in religion.

Little has been written about Hindu modernities, and I suggest that cinema, as a major arena of the religious and the cultural form mostly closely associated with modernity, seems a fruitful area to investigate. *Filming the Gods* makes some preliminary steps towards addressing this topic.

Film studies and religion

While few critics and film theorists have investigated religion in the cinema, one of the greatest film critics, André Bazin (2002), writes, 'The cinema has always been interested in God', usually with the most spectacular aspects of the history of Christianity. He argues that Catholicism has a 'natural affinity' with cinema with its formidable iconography and that these features have given rise to films that are successful but religiously insignificant because they have to work against these spectacular elements, focusing instead on the psychological and moral deepening of the religious fact, leading to a renunciation of the physical representation of the supernatural and grace.

Bazin's remarks are not applicable in the context of the Indian 'religious genres', in which I believe films are, in fact, religiously significant while also being highly successful commercially. Hindu iconography and its relationship of the image and the viewer have, perhaps, an even greater affinity with cinema and the conventions of Indian cinema, whether or not the operation of a melodramatic mode or its sequence of 'attractions' (see Dwyer and Patel 2002) subordinate the spectacular to the other requirements of cinema.

While it is widely acknowledged that the film itself has a mythological nature and is a creator of new mythologies, we also need to consider whether, as critics such as John Lyden (2003) have argued, cinema is almost a form of religion, as, like religion, it presents and examines images, relationships, ideas, beliefs, desires, fears, and brings to them its own specific forms such as the quasi-divine figures of the stars (see Lyden 2003). Cinema also has a certain mystical quality in that we may not understand films but we feel them and respond to their emotions. However, Hindi cinema's very disavowal of certain forms of realism and its unique modification of the melodrama allow the eruption of the religious, sometimes as images actively engage in the drama, often as a hierophany, that is the appearance of the religious in the everyday. Very few films show an absence of the religious, and many that seem to have some 'secular' patterning of divine order through the operation of fate, virtue and redemption reshape these into meaningfulness by their divine or superhuman qualities, while also emphasising the spirituality of the individual.

Film theory has also given little space to the study of religion. The concerns of many film critics are mostly with the modern and postmodern forms of subjectivity, audience and the dominance in recent years of psychoanalytic and feminist criticism. Scholars of Indian cinema have examined the form of film, its history, its social context and its relation to politics, in particular its relation with nationalism, but rarely discussed the spiritual realm; in fact there has been almost no research on religion in cinema in India.[9] This is not surprising given how little research there has been on religion and cinema in general.[10] Most books on religion and cinema are concerned with 'religious' films or with the depiction of spirituality in films, mostly drawing on Judaeo-Christian thought. This writing tends to focus on the image of Christ or on theology. There is yet to be a body of work that examines the non-Abrahamic religions in cinema.

My own reluctance to examine religion in Indian cinema has been due to wanting to avoid seeing religion as the essence of India, a Dumontian view of India's cultural difference. The idea of discussing religion and Indian cinema is usually taken to mean a study of representation of religious communities, religious nationalism and religious films, a political approach which I have discussed only where appropriate to the broader areas of my study. However, as there is interest in the current worldwide religious resurgence, which has been studied more in media other than cinema, it is likely that the academic study of the Hindi film will increase.

Religious films and their audiences

While religious studies has met with aesthetics in the area of historical forms (literature, music, song, architecture, dance and drama) it has not engaged with modern forms of art, again perhaps because of how modernity and

religion have been seen to be separate. Much modern Indian art is regarded
as derivative or kitsch and the art of the chromolithograph more so than
others.[11] Christopher Pinney's work has been pioneering in its engagement
with the religious aspects of photography and chromolithography.[12] So far
no one has defined a Hindu aesthetics, how Hindu art is defined by more
than its subject, the way they are practised and perceived. A study of a
Hindu enjoyment, aesthetic response and an emotional response to beauty
and morality as having religious functions seems to be an area ripe for investigation and I shall discuss this further in Chapter 4. The Islamic aesthetic,
which I discuss in Chapter 3 below, is much more clearly defined and is
consciously incorporated in Indian films, which take this to great extremes
in language, gesture, costume, location and so on.

David Morgan (2005: 5) argues that religious films in the west are seen
as B-movies, and Frank Burch Brown (2000) argues that much modern
Christian art in the west is viewed as kitsch. In India, the Hindi movies
themselves are often disparaged (see Dwyer 2000a), but the religious films
even more so:

> Mythology becomes a caricature of religion; it lacks sometimes the
> solemnity and the significance of religious literature and is often so
> mixed up with the grotesque as to be almost indistinguishable from
> the ludicrous. (RFEC: 176)

This question of taste and association with social class has been discussed
by Bourdieu (1984) and in the Indian context in Dwyer (2000a). It is
certainly true that the religious film is associated with women (RECFC:
182) and religious genres were until recently at least avoided by the elites
and fashionable youngsters.

There is little contemporary or historical ethnography of Indian cinema
(Dickey 1993 is an ethnography of fan clubs in Madurai, and Derné 2000
studies male audiences in north India). We see that, as in the west, audiences formed almost as soon as cinema was introduced but we do not
know much about how they viewed the films and their viewing practices.
Stephen Hughes (1996 and 2000) studies exhibition of silent cinema by
examining the licensing of cinema halls in Madras, while Bhaumik (2001)
examines the location of cinema halls and the films they showed to give
an idea of the Bombay audiences for silent films.

I have examined contemporary press coverage of cinema, including
reviews, reports and advertisements. There is some evidence from private
journals or interviews of what cinema viewing was like, but I have had
access to only a few of these although they will form an important part
of the history of the Indian cinema audience.

Some of the richest resources I found for the history of the Indian film
audience are the government enquiries into the film industry. The multi-

volume Rangachariar Report and Evidences (RICC and ICC I–V) is an invaluable document for the study of the silent film in India, and the Patil Commission (RFEC) is particularly useful for the workings of the industry while the Khosla Commission (RECFC) and the RWGNFP are the most recent I have seen.

The film industry in India has begun to compile publically available documentation through its work at FRAMES, part of the Federation of the Indian Chamber of Commerce and Industry. However, every producer and distributor imagines his or her audience and I have had close personal experience of this during my own association with the industry, critics and some audiences, over the last decade and a half (Dwyer 2002b).

The structure of the book: a question of genre

Filming the Gods draws mainly on textual and generic analyses of films and film history. Genres are ways of structuring the world, of making sense of it through the construction of narratives and signs (Frow 2006). While genres do not reflect a nation's thoughts at a given time (Neale 1990: 64), they are often associated with shifts in *mentalité* (Todorov 1984: 80–93), hence I have attempted to trace the attitudes of film makers, critics and audiences by studying these genres.

Filming the Gods is divided into four chapters. The first three look at genres which are labelled as explicitly religious, whether because of their origins (the mythological and the devotional) or because they are culturally marked as belonging to a religious community, hence the Islamicate film (often called the Muslim social). These genres are marked in that central to them is a clear religious presence, whether in terms of theology, ideology or culture, which is readily identifiable by the industry and the audiences, as they have been throughout the century of Indian cinema. The fourth chapter looks at the religious in other genres, mostly the social film that has dominated and absorbed other genres since independence.

With his first film, *Raja Harischandra*, Phalke created the mythological, one of the categories or genres of films that are unique to Indian cinema, all of which were established during the early days of silent films. Through this and the other religious genres, filmic ways of viewing religious symbols and practices became part of the visual culture of Indian cinema and indeed of Indian culture. The mythological was one of the most popular and productive genres of Indian silent cinema, which developed over the years and continues to be made, albeit very little in A-movies, until the present. Chapter 1 examines the mythological film's worldviews and values, rituals, religious power and moral values. It also looks at the impact of censorship, which allowed people to do things in the name of religion that they could not do as politics. It traces the evolution of the genre through the early days of the silent film, through its presentation of Indian history and culture, through the B-movies, to its revival as a family drama in film and in television, where it has mobilised political forces.

However, religious genres did not dominate the silent and the early talkies. Stunt films were hugely popular, and one of the major genres of the time. These films were centrally concerned with modernity and the modern world through the use of speed, energy, bodies in motion, the position of women and so on.

Chapter 2 examines the devotional genre, which had its greatest moment with the coming of the talkies in the 1930s and 1940s, when it was most closely associated with the freedom struggle and the reform of social practices sanctioned by religion. The chapter looks closely at the genre's association with political and social reformers such as M.G. Ranade and M.K. Gandhi.

A widely held and rarely contested notion is that mythological and devotional genres fade during this period. In fact it seems that they begin a slow move into B-genres, where they remain highly productive, in Hindi film, although they continue their A-grade status in other cinemas, notably Telugu, until a later date. (See the relevant chapters below.) The social comes to dominate, not so much in terms of the number of films made but the budgets and their prestige, and it is acclaimed in the elite English press, notably the *Times of India*'s film magazine, *Filmfare*, from 1951. Mythologicals continue to be made at roughly the same rate and often one is reviewed every fortnight in *Filmfare*.

Chapter 3 looks at 'Islamicate' genres, including the Muslim social, which flower in the 1940s and 1950s, alongside other popular 'secular' genres including the social-problem film, especially those which concentrated on being 'modern', while the historical remained productive. India's largest religious minority is the Muslim community, which numbers over 12 per cent of the total population of more than a billion people, making it one of the largest Muslim populations in the world. While Islam has many prohibitions on the depiction of the divine or its prophets in human form, and so much of orthodox Sunni Islam forbids 'filming the gods', Indian cinema may be said to have several genres which can be described as 'Islamicate' in their focus on Islam as part of culture and society. I examine these in Chapter 3, discussing the features that are seen to be Islamicate (language, literature, music, clothing) before looking at the genres particularly rich in depictions of an Islamicate world, namely the fantasy, historical, courtesan and Muslim social.

One genre which remains popular after independence is the historical, although its subject shifts from religious nationalism towards films that show a national integration of minorities, notably Muslims, mostly through presenting images of syncretic Mughal culture. It is in this context that I discuss the historical in Chapter 3.[13] The historical also suggests new myths of the nation – inventing the nation's ancient past – but begins to fade after ten years or so, only reappearing at the beginning of the 2000s, with films such as *Lagaan*, *Gadar* and *Asoka*, which explore non-Muslim histories (Dwyer 2002b).

Chapter 4 examines the standard Indian film history narrative; namely that as the films made in the colonial period are interested in nationalist issues, the post-independence film supports the ideas of Nehruvian secularism.[14] This may indeed be true of some of the greatest Indian film makers of these years (including Mehboob Khan, Raj Kapoor, Guru Dutt and Bimal Roy) and several stars become particularly associated with secular ideals, such as Dev Anand or Raj Kapoor. This argument fits in nicely with the idea of secular modernity, the exclusion of religion from the public sphere and so on, which was promoted by Nehru in the post-independence years. Yet if we look at the films of this time, the presence of the religious remains strong in the religious genres and even in the social genre itself.

This chapter looks at the ostensibly non-religious (therefore often nominally secular) films which are largely seen as non-generic, most grouped as the 'social' or 'masala' film. It discusses the direct depiction of religion whether of religious communities, festivals, ceremonies or divine intervention in these films before turning to ways in which religion is depicted indirectly in films through the raising and answering of questions which are central to religion such as virtue, suffering and redemption. It looks at the use of melodrama, language and music before examining these findings in the wider context of Indian religion and secularism.

The pervasiveness of religious imagery does not imply belief but is a way of constructing the world, an imagination. Mansukhlal Jhaveri (1906–1981) nicely puts his automatic response to religion in a Gujarati poem, *Haath jodaay jaay*, where even in the face of mockery from his friends, he says he cannot give up worship, which is automatic to him. This is the first verse from the long poem (my translation):

My hands join in prayer as my childhood habit.
If I see a god's temple or wherever I see a flag fluttering,
If I see red-ochre robes of an ascetic or the colour of pale saffron;
If my sight should fall on a river or a sacred ford of any of the rivers
Whose names I repeated everyday by heart
When bathing in my childhood;
When I get up from eating or in the evening when the lamp and wick are lit,
As soon as I see the line of the crescent moon, my hands join in prayer.
Even I don't know why my hands join in prayer.

My educated friend looks somewhat surprised
That my childhood habit remains.
As an adult, I haven't lost the habit, I still have it:
Automatically, without thinking, my hands join in prayer!

Terminology

Although the book is called 'Indian cinema', it will soon be clear to readers that I am talking mostly about 'Hindi cinema'. I use the term 'Hindi cinema' to cover the one with which I am most familiar, but should point out that before 1931 cinema was not language dependent, and during the time of the talkies I will also discuss Marathi cinema where some of the best of these genre films were produced. Although I mention the occasional film in other languages, I have little to say about India's other cinemas, which, however important they are at a national and a local level, are not part of the book I have written. To discuss them here would be to make the book unwieldy and to take it towards the encyclopaedic rather than the academic. I am more concerned about how much it is local, that is specific to India, and how much it is global, that is general to cinema and to religion, and I make my observations about religion in some forms of Indian cinema with this in mind.

The language of the films discussed in this book is (mostly) Hindi. However, Hindi cinema has another metalanguage, English, which is used for titles in films and for the considerable body of writing and discussion about this cinema both within the industry and other media. As this book is in English, I have drawn on the terms for religion used in English in this metalanguage as well as on the Hindi terms that have often been coined for religious vocabulary where no term previously existed. The word 'Hindu' is the most striking example of this as it is a word that was coined by the Persians to mean 'Indians' and then used, largely by the British, to group various religious beliefs and practices into one religion. Hindi and English are often used as equivalents when they are actually referring to different concepts. A good example is the word 'secular', which is discussed in Chapter 4, which, used in India in English, or in its Hindi 'equivalent', does not mean the same as in British English. This book is divided into genres which are well known in India by their English names, although they have Hindi equivalents too. Mythological and devotional films are usually called *dhaarmik* (approximately 'religious'), while mythologicals may be further distinguished as *pauranic* (literally 'coming from the *Puranas*' and epics); historicals may be called *aitihaasik* (literally 'historical'); socials, *samaajik* (literally 'social'). I am not aware of other generic terms used for the other film genres discussed in this book from the contemporary periodicals and publicity I read.

Note on transliteration

My aim is to be clear, rather than pedantic, and many Indian words and people's names have standard Roman spellings. Others vary greatly, film titles being notorious, and I have given priority to the actual spellings used by the texts and people themselves rather than being consistent. I have not used any diacritical marks, so vowel length is not marked in names like Rama or Sita. One ongoing dilemma is about inherent –a, which appears in the Devanagari syllabary as it is used in transliteration from Sanskrit but not modern languages such as Hindi and Gujarati. I have used –a with names of deities and Sanskrit texts, as I am more familiar with these sources. This means that I refer to modern tellings of the story of Rama (not Ram) as *Ramayanas* rather than *Ramayans*. I do not think this should cause undue difficulty to the reader.

As I am often talking about pre-independence India, I have kept the old names of the cities so Bombay (Mumbai), Madras (Chennai), Calcutta (Kolkata), Baroda (Vadodara), Benares (Varanasi), Poona (Pune) and so on. This is something of a habit for which I am often reprimanded and I apologise now for any unintended offence.

Chapter 1

The mythological film

Phalke states: 'I began the film industry in India in the year 1912' (ICC III: 869). In fact, the first film was shown in India in 1896 and, although screenings of these and other films were successful, it was seventeen years before Phalke's *Raja Harischandra*, the first entirely Indian film, was made.[1] However, the intervening years saw Indians working with non-Indians to learn about film making and Phalke's own training in other visual arts (see below) speaks volumes about the preparation that went into the formation of this cinema. Indian cinema's roots lie in so many of the arts (theatre, music, painting, photography, literature, dance, story telling) as well as in other aspects of culture that were stimulated by the colonial encounter and the new media that developed during the nineteenth century.

It would be fascinating to have more accounts of the beginnings of Indian cinema but apart from writings by Phalke[2] and J.B.H. Wadia's largely unpublished memoirs,[3] we have very little in the way of eyewitness reports. However, we have the extensive and invaluable source of the Indian Cinematograph Committee's Report and Evidences of 1927–8 (RICC and ICC I–V), which dates from the last years of the silent film in India and give us a great deal of information about the state of the industry, the cinema halls, the audiences and so on from across British India.[4] However, since the interviewees had to speak English, we only have the views of the elites and we know little about what the 'ordinary person' thought of cinema. We know which genres certain segments of the audience enjoyed but we do not have any information about why they enjoyed them and what they thought of them. We can reconstruct some of these views from advertisements in newspapers and specialist magazines but the former often ignored cinema while many of the latter publications have not yet been made publicly available, if they exist at all.

Reading the ICC Evidences, I was struck to find that so much of the discourse around cinema today in India is similar to that of almost a hundred years ago. Why has Indian cinema, which itself changed so much, been trapped by this discourse, which perceives it as backwards, inferior to the west, in need of censoring to 'protect' the lower classes, and in

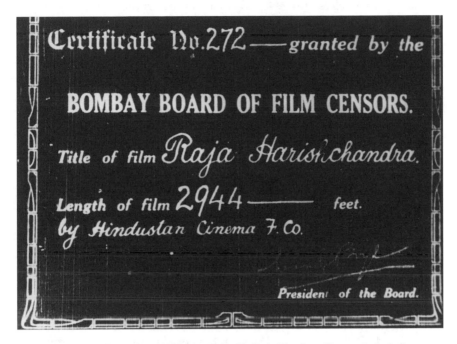

Figure 1.1 Raja Harischandra (1913, dir. D.G. Phalke). The first film made in India.

financial crisis and so on? Why does it focus on the failings rather than the success? Statistics quoted in Shah (1950) show the inexorable rise of cinema in India (1950, Ch. 3), although it remains relatively small in proportion to the population in comparison with the United States and Europe. However, by 1939 cinema was the eighth largest industry in India and the third largest cinema in the world (Shah 1950: 60). It has an audience throughout India, albeit concentrated in the urban centres, and was distributed in areas where the Indian diaspora were settled (East Africa, South Africa, Fiji, Mauritius, Federated Malay States, Iraq and West Indies (Shah 1950: 55).

Much academic writing on Indian cinema focuses on it as a major vehicle for nationalist discourses, but, although one or two of the interviewees refer to the nationalist movement and several film makers (such as J.B.H. Wadia) were actively involved with the freedom struggle, this topic is rarely mentioned in the Evidences. Indeed, the names of many of the companies (Imperial, Minerva) and the names of the cinemas (Albert, Coronation, Wellington) suggest a different view and I shall reassess the importance of nationalism in looking at these films.

As nationalism, cinema is often said to be a new religion (Lyden 2003). While there are striking shared features, the analogy should not be pushed too far.[5] Nonetheless, these features cannot be ignored and one of my concerns is to examine the universal and particular features of cinema in India. Hindu and Indian are often conflated (sometimes to dangerous effect), but given that Hinduism is almost exclusively associated with South Asia and its diaspora, this makes the analysis of the culturally particular relatively straightforward in the case of the mythological film.

The mythological among other genres

As feature films began to form into genres in the US, the religious film developed from the filming of Passion Plays[6] to Cecil B. DeMille's big-budget productions such as *The Ten Commandments* (1923) and *The King of Kings* (1927).[7] DeMille's much-quoted remark that 'God is box office' was certainly true of these and other films, whose attractions included great spectacle and often special effects for miracles as well as providing audiences with religious experiences.

The first films made in India before Phalke were by Harishchandra Sakharam Bhatavdekar (1868–58), better known as Save Dada. He made several shorts including one of a wrestling match in the Hanging Gardens, Bombay and another on monkeys (both 1899), as well as some actualities including the return from Cambridge of a famous mathematician (*Sir Wrangler Mr R.P. Paranjpye*, 1902) and the celebrations of the coronation of Edward VII (*Delhi Durbar of Lord Curzon*, 1903);[8] while Hiralal Sen (1866–1917) shot plays from Star Theatres and Classic Theatre, Calcutta from 1898. However, the first all-Indian feature film, *Raja Harischandra*, was a 'mythological', a genre which is unique to India.[9] The mythological has been given prominence in India as its founding genre and because of Phalke's eminence (and the survival of so much of his output) but it has always been perceived to be in decline and many other genres were popular during the silent period in Bombay including the stunt or action film, the historical,[10] the Arabian Nights Oriental fantasy (see Chapter 3) and the social (see Chapter 4). (Other regions preferred different genres; for example Bengal, with its rich literature, preferred more intellectual and social themes drawn from novels or filmed stage plays.)

Some sources give early genres as mythological, religious, historical and stunt (Shah 1950: 43), with some distinguishing the mythological from the folkloric while others regard them as the same, and yet others separate the devotional and religious (Shah 1950: 116). The RICC (p. 34)[11] notes the major genres as mythological or religious, historical and social dramas, before saying that there are two or three companies which specialise in mythological films.[12]

The advertisements of the early periodicals are not consistent in their generic categories. For example, Variety Film Service, in its magazine advertisements, lists its 1931 and 1932 releases as: Special exclusive (included

Biblical themes such as *Sodom and Gomorrah*, *Judith and Holophernes*); social; jungle; Oriental, romantic (including *Sampson and Dalilah*, *INRI*) and semi-Oriental; stunt and fighting.[13] The Gujarati journal *Mauj Majah* during the 1930s refers to *pauranik* films, which could mean literally from the *Puranas* (Hindu myths) or could mean more broadly mythological/ legendary. The Hindi journal *Rajatpat* of the late 1940s has adverts for *samaajik* ('social'), *dhaarmik* ('religious'), *aitihaasik* ('historical') and stunt.

Kusum Gokarn devotes a whole chapter of her study to a discussion of the discreteness of the mythological and devotional to conclude that there is just one genre (Gokarn n.d.: 86–92), the 'religious' film, but I am maintaining the division here between the two types as it seems to me that they are differentiated by their production houses, their style and content, their advertising and reception.

Although the genres of early Indian cinema were recognised by the film makers and the audiences, no generic category is watertight and Indian cinema's notoriously fuzzy genres are even more porous than most. However, I define the mythological, the founding genre of Indian cinema, and one of the most productive genres of its early cinema, as one which depicts tales of gods and goddesses, heroes and heroines[14] mostly from the large repository of Hindu myths, which are largely found in the Sanskrit *Puranas*, and the Sanskrit epics, the *Mahabharata* and the *Ramayana*. The early mythological genre drew on a wide range of the modern and the traditional to create its own distinctive hybrid style, with strong connections to nineteenth-century Indian popular or middlebrow public culture as well as with other forms of cinema that were emerging at the same time in other places in the world.

Some films blur these generic boundaries, notably the much-discussed *Jai Santoshi Maa* (see below), which has many elements of the social (the heroine is fictional and lives in some vaguely contemporary world) or the devotional (the film concentrates on her devotion to the goddess), but, I argue, the actual manifestation of the gods in human form separates it from the social where the miraculous is usually shown as acting through an image or other medium, and is distinguished from the devotional, which focuses on the life of a human devotee who is presented in historical time. Of course, for many devotees of Rama, the *yuga* (aeon) in which he was on earth is historical time and he continues to live in the present time, but I am referring to the narrow, academic definition of historical time. In many devotional films, the historical figure of the devotee enters into divine time and space, so Narsi Mehta witnesses the Vrajlila (episodes from Krishna's pastoral idyll), but the film's focus is on Narsi and his devotion. The mythological is defined by the stories of the gods and goddesses – or heroes and heroines – themselves, so *Jai Santoshi Maa* also tells the story of the goddess herself, how she is born and how she gains recognition among the older goddesses.

The mythological genre is defined largely in terms of its narrative. It may recount the story of gods and goddesses, whose oldest versions we have in the Sanskrit *Puranas*,[15] which have been retold over the centuries.[16] Each *Purana* contains the stories associated with particular deities, so Krishna's *lila* or 'life' is told in the *Bhagavata Purana*. However, the films have drawn more closely on India's two great epics, the *Mahabharata* and the *Ramayana*.[17] While these texts are traditionally the work of single authors (Vyasa and Valmiki respectively), historical analysis finds them to be the result of oral composition and as such there is no original text of either, nor is there one single, correct version but there are many versions of each epic (Richman 1991). Their origins are at least non-Brahminical, judging from the names of the characters and given that the *Ramayana* story is first found in Buddhist sources. However, they have been fully incorporated into Hindu religious literature, as key characters are seen as incarnations of gods, the *Mahabharata* now being called the 'fifth Veda'. Although these Sanskrit texts are the oldest extant versions we have of these stories,[18] and are still sources of powerful narratives and imagery, they have no claim to primacy and they should not be read as 'original', because of the plurality of traditions in India. We should also note that the Sanskrit tradition is predominantly the culture of the male and the high caste, while other tellings are found among women, Dalits and other subaltern groups. There are still many other tellings of episodes from these epics, whether sung by bards, performed in plays, depicted in comics, made into films and television dramas or simply told as household tales.

The core of the *Mahabharata* was composed around the second or third century BC, although some sections are much older. Various episodes, stories and even whole texts (such as the *Bhagavad Gita*) have been interpolated, with it reaching its present form of around 100,000 stanzas, some time around the fourth century AD. The central story is the dispute over the throne between the descendants of King Bharata, the Pandavas and the Kauravas, which ends in a great war. Although some films cover large parts of the stories, most concentrate on a single episode which they narrate in some detail and adapt to suit the narrative conventions of cinema.

There is no one original version of the story of Rama, the *Ramayana*, there being many tellings in genres ranging from folktales to texts to television serials in India and in South-east Asia, in Hindu traditions and among Buddhists and Jains. There are several key versions, each of which has become the hegemonic version in particular times and places: the Sanskrit *Ramayana* of Valmiki (composed between the second century BC and the second century AD), the Tamil *Iramavataram* of Kampan (ninth century) and the Hindi (Avadhi) *Ramcharitmanas* of Tulsidas (sixteenth century),[19] and the staging of the *Ramlila*, which has contributed to making

Rama the most popular deity in northern India (Kapur 1993b: 85). The story is roughly the same and while many films tell the whole story (the *Sampoorna Ramayana* or 'complete Ramayana'), others may do so while foregrounding certain episodes.

Sita's hand is won by Rama, eldest son of Dasharatha, king of Ayodhya. When the king abdicates, he is tricked by his youngest wife into banishing Rama and handing his kingdom to her son, Bharata. Rama, Sita and his brother Lakshman go into fourteen years of exile in the forest. A demoness, Surpanakha, repulsed by Rama when she tries to seduce him, attacks Sita, provoking Lakshman to mutilate her to punish her for her erotic desire. Her brother Ravana, wishing to avenge his beloved sister and enticed by her tales of the beauty of Sita, carries Sita off to his kingdom of Lanka. Rama's devotee, Hanuman, finds Sita, sets Ravana's city ablaze then brings Rama and his armies to rescue Sita. Rama takes Sita back only after she has undergone a trial of fire to prove that she is pure after living in the house of another man. Rumours persist in Ayodhya, where Rama is restored to the throne, and Rama banishes the pregnant Sita from his kingdom. She gives birth to twin boys, Lav and Kush, in a hermitage. She asks the earth to open to allow her to return; Rama ascends into heaven.

These stories from the *Puranas* and the epics have long been mediated by pre-existing genres and media, ranging across Sanskrit texts, narrative retellings, folktales, songs, poems, music paintings which had already established a combination of visual, musical and dramatic conventions before the new nineteenth-century forms of urban theatre, photography and chromolithographs.[20]

The early genres – the mythological, the devotional and the historical – drew for their idea of clothes from art, chromolithography, religious processions and performances, folk and urban theatre, and foreign cinema. These were often anachronistic, so the *choli* ('blouse'), which became popular only in the nineteenth century, was worn in many films for the sake of modesty.

The folk theatre was also a rich source of narrative, with *Ramlila* and the *raslila* as well as *yakshagana*, *bhavai*, *nautanki* and others. However, during the nineteenth century, the *Puranas* and epics were foundational to various new theatre traditions that developed in India, which had important influences on local films. For example, the Telugu Surabhi Theatres took local traditions such as that of Andhra leather-puppet shows, and the *Harikatha* whose performers adapted the epics to the stage. The many companies that flourished in the area in the early twentieth century provided the Tamil and Telugu cinemas with their repertoire and their stars. In western India the Marathi Sangeet Natak, which blended traditional elements from Tanjore and (modern) Maharashtra with western-style painted backdrops, performed from a wide repertoire including Shakespeare and

Sanskrit plays set to music. Among the most famous groups were Bal Gandharva's Gandharva Natak Mandali and Govindrao Tembe's Shivraj Natak Mandali. Gandharva as an actor and Tembe as a music composer were key figures in Prabhat Films alongside other Sangeet Natak associates including V. Shantaram and Vishnupant Pagnis (see Chapter 2), while Baburao Painter, né Mestri, later of Maharashtra Film Company, gained his name as a professional painter of backdrops (see Rajadhyaksha and Willemen 1999: 205–6).

However, the most important form was the Parsi theatre,[21] named after the Zoroastrians, or Parsis, who founded it in the nineteenth century. Many groups in Bombay with names such as the Empress Victoria Natak Mandali and the Alfred Co. Groups soon became fixed in other cities such as Karachi, Hyderabad, Lucknow and Lahore.

Parsi theatre was important for cinema in numerous ways, in language, music, style, scenarios, stories, genres and personnel. Several Parsis were key figures in early cinema, notably the Madan brothers of Calcutta, Ardeshir Irani of Imperial Film, Sohrab Modi of Minerva Movietone and the Wadia brothers of Wadia Movietone. The Parsi theatre produced professional full-time writers, who published their plays. Some of the most famous of these became writers for cinema, including Aga Hashr Kashmiri (adapter of Shakespeare, and Arabian Nights stories as well as later writing mythologicals and devotionals such as New Theatre's *Chandidas*), Narayan Prasad Betaab (who later wrote for Ranjit Studio among others, where he was a great promoter of Hindi) and Radheshyam Kathavachak (another promoter of Hindi and a great writer of mythologicals, drawing on his family's background in the *Ramlila*) among others.

Genres of Indian cinema inherited from Parsi theatre included the historical, the romance, the Arabian Nights fantasy (see Chapter 3) and the mythological.[22] Cinema sometimes directly adapted popular plays such as *Raja Harischandra* and Parsi and Iranian legends such as Rustom and Sohrab, and Shirin and Farhad.

The continuing popularity of the Parsi theatre set the style for silent films as well as for the talkies after 1931 (see Kapur 1993a, 1993b). Although the early cinema was 'silent' in the sense that it had no recorded sound, it often had a musical accompaniment in the style of the theatre and it adapted its sets, costumes, performance styles and gesture. It was not until the talkies that its mixture of dialogue and music became a hallmark of Indian popular cinema, but the influence of other performance styles cannot be discounted. Parsi theatre was originally in English, then Gujarati, the language of the Parsi community, but by the late nineteenth century it shifted to Urdu or Hindustani.[23]

The nineteenth century in India saw a proliferation of cheap, moveable images which clearly influenced moving pictures. Early Indian cinema drew on the visual regime established in the nineteenth century in art, notably in Ravi Varma's painting, which was developed by the new technologies of chromolithography ('calendar art') and photography (see Pinney 1997, Rajadhyaksha 1993). These in turn showed developments from conventions of miniature painting via the Company School.[24] Phalke was a maker of chromolithographs as well as a photographer (see below) so was also familiar with these iconic images; it is not surprising therefore that the imagery of the mythological film is so closely enmeshed with these other visual forms, in particular the representations of 'calendar art', that is popular prints of gods and goddesses, produced in the new medium of chromolithography, which in turn had drawn on the new national art, both of which had earlier affected stage presentations (Pinney 2004).

Geeta Kapur argues that the films use iconicity and illusionism to compensate for descent of gods into realism (Kapur 2000). This iconicity is reinforced by the manifestation of premodern ways of looking in the cinema, notably that of *darshan* ('seeing').[25] The narration invites *darshan* by its use of tableaux, a feature that has long been seen in forms of worship such as the *jhanki* or tableau of the gods that the devotees view in the north Indian *raslila* and the *Ramlila*, and these mixed codes exist side by side in cinema as they had for decades in the other mass arts.

Christopher Pinney (2004: 193) argues for a corpothetics, a way of engaging the whole body through the eye. *Darshan* is dissimilar to elite western 'disembodied, unidirectional and disinterested vision, but not strikingly unlike a whole range of culturally diverse popular practices that stress mutuality and corporeality in spaces as varied as those of religious devotion and cinematic pleasure'. Pinney argues that in *darshan*, the exchange of looks, the eye is an organ of tactility that makes the connection. Linking the idea of seeing and being seen with Merleau-Ponty's 'double sensation' of touching and being touched, and picking up on Benjamin and Taussig, he argues that one should think of the corpothetics (sensory, corporeal aesthetics) of the encounter: a desire to fuse the image and the beholder with a focus on efficacy of the image, rather than of aesthetics, with a separation of the image and the beholder. He links *darshan* with popular visual practices elsewhere. This corpothetics is also suggestive for thinking about engagements with cinema and religious devotion in India and in the west, leading to a reconsideration of *darshan* as 'less than universal and more than local' (Vidal 2005).

Another way the mythological distances itself from the everyday is by its use of the special effect. While the religious image is held to be efficacious in films as it is elsewhere, cinematic special effects of beams of vision and of light moving from eye to eye emphasise the very nature of the religious image whether in the mythological film, such as *Jai Santoshi Maa*, or in moments in other films where images become efficacious, such as *Amar, Akbar, Anthony* (see Chapter 4).

As Sean Cubitt has noted (2004: 53), the cinema drew on the use of special effects in theatre. He points out that the great master of the special effect, Méliès, had worked in the melodramatic theatres of Paris, which were 'majestically devoted to earthquakes, waterfalls, railway crashes, airborne apparitions, imaginary journeys, stampedes, battles, and mythical beasts. The apparatus of traps and projections, prestidigitation, wire acrobats, wrangling, massive and mobile sets, lighting and sound effects put it on a par with the 1990s music theater of Andrew Lloyd Webber'. Cubitt also observes that, 'As the technologisation of spectacle accelerated, its thematics moved bizarrely in the opposite direction: to folklore ... the gothic ... the melodramatic grotesque ... and the spectacle of the exotic (Cubitt 2004: 54). A similar history can be traced in Indian cinema, where the special effects of Parsi theatre and its various mechanisms for depicting flying gods and other astonishments (Kapur 1993a), were drawn on in cinema, where they were augmented by trick photography, particularly in the mythological film rather than in the films which dealt with contemporary issues such as the social and the stunt.

Silent mythologicals: the makers and their films

Far from being some sort of 'backward' types, nearly all early film makers were educated in British institutions in India, whether art colleges (Phalke, Dhiren Ganguly of New Theatres) or universities (J.B.H. and Homi Wadia). Many of them were from elite families, notably the Wadia brothers whose ancestors were master shipbuilders to the British Navy, and most of the founders of New Theatres (B.N. Sircar's father was Advocate-General of West Bengal; Debaki Bose was the son of a lawyer; P.C. Barua was from a royal family, Nandy 2000) and Himanshu Rai and Devika Rani were from wealthy families and educated in London. Among the makers of mythologicals, several were from the traditional elite of Brahmins, such as D.G. Phalke and Vijay Bhatt. (Interestingly, the film makers at Prabhat were nearly all technicians and came from a wide range of social backgrounds.)

Fewer than twenty of India's silent films have survived to the present and these are mostly in the collection of the National Film Archive of India in Pune, Maharashtra.[26] For example, we do not have a single film made by the Maharashtra Film Company, several of whose personnel later formed Prabhat. Painter's company specialised in overtly nationalistic historical films according to all accounts, but also made a story from the *Mahabharata*, *Sairandhri* (1920), for which Tilak (the nationalist leader from (modern) Maharashtra) congratulated Painter. This story had been linked to depictions of Indians in servitude in chromolithographs and its resonances may well have been recognised by the audience as they were by Tilak (Dharap 1983: 82, Pinney 2004: 68–71). However, there are some mythologicals including several by Phalke among this collection (see below) and also Phalke's *Tukaram* (1921, 498 feet)[27] and *Bhakta Prahlad* (1926, of which 501 feet survive) [28] and the Indo-German co-productions such as *The light of Asia* (1925, see below).[29]

One type of mythological was also made during the silent period, that was aimed less at a religious audience was about Buddhism (such as Phalke's *Buddhadev* in 1923), which was largely no longer practised in India, or was aimed at Europe and beyond, which used the special effects and the aesthetic of astonishment, but showed Indian culture and history. We know little about *Savitri* (1924), which Madan Theatres made in collaboration with Union Cinematografia Italiana of Rome and produced in Italy under supervision of Artur Ambrosio. However, we do have copies of Himanshu Rai's collaborations with Emelka Studios in Munich, including *Prem Sanyas/The light of Asia* (1925), directed by Franz Osten, a team which is something of a precursor to Bombay Talkies (although they never made a mythological). It was edited and processed in Germany and given English titles. It ran for only two weeks in India but ran in London for ten months (Shah 1950:23). *The light of Asia* was much discussed in the ICC though largely as the testing ground for possible cooperation between Indian and overseas film makers.

The light of Asia was adapted by Niranjan Pal from Sir Edwin Arnold's epic poem *The light of Asia or the great renunciation (Mahabhinish-kramana), being the life and teaching of Gautama*, first published in 1861. The film is largely in the style of the historical – with calendar art historical depictions. The film does not worry about anachronisms, so it shows many Muslim buildings as part of classical India's heritage (while Vijay Bhatt's mythological films show contemporary styles such as Art Deco). The film is keen to assert its high status, the opening credits telling us it was 'Shown by royal command at Windsor Castle, April 27 1926' and that they received great help from the Maharaja of Jaipur. The credits also tell us that the makers gave up their careers (a doctor, a lawyer, an engineer, and a professor) for the sake of Indian dramatic art.

Osten's film shows spiritualism as the essence of India. The film begins with shots of western tourists in Bombay who then travel around India to Delhi, Benares, Gaya and then Bodh Gaya (the scene of the Buddha's enlightenment). There they meet an old man who tells them the story of Siddhartha Gautama from his birth to his leaving the palace, his wife and child, the *mahabhinishkramana* ('the great setting forth'), his moment of renunciation on his path to becoming the Buddha and the beginnings of his conversion. The scenes of the court were filmed in Rajasthan, which anachronistically passes for ancient India, largely because the Maharaja lent his elephants and collection of antique clothes to the production unit.

Phalke: art and technology in the mythological

Dadasaheb Phalke (1870–1944) dominates the history of early Indian cinema, not least because the major body of work from that period which survives is his (cf. Rajadhyaksha 1994), but also, because of his writings in *Navyug*,[30] his interview with the ICC, and recent research,[31] we have much information about his training and background in the industrial arts of his time. The surviving parts of his films were assembled in 1956 for the Indian Motion Picture Producers Association (Barnouw and Krishnaswamy 1980: 19).

Dhundiraj Govind Phalke, known as Dadasaheb Phalke ('respected grandfather Phalke'), was born in the sacred place Tryambakeshwar near Nasik in 1870.[32] His family intended him to follow his father as a Sanskrit scholar but when the latter moved to teach in Bombay, the son joined the J.J. School of Arts then went to study at Kalabhavan, Baroda, where he first became interested in photography. He trained as an amateur magician, then after working as a photographer, a scene-painter and draughtsman, he worked in Ravi Varma's Lonavala Press from 1901 to 1911, which was after Ravi Varma had sold up, the firm now being run by a German, Schleicher. Phalke then managed his own business in Bombay, namely Phalke's Engraving and Printing Works, Dadar. He went to Germany in 1909 and on his return renamed his company the Lakshmi Art Printing Works setting in new premises in Byculla. One of the few presses to do colour printing, they produced a series of illustrated booklets, the *Suvarnamala*, for major festivals (Pinney 2004: 72).

Already a photographer, magician and lithographer, Phalke decided to become involved in films after seeing *The life and passion of Christ* in 1910.[33] He made some short films, then in 1912 went to London to buy film-making equipment and met the editor of *Bioscope* and Cecil Hepworth. Film making was very much a one-man effort as Phalke told the ICC that he had to direct, write, photograph, print and edit. Phalke used complex editing and was clearly a master of special effects; however, his films are driven by narrative as much as by spectacle.[34]

Raja Harischandra was premiered on 3 May 1913 at the Coronation Cinema, Bombay, where it ran for twenty-three days, six times the usual run of films (Dharap 1985: 38). Phalke's first version of the film has disappeared but he remade it in 1917 and 1,475 feet of this later version have survived.[35] This is a story transmitted from ancient Vedic *Brahmanas*, through the *Mahabharata* and various *Puranas*. It was a staple of the Parsi theatre, its most famous version being that performed by the Victoria Theatre Group, although Bharatendu wrote a version in Hindi, *Satya Harischandra* (1885). The story was also the subject of a painting by Ravi Varma and then a popular chromolithograph of the Calcutta Art Studio (Pinney 2004: 72). King Harischandra goes on a hunting expedition, when he finds that the sage Vishwamitra has trapped the three powers (Trishakti) and Harischandra releases them. The sage is angered and the king appeases him by giving him the kingdom. Harischandra, Queen Taramati and the prince go into exile. The son dies and Queen Taramati is accused of his murder. Shiva appears to save the situation and the family are restored to the throne.

Even though men performed women's roles in many forms of theatre, Phalke felt that film with closer shots needed women to act. However, he was famously unable to get any women to perform in his film, despite the mythological theme. He even placed an advertisement and approached prostitutes but no one was willing to appear. In the end he took an effeminate waiter, Anna Salunke, to play Queen Taramati (Barnouw and Krishnaswamy 1980: 13–14). Salunke also acted in Phalke's *Lanka dahan*, where he played hero (Rama) and heroine (Sita).

Phalke moved to Nasik and soon made his second mythological, *Mohini Bhasmasur* (1914), soon followed by *Savitri Satyavan* (1914), neither of which has survived. *Mohini Bhasmasur* is noteworthy for having the first woman to act in Indian cinema. Kamalabai Gokhale, née Kamat (1900–97), was an actor on the Marathi stage, often appearing along with her mother, Durgabai. She played Mohini when she was thirteen then returned to the stage, paradoxically, often acting in men's roles.[36]

The success of these films allowed Phalke to buy more machinery but his plans of showing his films abroad were held up because of the war. Facing problems with the freeze on imports, Phalke kept the studio open on a shoestring and made many shorts – comedies, cartoons, topicals and educational shorts, and a film of himself performing magic tricks. After further setbacks, Phalke made new versions of *Raja Harischandra* (this is the version of which some has survived, see above) and *Lanka dahan* (*Lanka aflame*, 1917), the story of Hanuman setting fire to Lanka with his tail. Of the latter, 501 feet have survived[37] showing Sita in captivity and scenes with Hanuman and Ravana. This was Phalke's most popular film, and it met with huge success. This story from the *Ramayana* was a popular theme even before Phalke for chromolithography[38] and Hanuman films have continued to be some of the most popular mythologicals.

Other mythologicals of Phalke's which have survived are *Shree Krishna Janma* (*The birth of Shri Krishna*, 1918), which shows well-known episodes from Krishna's childhood. In the 576 feet that remain[39] is the sequence where Krishna rises from the River Yamuna on the demon snake Kaliya with the famous shot framed by his devotees. Other sequences included Krishna with his mother, Yashoda, in which she sees him as god, and also a sequence where Krishna's wicked uncle, King Kamsa, imagines his head being cut off (and the wonderful throat rubbing he does afterwards). The final title-card reads, 'May this humble offering be accepted by the Lord.'

Figure 1.2 Shree Krishna Janma (1918, dir. D.G. Phalke). Krishna's devotees take his *darshan* within the frame as he rises from the River Yamuna (formerly named Jumna).

Of Phalke's *Kaliya Mardan* (1919), 4441 feet[40] remain, including Mandakini Phalke, who had also played Krishna in *Shree Krishna Janma*, showing various expressions of her acting. The surviving episodes show his pranks as a child – stealing butter and tying a man's beard to his wife's hair, and the underwater fight with Kaliya, after which Krishna emerges triumphant.

Phalke wrote some articles about film making for *Navyug* (see Rajadhyaksha 1993) and set up his studio in Nasik on a more secure footing. About 100 people worked there (ICC III: 875), all family and quasi-family. However, he retired at this point, with only occasional film making thereafter. In the end he had made 100 feature films and thirty shorts (Dharap 1985: 46).

Although Phalke filmed his first *Raja Harischandra* in Bombay, when there were still wooded hills in Tardeo, he then moved to Nasik where he made all his later films. There were sacred places in Nasik and it was cheaper to run his company there, but also, even though when I visited (2003) Nasik was very industrialised, the beauty of the older city was still clear. Cubitt notes that Phalke's films were shot on location – in our everyday space, not in studios (2004: 57). However, space in Tryambakesh-war and Nasik is not everyday but divine space. The former is sacred,

Figure 1.3 Kaliya Mardan (1919, dir. D.G. Phalke). Phalke's use of special effects to show that the divine is dramatic can be seen in this image of Krishna being worshipped as he rises from the Yamuna.

marked by one of the twelve Jyotirlingas (forms marking the sacred places) of Shiva and the source of the River Godavari. Nasik contains Panchavati, where Rama, Sita and Lakshman lived during their exile in the forest. However, the space inbetween these two was the British military base of Deolali, a constant reminder of the colonial presence. This space was therefore marked as a place of myth, of colonialism and of the nationalist, *swadeshi* (the movement adopted by the Indian National Congress to boycott foreign goods) vision of Phalke himself.[41]

The audience

Before we can examine how the audience viewed these religious films, we need to place them in the wider context of film viewing during the silent period. One of the very few accounts we have is by J.B.H. Wadia (1977), who writes about cinema going in his memoirs. In Chapter 1, he describes how he and his school friends went to the cinemas every Saturday and Sunday, seeing around four or five films over the weekend. Their staples were Hollywood serials, westerns and slapstick comedies. They could not afford trams so they walked to cinemas in the periphery of Fort, Opera House and Charni Road Junction. Their cinemas ranged from the upmarket

Excelsior Theatre to Lohar Chawl where the Alexandra Cinema was a rough structure with a tin roof.

Wadia describes these cinemas as chaotic and overcrowded. The stalls were no more than wooden benches, while the balcony viewers were sprinkled with rosewater. Once the film began there was no silence, as there was the 'clapping, whistling and shouting of the excited audience in the cinema hall itself', and when the hero appeared, they shouted '*Dey dey – maar saaley ko!*' ('Go on, hit the bastard!'). There were intertitles for films, but all in English. Wadia writes: 'Those few fortunate ones who had a smattering of the language would read aloud and translate them in a Babel of their respective vernaculars for the benefit of those who did not know the common language of the British Empire.' Meanwhile the *pista-badamwallas* (nut-sellers) shouted out their goods during the film.

However, Wadia saw Indian films infrequently because, as an educated Parsi, 'I was still out of tune, more or less, with the Hindu way of life – in fact the overall Indian way of life' (1977: 26). He found the Indian social film full of male chauvinist ideology, citing Madan's *Pati bhakti* at the old Imperial Cinema. 'Patience Cooper (Jewish) was the heroine and Signora Minelli was other woman. Patience Cooper was the "adarsh abla", ideal Hindu wife. Cooper's words in subtitles to the effect "Please don't. He is my pati dev [husband like a god]."' 'The bathos of the melodramatic sequence was beyond my endurance'. However, he enjoyed Baburao Painter's film, saying, 'No anthology of the Indian film can be called complete if it did not include "Savkari Pash"' (Wadia 1997: 29).

As the other ICC interviewees, Wadia describes the audiences as being divided by class, with cinemas catering to specific audiences. For example, the Super Cinema, Charni Road Junction, owned by Seth Ruttansha Dorabji aka Bawaji and his brother Seth Rustomji (the Wellington brothers), even gave rosebuds to patrons. Bawaji wore a respectable Parsi long coat, black necktie and Parsi *pughri* (headdress). Patrons would always come to his films, even Parsis who were mostly not interested in film. Chinese men and women from the Red Light District at Playhouse and its unique White Lane also attended.

J.B.H. Wadia notes the aversion of the intelligentsia to films (1977: 75), and in particular the stunt films, 'derided at by clever film critics and discerning cinegoers' (1977: 78). Yet although he was from the elite Wadia family and highly educated, Wadia himself made mostly stunt films, while his brother Homi later made mythologicals (see below), thus going against the class and educational divides which seem to be so widely accepted:

> Money makes the mare go and I jumped on the obliging steed joyously and kept galloping for some years. In the process thereof I had forsworn whatever dreams I had secretly nurtured to reach 'the cloud-capped towers, the gorgeous palaces' in the realms of Socials and Musicals.

Lest I be misunderstood let me make it clear that I have enjoyed making stunt films as much as Socials, Mythologicals etc. Those who look down upon the Stunt film forget that it, too, has merits of its own. Its special attribute of providing Thrill and Suspense has been unhesitatingly appropriated by all types of film makers. A film maker worth his salt will not make a film if his heart is not in it. (Wadia 1977, Part 2, 1993–41: 2)

In the absence of other such eyewitness accounts we have to use other materials to retrieve some idea of what the audiences thought of early cinema. Film reviewing starts late (the *Times of India* begins reviewing films only with the coming of sound in the 1930s), the early papers and film magazines gave mostly press releases about the films as they feared critical reviews would lose them valuable advertising revenue. There are some advertisements and features about the industry but I have found few dating back to the silent period. For this period, the most valuable source is the ICC Report (RICC) and the accompanying Evidences (ICC I–V).

The audiences for the different genres were quite clearly segmented.[42] The cinemas each catered for specific audiences and showed different types of films with this intention. Since people largely lived in areas according to their race (European or Indian) and class, these divisions were fairly straightforward. For example, in Bombay the Fort area had cinemas for Europeans and educated Indians that show mostly foreign films; middle-class Indians go to cinemas in the Grant Road area while the lower-class audience goes to the cinemas in the mill areas.

The audience was also divided by religious group: 'Only Hindu audiences appreciate Indian pictures. Parsis, Muhammadans and Europeans and Anglo-Indians like foreign pictures' (ICC I: 123). Within these groups, Hindus preferred mythologicals while Muslims liked love and romance from Muslim and Persian sources and historicals about Muslim rulers (ICC I: 561). However, even a religious film attracted a wider audience for other reasons. Dorabji, the owner of the Wellington, notes (ICC I: 357) that in a film that showed the Exodus from Egypt, the parting of the Red Sea was very popular with the audience for many days, although eventually even its popularity wore off.

Gender was another divide as, although male and female Parsis went together to see mostly foreign films, fewer Muslims went to the cinema and among them, only men; while among Hindus, mostly men attended (ICC I: 560). Some see the audience as being divided by education, with the English-educated going to cinemas that show foreign films; whereas most of the educated classes, and some Europeans and Parsis, did not like to see a Hindu film relating to mythology as they preferred history and social dramas (ICC I: 17). The working classes preferred stunts, romance and comedy; while the 'illiterates' preferred mythologicals and folklore romances (ICC I: 24).

There were also important regional differences in taste, beyond the question of the language of intertitles, and styles of clothing. It was often mentioned that the mythological was more popular in Madras (ICC I: 865), whereas historicals, especially those which were about the Great Maratha, Shivaji, were much more popular in Bombay, where the mythological was only really popular at festival times (ICC I: 377). In the north, Muslims, who were known to object to depictions of their own prophets, demonstrated against the film *The moon of Israel* even though the film did not show Muslims. Films showing the Buddha in human form were often banned in Buddhist parts of South Asia, so *The light of Asia* was banned in Ceylon and also the Malay states. Some Hindus objected to scenes showing Krishna and the Gopis as these were felt to be inappropriate to modern sensibilities and should not be shown to the uneducated. Yet the summary in the Report (RICC: 34) says: 'These mythological films are less affected by provincial differences than the social dramas; they have an especial appeal for the uneducated people, and, if they are of good quality, they appeal to the deep-rooted religious instincts of all classes.'

There was little interest in Indian cinema from the elite (European and educated Indian) audiences, and Indian films were not reviewed in the English-language newspapers. However, Phalke must have thought he might attract some of the elite to his films for which he had a high rate of admission, by placing an advert for *Raja Harischandra* in the *Bombay Chronicle*, 3 May, 1913.[43] However, he thought it was still restricted as he says the film is 'Sure to appeal to our Hindu patrons.' It was screened at the Coronation Cinematograph and Variety Hall, Sandhurst Road, as part of a variety programme with 'Miss Irene Delmar, in a duet and dance; the McClements, Comical sketch and Alexandroff, the wonderful foot-juggler.' This does not suggest the overall effect of the screening was a pious occasion but part of a broader programme of entertainment.

We know that Phalke's films were phenomenally successful in India as this was reported in the Evidences (ICC III: 280, ICC I: 356) and that they were shown in Burma, Singapore and East Africa (ICC II: 874). As we saw above, *Raja Harischandra* ran for a record twenty-three days, while *Lanka dahan* was Phalke's most successful film. It was screened at West End Cinema, Girgaum, Bombay, where it was shown every hour from 7 a.m. to midnight to allow the crowds to see it and it collected Rs 32,000 in the first ten days (Dharap 1985: 38). There were similar reactions in Poona, where the crowd nearly broke down the doors, while in Madras the takings had to be carried in a bullock cart with police protection (Dharap 1985: 43).

J.B.H. Wadia writes in his memoir:

> [*Lanka dahan*] was tagged to an American feature film at the old
> West End Cinema of Seth Rustomji Dorabji Wellington situated just
> behind the Girgaum Police Court. The roadside and the compound
> of the cinema used to be chokeful with bullock carts in which devoted
> people from small towns and villages nearby – Bombay came to have
> a 'darshan' of their beloved gods, Shree Ram and Shree Hanuman.
>
> As a westernized Parsee youngster I had a hearty laugh at the sight
> of a muscular Seeta played by a male artiste (Salunke) as also the all-
> powerful tail of Shree Hanuman made of rope. But I was stunned by
> the spectacular burning of Lanka and the thrilling flight of Ram Bhakt
> in the sky with every shot of the divine flier becoming progressively
> smaller and smaller to heighten the effect of the sequence. (Wadia
> 1977: 25)

Phalke's films were clearly seen as both part of a religious experience and
a major attraction. His genius in special effects and his skill at storytelling
were enough to attract non-religious viewers, who could also enjoy the
awe and wonder of these skills and of seeing the chromolithographs move
and come to life. Yet Phalke never allows these attractions to distract
from the strong narrative line of his films, in which heroes and gods come
alive on the screen. His films, which he called nationalistic (*swadeshi*),
and his use of special effects created a new form of modernity around
religion, which reached an enormous audience and he is rightly called 'the
father of Indian cinema'.

The mythological after the silent film

It is said that the coming of sound led to a rapid decline in the number
of mythologicals, but a reading of the statistics (Gokarn n.d.: 83) shows
that the number of religious films does not change but that the number
of other genres made increases. In the silent period, mythologicals were
around 20 per cent of the silents made from 1913–34 (Dharap 1983: 80).
They were around 70 per cent until 1923 when they fell to around 15
per cent, rising towards the end of the silent period to 40 per cent total
output in 1931–3 (Dharap 1983: 80), falling to 22 per cent in 1935 and
then down to 10 per cent over the next four decades, to 3–9 per cent in
the 1970s (Gokarn n.d.: 82).

The silent films had found different audiences for different films (see
above), with the mythological being more popular in the south than elsewhere. However, apart from the Sanskritic *smarta* deities (Vishnu-Krishna,
Shiva, Durga, Ganesh and so on), many deities in India can be said to
be localised, so Skanda is not worshipped much in the north but, called

Murugan, he is one of the most popular deities in the south. Some deities had a more local following but have now spread, for example, Lord Venkateshwara of Tirupati in Andhra now has many devotees in the north.

Language was already an issue which divided audiences, even in the silent films by the choice of language for the intertitles, something much discussed in the ICC. Once the talkies begin, this makes the divide all the clearer as a Tamil film is not going to be a hit in the north unless it is dubbed. Even for an audience used to silent films and knowing the stories of the mythologicals, the style of music, of costume and so on always has marked regions and there has been little interest in films about other regions.[44] When Prabhat made bilingual films (see below), the late Mr A.V. Damle (son of one of the founders, V.G. Damle) told me that they used to change costumes for Hindi versions to look more north Indian. Bombay Talkies (whose predecessors made *The light of Asia*) had many Bengali personnel (Himanshu Rai, Devika Rani and later others) and created the first generic north Indian look, with little regional identity.

Nearly all the early talkies with a regional flavour, apart from the Hindi films, were mythologicals, devotionals or historicals. Telugu had *Bhakta Prahlad*, Tamil *Kalidas*, Marathi *Shyamsundar*, and Gujarati *Narsi Mehta*. The film language of Hindi/Urdu is largely taken from the Parsi theatre, the mythologicals showing a striking use of Sanskritic Hindi, while avoiding Persian/Urdu. (It is perhaps ironic that this style of Hindi that continues to be used by later mythologicals, which are mostly B-movies, is that promoted by the government and its official media such as Doordarshan – state television – and AIR – All India Radio, state radio.) Many later social films mock this style of speaking, such as *Chupke chupke* (1975, dir. Hrishikesh Mukherjee).

The makers of these talkies mostly made all genres, rather than special-ising in the mythological. Shantaram directed several mythologicals and devotionals at Prabhat before concentrating on social films. Some makers found that the communalism that was being mobilised by politicians in the 1930s made it hard for non-Hindus to make mythologicals, although several of the film makers (Wadia, Fattelal) and actors (Shahu Modak, Gohar) were non-Hindus. Even though Parsis were not involved in the communal problems, J.B.H. Wadia ran into trouble with his only mytho-logical, the 1934 film, *Vaman avatar*. He writes:

> In the first two decades of the Talkie Era, producers were often harassed by self styled protagonists of Hindu and Muslim culture. They had raised themselves to the stature of super-censors but more often than not it was just blackmail . . . . My first two talkies happened to be set in the backdrop of ancient Muslim history. Some orthodox Hindus in their anxiety to defend their ancient culture condemned me

as a Parsee who was not only pro-Muslim overtly but also pro-Pakistani covertly. Little did they know that I was a freedom fighter and selected by the Indian National Congress as one of the Congress Dictators during the second Civil Disobedience Movement .... . To prove my non-alignment I chose to make a Mythological as my third film. The ever-resourceful Joseph David had a story on Vaman Avtar in his handwritten books .... . But when the film was released in Super Cinema of Seth Ruttonsha Dorabji Wellington, affectionately known as 'Bawaji' I was simply flabbergasted to find opposition to my effort from some orthodox Hindus themselves.

The scriptured Bali had humiliated Indra and conquered Swarga by performing marathon yagnas. With the help of his great Guru Sukracharya he had become the lord of Trilok – Swarga, Mrityu and Paataal. He has been generally depicted as an evil entity, say, like Ravan. However, Dada and I had portrayed him as a virtuous Danava and not as an asura. Dada suggested we go and see the High Priest of the Bhuleshwar temple. He wouldn't see the film ... so I told the story. [He approved.]

Delhi – UP circuit .... . editor of Hindu newspaper started a virulent campaign against the film. [Vaman Avtar of Vishnu shouldn't be played by Parsee ... needed [someone] not only Hindu but Brahmin.]' (Wadia n.d.)

The first Marathi talkie, *Shyamsundar* (1932, dir. Bhalji Pendharkar) was probably such a novelty that it crossed linguistic and religious boundaries in Bombay. A review says, 'The singing of Balgandharva and Master Modak drives everyone – Hindu, Parsi, Muslim – crazy – whether they half understand Marathi or not.'[45]

Prabhat's early productions were mostly bilingual (Hindi and Marathi) as were those of New Theatres (Hindi and Bengali). Their first talkie was a version of the story of Harischandra, *Ayodhyache raja/Ayodhya ka raja* (1932, dir. V. Shantaram). Although this film is important as it is the oldest surviving talkie, it is rather dull, but it has all the technical qualities of a Prabhat film, with spectacles of processions of elephants, dances, an ornate palace and court, and music by Govindrao Tembe. Alongside Tembe and Durga Khote are Baburao Pendharkar and his stepbrother Master Vinayak, both of whom had long careers in Shantaram's films.

The second Prabhat talkie to come out that year, also directed by Shantaram, was the much more striking *Maya Machchindra*, again in Hindi and Marathi. This film, though a mythological, is set in the somewhat more remote (and somewhat confusing to this viewer) world of Nath yogis, the sect of which Shiva himself was the first yogi, Adinath, the second being Macchindrinath. Macchindrinath shows his disciple, Gorakhnath, that the world is *maya* (approximately 'illusion'), which allows for the showing of miracles such as beheading and restoration of the head. Far more spectacular are the wonderful sets and costumes of Fattelal showing this world of women who hate men. A spectacular set shows the queen in a room with a giant lion's head, whose jaws open to reveal a throne, while the floor has tigerskins and a real leopard wanders around in a most alarming manner. It is shot with a static camera, nearly all full shot, with no close-up or shot-reaction cuts, giving the film a very theatrical feel. The film seems to have little of the religious to it, being much more about spectacle than piety.

One review mentions that the Urdu diction is not very good,[46] while an advert in Gujarati (not one of the languages of the film) proclaims, 'Prabhat sinetonni sarvottam pauranik bolti philm: Maya Macchindra (Marathi). Uttam sangit! Uttam samvaad! Uttam abhinay!' ('Prabhat Cinetones' ultimate religious talkie: Maya Macchindra (Marathi). Best music! Best dialogue! Best acting!')[47]

Shantaram then directed another Hindi/Marathi film, Amritmanthan (1934), based on a Marathi novel by Narayan Hari Apte (1889–1971).[48] Although set in mythological times, the film has the political feel that was to become Shantaram's hallmark. Again it uses spectacle to great effect, once in the extreme close-up of the priest's eye and in the showing of the amritmanthan (the mythological story of the gods' churning of the ocean to extract nectar), where the special effects show a huge snake, Shesha, who appears to be using Mt Meru as the churning pole.[49] It was a huge hit, largely for the technical qualities of Prabhat that are by now clearly established.

THE QUESTION WHY?
HOW is it that Amrit Manthan which is now running for the 9th week, note that this is the 9th week the Krishna Talkies is drawing those very crowded houses which are generally expected at the first or at the most the second week of any good picture; as also the SECOND question WHY is that Prabhat's Indian Talkie Picture Amrit Manthan is being so enthusiastically patronised by that HIGH CLASS COSMOPOLITAN PUBLIC OF BOMBAY who attend only the English picture houses. Now these are the answers. (1) Prabhat's Amrit Manthan is drawing even after eight weeks run crowded houses as if it were just released because it is a picture that is SUPERBLY PRODUCED, DIRECTED AND ACTED. No wonder then that it has even after eight weeks continuous run kept up its popularity which is not at all diminishing even when the number of weeks is increasing with the flow of time. (2) The convincing reply to the question why is already given by such notables as – SIR AKBAR HYDARI, SIR PHIROZE SETHNA, SIR CHUNILAL MEHTA, and many others like them. And we have all proclaimed that AM is a very very NICE

picture which can safely be compared to any good western one. THEN
WHAT WONDER is it that even with increase in weeks, the popularity of AM is also on the increase? Miss not therefore to see this
super epic musical, Amrit Manthan, with the divinely delicious Shanta
Apte, and be convinced yourself.[50]

And:

IN THE STUDIOS – ON THE SCREEN
Amrit Manthan at the Krishna: The Western India Theatres Limited
are proud to announce that Prabhat's Amrit Manthan has now reached
the highest record figure, 15 weeks of continuous run, reached by any
picture (foreign or even Indian) released in Bombay during the last
two years on 1933 and 1934.[51]

And:

IN THE STUDIOS – ON THE SCREEN
Amrit Manthan, 16th week ... A visit to the Krishna shows that
Hindus, Parsis, Mahomedans, Jews, Christians and even Europeans
make a liberal rush to see Amrit Manthan.[52]

An advertisement for *Amritmanthan* says:

Amrit Manthan has been appreciated not only in India but all over
the world. The Illustrated London News – 'India is on the way to
becoming a serious competitor in the film-producing world, to judge
by these interesting photographs taken in the new establishment of
Prabhat Cinetone at Prabhatnagar, Poona, near Bombay ... claimed
to be the largest and the only self-contained studio in India, with high
reputation both among Indians and Europeans. As our illustrations
show, the studio is well equipped with modern technical apparatuses
while the skill of the Indian artist and craftsman shows to great advantage in the sculptural and architectural work. The examples illustrated
and the big set on the full page opposite, belong to a new picture on
the grand scale entitled Amrit Manthan. It is a drama of the Vedic
period.'[53]

The film had a silver jubilee (25-week run) and Prabhat's next film, also
directed by Shantaram, *Chandrasena* (Hindi, Marathi and Tamil), an
episode from the *Ramayana*, full of special effects, profited from this.

IN THE STUDIOS – ON THE SCREEN:
Chandra Sena at the Minerva: Prabhat's new mythological picture,
Chandra Sena, which was released at the Minerva Talkies Friday last

has been as was anticipated, a tremendous success. It is said that the box-office collections of the opening night have broken all records of any Indian or foreign picture so far released in Bombay. The Minerva has been drawing capacity houses at each show for the last eight days. From the popularity which the picture has achieved in its first week it may be safely predicted that it will enjoy a run of several weeks like Amrit Manthan. Nailini Turkhad does justice to her role as Chandra Sena. As the abducted maiden she is irresistible and sings songs that delight the audience ... a prominent feature of Chandra Sena is the novel type of orchestral music which serves as a delightful background. Another outstanding feature is the wonderful setting of patal lok.[54]

Other films seemed to be of more interest for their religious context and attracted interest from various Hindu leaders.

BOMBAY FILM DIARY: RADHIKA AT PATHÉ.
Leaders of the Hindu community, like Dr P. Varadarajulu Naidu, general secretary of the Hindu Mahasabha, Swami Sambudhananda of the Sri Ramkrishna Ashram, Mr N.V. Tampi, president of the theosophical society, Bombay, have given Radhika their unanimous opinion that it is a picture of a high order and higher ideals that every Hindu man as well as woman should make it a point to see. The president of the theosophical society remarks that the picture shows once again that to the truly pure in heart, no danger can ensue and that our surest and safest refuge in weal and woe is God. Swami Sambudhananda remarked that the central theme of the picture is the immortal teaching of Lord Krishna.[55]

Mythologicals as Indian heritage

One of the great makers of the mythologicals was Vijay Bhatt (1907–93)[56] who made films in Hindi, Marathi and Gujarati. He made Gujarati plays and stories into silent films, working with many companies. Trained by Ardeshir Irani of Imperial, he and his elder brother, Shankar Bhatt, the writer of Gujarati plays and later screenplays, founded their own silent film company, Royal Film Company. Vijay worked as a director with Kadar Studios then founded Prakash Pictures, later Prakash Studio (1933–71), in which Nanabhai Bhatt also worked. Prakash's motto was taken from Cardinal Newman: 'Lead kindly light', and they made around sixty-four films. They discovered many stars, including Jayant (Zakaria Khan, father of Amjad), Meena Kumari and the music director, Naushad. Prakash also made action films,[57] fantasies and an occasional social (*Poornima*, dir. Balwant Bhatt, 1938, by Ramanlal Vasantlal Desai, the famous Gujarati writer; *Hariyali aur raasta*, 1962), before moving into devotionals (see Chapter 2), and mythologicals. Bhatt's interest in Indian historical culture and history were seen in his films such as *Vikramaditya* (1945) for the two-thousandth anniversary of the Vikram Samvat (the major Indian calendar), starring Prithviraj Kapoor as the monarch who saved the nation. He made celebrated films about Indian musical culture, including *Baiju Bawra* (1952) and *Goonj uthi shehnai* (1959).

Two of Vijay Bhatt's films were mythologicals based on the *Ramayana*. The first was *Bharat Milap* (Hindi)/*Bharat Bhet* (Marathi) (1942), with titles and intertitles in Devanagari (Hindi and Marathi), English and Urdu. Much research went into the film, and the credits mention sources as both Maharshi Valmiki's *Ramayana* and Goswami Tulsidas' *Ramcharitmanas*.

Rama's brother, Prince Bharata (played by Shahu Modak), is celebrating his birthday in Ayodhya and an *aarti* (worship with lights) is performed. Rama (Prem Adib), Sita (Shobhana Samarth) and Lakshmana come to wish him a happy birthday. Rama's mother, Queen Kaushalya, gives him an image of Rama with which Bharata is thrilled. Queen Kaikeyi, Bharata's mother, is shown with King Dasharatha. Manthana, the wicked servant, encourages Queen Kaikeyi to be envious of the king's love for Rama, even though Bharata is such a devotee of Rama that the latter's image appears on his chest.

In a grand song sequence, a group sings, '*Aaya Raam Raajya*' ('Rama's rule has come'; 'Ram Rajya' was a term used by Gandhi for India restored to rightful rule) and lights spell out '*Aaya Raamraajya tyauhaar*' ('The festival of Rama's rule has come').

Queen Kaikeyi asks King Dasharatha for a boon. He agrees and she asks him to exile Rama for fourteen years. The crowd rebels against the king, but Rama says he has to follow his father's order and leave, he takes his leave of Ayodhya with sadness, going into the forest with Sita and Lakshman.

The great emotional moment of the film is the reunion of the brothers. Bharata is thinking about suicide, when Rama appears and saves him. Bharata returns to the kingdom where he puts Rama's shoes on a throne, and images of Sita and Rama appear on them. After the exile is over, Rama, Sita and Lakshman return with Hanuman leading. The three queens welcome them back while everyone sings, '*Raam Raam Raja Ram*' ('King Ram').

This is not a film with many miracles nor with swashbuckling heroism, but it is about the brothers' love for each other and the virtues of patience, endurance, forgiveness and loyalty. The emotion is very well handled and the image of gentle, righteous Rama is projected, rather than the angry warrior we have seen in recent years. The film was a huge success:

THIRD WEEK OF BHARAT MILAP – FILM BASED ON EPIC RAMAYANA PROVES IMMENSELY POPULAR.

Prakash's Bharat Milap that has taken Bombay cinegoers by storm now makes its triumphant entry into third week at Majestic. It is a gorgeous

Figure 1.4 Bharat Milap (1942, dir. Vijay Bhatt). Bharata takes Rama's sandals to keep on the throne to show he is king in absentia.

picture full of architectural grandeur and costumes of the days of the Epic Ramayana, as well as scenes depicting deepest love and fiercest jealousy. The picture depicts how Shree Ramchandra in the idol of Ayodhya and the beloved son of Raja Dasaratha, declining the offer of sovereignty willingly embraced banishment in the wilds for fourteen long years to honour his father's words to one of the junior queens. It shows also how Ramchandra's brother Bharata refuses the gift of throne out of his love and respect for Ramchandra and the traditions of the royal house of Raghu. The picture depicts also the graceful and gracious Seeta suffering ungrudgingly with her lord as a dutiful Hindu woman who finds joy in the pleasures of her husband, grief in his sorrows and unbounded sympathy in his predicaments, thus proving that for her, there is none greater than her lord. *Bharat Milap* has also a Marathi version entitled *Bharat Bhet*. The picture, which is a product of devoted study and strenuous labours, is directed by Vijay Bhatt who has carved a niche for himself in film-history.

[Advertisement] Prakash Pictures Divine Message to Humanity, Bharat Milap. A golden page from great epic Ramayana, a picture of ancient art and culture, a gorgeous picture that recaptures the glory of ancient days on screen, see at Majestic.[58]

It was premiered by Dr Radhakrishnan at the Majestic Cinema, who enjoyed the film. The guest of honour at the Calcutta premier was a minister, Dr B.C. Roy. The film had silver jubilees all over the country, attended by Dr K.M. Munshi and other dignitaries.

CRIPPS ASKED TO SEE BHARAT MILAP.
The last and current weeks have been particularly good for Bharat Milap in all the 30 stations it has been released. Hindus in North and South India have been celebrating the Jayantis of Ramchandra and Shri Hanuman and none who could has missed seeing the life of Ramchandra on the screen at Majestic Cinema in Bombay, all the shows have been crowded. Mr Bhadrakumar Yajnik, Publicity Officer of Prakash Pictures, who has produced BM has done well to invite Sir Stafford Cripps to find a little time to see this picture in Delhi at Moti Cinema, reminding him that it breathes the true spirit of Indian culture and telling him that such eminent Hindus as Dr Radhakrishnan, N.C. Kelkar and K.M. Munshi have liked the film very much.[59]

Vijay Bhatt's next film, *Ram Rajya* (1943), was also a Hindi Marathi bilingual. It takes up the story of *Ramayana* after the return from Lanka. Rama (Prem Adib) and Sita (Shobhana Samarth) are back on the throne but Rama hears a washerwoman ask how Rama knows Sita was faithful to him in Lanka. Rama sends her to Valmiki's ashram in the forest, where she gives birth to Luva and Kusha. Rama performs the vedic *ashwamedha* sacrifice, where a king sets a horse loose to wander for a year and, unless anyone challenges it, the land is the king's. Luva and Kusha stop the horse and Rama has to fight them. This is an episode from the *Ramayana* that some people nowadays find hard to digest but one that has particular resonances for women who have been brought under suspicion, even though they are innocent of any wrong-doing.

Picturpost mentions it ran for eighty-eight weeks, the longest in history;[60] it later ran in some cinemas for over 100 weeks. Vijay Bhatt was honoured by politicians and others, but the greatest honour this film received was that it was the only film that Gandhi ever saw. Gandhi's low opinion of cinema was recorded in the ICC:

Even if I was so minded, I should be unfit to answer your questionnaire, as I have never been to a cinema. But even to an outsider, the evil that it has done and is doing is patent. The good, if it has done any at all, remains to be proved.[61]

Figure 1.5 Ram Rajya (1943, dir. Vijay Bhatt). Cover of song booklet. 'The Kingdom of Ram' was a term used by Gandhi for the ideal Indian polity.

Figure 1.6 Ram Rajya (1943, dir. Vijay Bhatt). Shobhana Samarth as Sita.

However, when Gandhi was convalescing in 1945, Bhatt was asked to show him forty minutes of the film but he watched it for over an hour and a half.

Despite the fame these films brought Vijay Bhatt, when Prakash Pictures wanted to make a life of the Buddha there were objections in Sri Lanka where a meeting to discuss the idea was disturbed by protestors.[62] The writer says, 'We are not aware of even one film dealing with the Hindu gods that has been well portrayed as to reflect credit on Hinduism.'[63] The writer uses the word 'exploitation' several times in the article before admitting that Prakash's films are better than most, in that they are sincere, but that they are still not good films, which should be about 'plain-living and high-thinking'.

In 1947, Bhatt went to the US to show his films (*Bharat Milap, Ram Rajya* and *Vikramaditya*) and to see if he could find a co-producer for this film on the Buddha, which was written in English. However, it seems he had no luck as it was more than fifteen years later that Bhatt made a film on the Buddha, not on Gautama himself but on a convert, Angulimala ('The one who wears a garland of fingers'). Released in 1960, *Angulimala* was produced by the Thai Info Service for the 2500th anniversary of the Buddha's *mahaparinirvana* ('attainment of nirvana').[64] However, the film has hardly anything about Buddhism, concentrating instead on Angulimala's upbringing, his romance, how his 'friends' destroyed him, leading him to become a fearsome murderer before encountering the Buddha (shown as a lotus and then as a human figure, but in fragmented shots to distance him from the human world). The film shows Angulimala's conversion and his elevation to sainthood.

Independence and beyond

It is not the case that the mythological faded after independence as is the widely held view often voiced in the context of the phenomenal success of *Jai Santoshi Maa* in 1975 (see below). Gokarn's figures (Gokarn n.d.: 82–5) on religious films (her statistics combine the devotional and mythological) show that their numbers remain fairly standard as long as her figures run (up to 1982). However, some striking features can be noted. In the 1930s, the religious films formed a higher proportion of films produced, at their maximum in the last days of the silent movie, when they formed as much as 40 per cent of the annual output (1931–3). However, when the number of other films being made begins to increase, as sound allows the social and other more literary and verbal genres to flourish, the religious genre carries on being made in the same numbers, but is proportionately much lower. The figures of the number of religious films made in a year vary over the years from 1 to 4 on average with the occasional higher figure (maximum 11 in 1979). The only notable clusters are the higher numbers in 1953–57 (for no reason that I know, but maybe due to the search for myths for the new nation and pleas for communal harmony) and 1975–83 (which I would attribute to the success of *Jai Santoshi Maa*, were it not for the fact that 1975 itself saw an increase to 6 films after a decade averaging 2.4, that is before this film met its phenomenal success).

Gokarn's statistics end in 1982 and there is no other source available for the last two to three decades on the number of religious films made annually. However, these would not be comparable because we would have to factor into our accounts the phenomenal audiences for religious programmes on television, such as Ramanand Sagar's *Ramayana* and B.R. Chopra's *Mahabharata*, as well as the screening of religious films. We should also have very incomplete data on the rise of non-cinematic viewing (VHS, VCD and DVD), which only became possible during this time and is now a major part of any Indian film's distribution. I have a strong impression from viewing the stock in music shops in Mumbai and Pune and talking to sales staff, as well as viewing websites selling Indian films,[65] that these genres remain very popular and old films are constantly recycled but there are no hard statistics on numbers sold, audiences reached and piracy.

The religious films were in decline in the sense that few were major hits or made on large budgets, but they remain a staple of the B-circuit. However, the audience for these films is not necessarily downmarket as many of the films circulate through the Internet and are found in fairly upmarket shops (Alunkar in Pune; Rhythm House in Bombay), though admittedly richer sources are found in more downmarket shops (Grant Road, Lamington Road in Bombay). Religious films are also popular among the diaspora as can be seen in shops, Internet sites, the South Asian cable channels and my conversations with friends. The religious films have remained popular in 'regional' languages but, apart from a very brief discussion below, this lies outside my area of knowledge and the scope of this book.

Stars as gods, gods as stars

Some of the earlier stars were particularly associated with their mythological roles, so Shobhana Samarth was best remembered for her roles as Sita, and Shahu Modak for his Krishna (and there are many similar famous examples from devotional films, notably Vishnupant Pagnis, see Chapter 2). Other stars, like Durga Khote, acted in many major films from different genres and never came to be associated with their religious roles, and Bharat Bhushan was regarded as a safe bet for any kind of film, mythological, devotional or Muslim social. Perhaps one of the last figures in film to be associated with her roles in religious films was Nirupa Roy. Her films, even folktales like *Naag Panchami* (see below for more on 'snake films'), get good reviews in *Filmfare* as late as 1954.[66] This is a much-loved story set in Shankara's heaven, the snake queen's court, and an earthly court. The snake queen is angry when King Chandradhar and Queen Sanka (Durga Khote) will not worship her so she kills their six sons, giving them another, Lakshmendra, who is destined to die by snakebite on his wedding night. His bride Behula (Nirupa Roy) pleads with Shankara for his life.

Roy became regarded as a semi-divine figure, and she reports that when she goes out in public, people sing her *bhajans* and touch her feet.[67] Roy was particularly admired for her roles with Trilok Kapur as the divine couple. A photo caption of them in *Filmfare* says, 'He takes great pains to portray the Gods correctly' (whatever that means) and of her 'The halo that she dons for her work surrounds her with a serene glow off-screen too.'[68] His divine look was remarked on elsewhere: 'Trilok Kapur looks every inch Lord Vishnu.'[69]

In her later years, Nirupa Roy became most famous for playing Amitabh Bachchan's mother in the 1970s and 1980s. Many viewers, familiar with her divine role, may well have felt that this added to the view of him as a demi-god. (For more on stars and divinity, see Chapter 4).

Mythologicals as stunt movies

The mythological, always regarded as a downmarket genre, becomes firmly established in the B-movie circuit after independence.[70] While this seems largely due to the rise of the social genre (see Chapter 4), the mythologicals were made on lower budgets (often recycling sets and costumes), with B-grade actors and so on. Somehow the mythological in colour has what Christopher Pinney calls a 'sticky mutuality', where the involvement the viewer has with the image becomes less aesthetic, as the image looks newer, brighter and more cheerful (Pinney 2004: 156).

One of the leading exponents of this genre was Homi Wadia's Basant Pictures, which made around 152 films, most of them mythologicals, between 1942 and 1982 from its base in Chembur, Bombay. Some were directed by Homi, some by others including Babubhai Mistri. They made many grades of films among them some A-grade (including the old staple of Parsi theatre, *Hatim Tai*, 1956, dir. Homi Wadia) but many B- and even C-grade films. Homi kept costs down by recycling. For example, he had fifteen sets on *Hatim Tai*, but he then reused these for junior film-makers to film *The thief of Baghdad*.

J.B.H. Wadia founded Wadia Movietone in 1933 with his younger brother, Homi (1911–2004). Although they made versions of Parsi theatre classics (*Lal-e Yaman*, 1933, and *Baag-e Misr*, 1934), they were most famous for their stunt films, in particular those which Homi directed, starring Mary Evans, better known as 'Fearless Nadia', later his wife. Homi left Wadia in 1942 to start Basant Pictures when J.B.H. decided to focus on socials, documentary and newsreels. Wadia Movietone made just one mythological, *Vaman avtar* (1934), so it was surprising that Basant, in addition to the expected stunt films, was most famous for its mythological films. I assume that Homi made these films not for religious purposes (he was a Parsi, a humanist) and I guess he found the pictures amusing and awe-inspiring as did his brother, J.B.H. (see above). (Several other non-Hindus were active in making mythologicals, including Babubhai Mistry – see below – also a Parsi. Mistry also made mythologicals for other producers, including A.A. Nadiadwala, a Muslim.)

These films are more about trick camerawork (flying, changing shape and size, burning buildings and so on), stunts and wrestling, than about devotion. Devotion may appear in songs, and is coded in gesture and behaviour but it is definitely secondary to stunts and thrills.

Some of these films received quite a bit of press coverage and became box office hits, such as Basant's 1950 *Shri Ganesh Mahima*:

> LIFE OF SHREE GANESH:
> Basant pictures who have specialised in mythologicals in the past are now going to present the life of Shree Ganesh. Noted for the production of Shree Ram Bhakta Hanuman and the Life of Ghatotkach,

Basant Pictures have engaged a strong cast ... The lives of practic-
ally all the characters of Mahabharata have been screened but not
that of Ganesh, a god who is a household word in every Indian
home.[71]

Ganesh Mahima at two theatres next week: Ganesh Mahima is the
work of a team that has specialised in turning out mythologicals. The
story is not too literal transcription from the classics, and deals with
the great power that Ganesh is supposed to have held. Though
ostensibly about Ganesh, the film actually deals more with incidents
from the life of Krishna and the bulk of the footage is Krishna's
feverish attempts to clear himself of charges that have been falsely
laid at his door.[72]

Ganesh Mahima at three theatres: Shree Ganesh Mahima which is
now showing at Lamington, Kismet and Edward deals more with
Krishna than with the Ganesh of the title. The plot is based on the
old curse of Ganesh that anyone who looks at the moon on Ganesh
Chaturthi would fall prey to various forms of calumny. Poor Krishna
accidentally has a peek and is forthwith doomed to slander. The film
being a mythological one and Lord Krishna being what he is, every-
thing works out to everyone's satisfaction .... A few of the more
miraculous scenes are a little overdone but pleasant enough to the
hoipolloi.[73]

Ganesh Mahima a box office hit: Shree Ganesh Mahima topped
the list by breaking box office records of all pictures at the Kismet
Cinema. The picture is produced and directed by Homi Wadia.[74]

People say that mythologicals appeal only to a particular class of
audience, but the thousands that throng the Lamington and Kismet
to see Basant Pictures' Shre Ganesh Mahima prove that mythologicals have an all round appeal to every class and the reason for
this lies in the polished production, the deft direction by Homi Wadia
and the natural acting by Meenakumari, Mangala and Tripathi.

Wadia's next devotional: Basant Pictures creators Shree Ganesh
Mahima are due to release their next production Hanuman Patal Vijay
next week. Built around the devotion of Hanuman, the direction of
the film is by Homi Wadia, who within the rather limited confines
of the mythological form has managed to produce what is claimed
to be an entertaining picture.[75]

They sometimes had A-grade actors in the films. Meena Kumari appeared
in several of them, including their 1951 *Hanuman pataal vijay*, just a year
before her first huge hit, Vijay Bhatt's 1952 *Baiju Bawra*.

Wadia's new tale of Hanuman: Homi Wadia, producer of several
mythologicals in the past, is releasing his latest offering Hanuman

Patal Vijay this week. The film tells the story of the two demon brothers Ahi and Mahi who ruled over Patal and also shows the great devotion that Hanuman had for Ram. Meena Kumari is the star of the film and she is supported by SN Tripathi who plays the role of Hanuman.[76]

Nanabhai Bhatt (Mahesh Bhatt's father) worked in Basant Pictures for a short while before founding his own Deepak Pictures (1946). His speciality was lower-budget mythologicals than Vijay Bhatt (with whom he had worked earlier) made alongside Arabian Nights fantasies, with the use of dramatic special effects.

Another of the Basant team had a longer and more famous association with Vijay Bhatt, namely Babubhai Mistry (or Mistri) (1919–) from 1933–7. Mistry trained with Bhatt as a special effects director, then became a director and a cameraman. However, it was for his special effects that he remained most famous, in mythologicals and fantasies for Nanabhai Bhatt (*Khwab ki duniya*, 1937) and Basant (*Hatim Tai*). Mistry worked on Ellis Duncan's *Meera* (see Chapter 2) and directed many mythologicals himself, the most famous being 1961 *Sampoorna Ramayana*, and he was consultant for Ramanand Sagar's TV *Ramayana* (see below). However, computer-generated images saw the end of the need for his talents, which had stretched from the silent film, through the black and white era to the end of the century. He was honoured with the Kodak Trophy for Technical Excellence at MAMI 2005 for the sixty-three films he has made.

Mistry's *Sampoorna Ramayana* ('Complete Ramayan', 1961) was very popular, with its dazzling effects and its slightly strange style (Hanuman and his army sing '*Bolo sabhi jai Ram*'/'Everyone sing long live Rama', when building the bridge to Lanka but do so to a calypso tune). My efforts to obtain a copy on VCD met with bemusement about why I did not want a copy of Ramanand Sagar's television series, which was seen as 'better' and more technically proficient. As with oral tellings of the epics, the older films are eclipsed by 'better' versions.

Mistry's *Mahabali Hanuman* (1980) has many scenes that are very similar to those from the *Sampoorna Ramayana*. The film has very popular special effects, such as when Shabari, the 'Untouchable', sings a song that Ram is everywhere, then the flowers are shaken from the tree to form into the name of Ram. There are some dramatic special effects, of monsters changing form, Hanuman flying and changing size, and a river turning to blood, although they look rather dated.

Mistry also made a version of the *Mahabharata* in 1965, which has also been eclipsed by a television version, namely that of B.R. Chopra (see below). The film has Dara Singh as Bhima. (Dara Singh became a great B-movie star, his most famous roles being Tarzan, Hanuman and Bhima.) The episodes are very much as they are depicted on the standard chromolithographs, but the film has a surprise happy ending, the final scene showing Yuddhishthira on the throne while a verse from the *Bhagavad Gita* is recited.[77]

The VCD of Joy Films' *Bajrangbali* (1976, dir. Chandrakant[78]) has music by the giants of Hindi film, Kalyanji-Anandji. The cover shows the film's emphasis on action and special effects as it has pictures of a four-headed Ganesha with his trunk wrapped around a Hanuman with extra heads. The film has a well-known cast, mostly in B-movies by this time: Dara Singh, Premnath, Mehmood, Mausmi Chetterji [*sic*], Sahu [*sic*] Modak, Durga Khote, *et al.*

The movie has some very bad props and there are some disconcerting moments, such as Shiva and Parvati miming playback singing while flying through the air on a papier-mâché Nandi. Premnath, well-known as a villain in Hindi films, plays Ravana as a pantomime villain, with his catch-phrase '*Main Lankesh hun*' ('I am the king of Lanka') reiterated constantly. However, Hanuman himself is sympathetic, his devotion moving and he has a great sense of humour in part resulting from the juxtaposition of his animal and human qualities. His fights can verge on the slapstick and he uses his tail, always a popular special effect, in the film. He ties people up with it, grows it to several metres and sits on its coils as if on a throne that makes his position higher than Ravana's, and, when the Lankans set fire to his tail, he in turn sets fire to the palace. The film certainly carries religious sentiment, although for the neophyte perhaps it will remain strange as an online review shows:

> Bajrangbali: If you think Americans invented Superman, you've never seen a Hanuman film. This monkey god star of the epic Indian poem Ramayana has all the super hero moves without having to moonlight at the Daily Planet. Bajranbali is in color and the extra-special effects will compensate for the hard to assimilate myth. Do not watch this movie under the influence of mind altering drugs, it could prove fatal. Starring the incomparable Dara Singh 175 minute Unrated Hindi w/subtitles on DVD/VHS.[79]

So although the film is rather good the cover of the VCD shows a range of mythologicals (*Tulsi vivah*, *Hari darshan*, *Har Har Mahadev*, etc.) that are firmly part of the B-circuit, along with horror films (*Draculla*, *Chudail no 1*, *Shaitanon ka honeymoon*) and sex movies (*Drugs and AIDS*, *Sexy girl*, *Hello doctor*, etc.).

Jai Santoshi Maa: mythological as family drama

Jai Santoshi Maa was a surprise hit film in 1975. It was one of the three biggest hits of the year, alongside *Sholay* (dir. Ramesh Sippy) and *Deewaar* (dir. Yash Chopra), which starred the 'Angry Young Man', Amitabh Bachchan, securing his subsequent domination of the box office and god-like status. This film is a generic mixture of the mythological, devotional and the social in the manner of a *vratkatha* or story about a fast to propitiate a specific deity rather than a story from the Sanskrit repertoire. In this film, a young woman, Satyavati (Kanan Kaushal), is victimised and bullied by her in-laws and is helped by Santoshi Maa (Anita Guha), a mother goddess, and is finally restored to her husband (Ashish Kumar).[80]

It is often said that Santoshi Maa was a new or local goddess who became popular as a result of the film but there seem to be popular images of her from the 1960s by the well-known firm, Sharma Picture Publications (Pinney 2004: 154–5). Although there are *vratkathas* associated with Santoshi Maa, her origins are not clear. These Hindi and Marathi book versions are somewhat different, the more detailed Hindi version being more like the film, although with some major differences. Kusum Gokarn shows that the film is adapted from a prayer book, *Shri Santoshi Mata puja va vratakatha*, in Hindi, published by Vijaya Balwant Kaushik.[81] The book does not mention any persons or places, thus suggesting this is not necessarily a local goddess. In the film, of course, the characters are given names and these have religious implications. In the book the husband is lazy and does not work, whereas the film makes him a poet and singer, not just to

Figure 1.7 Jai Santoshi Maa (1975, dir. Vijay Sharma). Satyavati (Kanan Kaushal) pays her respects to the goddesses Brahmini, Lakshmi and Parvati.

raise his moral status, but also to give an excuse for more songs. His mother is a new figure in the film and the film loses Satyavati's son.

Santoshi Maa is not the daughter of Ganesh in the Hindi book as she is in the film. Gokarn mentions a Marathi version of the *vratkatha* in which she is an incarnation of Mahalaksmi but Ganesh seems to have been added as a popular figure. In the film, Lakshmi is a rival of Santoshi Maa, but Gokarn points out that the *vratkatha* does not give the names of the three jealous goddesses (Brahmani, Lakshmi and Parvati), nor does it have the curse to make a husband forget his wife, which allows the typical film device of the 'other woman'. Narada is also introduced in the film as a busybody; the *vrat* is cut from sixteen consecutive Fridays to twelve.

In the *vratkatha*, the children eat sour food and Santoshi Maa becomes angry with the family. However, the great denouement of the film is the *udyaapana* ceremony (final ritual after fast), when Satyavati invites her nieces and nephews for food. This becomes the occasion for an elaborate *garba* dance (round dance sacred to the mother goddess) in which the sisters-in-law put lemon in the *kheer* ('rice pudding') to spoil it, children die, the sisters say Satyavati poisoned them so Santoshi Maa appears, restores the children and deforms the sisters-in-law until Satyavati prays and they are restored, becoming devotees of Santoshi Maa themselves.

Although the film is set in some vaguely north Indian village in roughly contemporary time, the cult of Santoshi Maa has become strong in the cities, in particular for lower-middle-class women, for whom this is a fairly easy *vrat*, as it requires only the avoidance of sour foods and removes the need for intermediaries and large expenses.[82] The story of the goddess is also appealing to women as it takes up the popular theme of *saas-bahu* (mother-in-law and daughter-in-law), which has become a staple of television soap operas.

Although *Jai Santoshi Maa* was the biggest hit of its type it should be contextualised in a series of mother goddess films based on *vratkathas* which became popular from the 1960s onwards. Many of these were about localised village mother goddesses, 'Maa', or, further south, 'Amma' figures. Most of these films had many special effects, mostly involving trident-hurling but the *vratkatha*-type performances were more popular. Veena Das (1981) shows that *Jai Santoshi Maa* is a modern version of the goddess story, in which the goddess is not a form of *shakti* ('power') as she does not fight nor does she want anyone destroyed, but is a benevolent figure who only requires the suffering of a single devotee as her sacrifice. Satyavati is a *sati* figure, whose sacrifices and *vrats* ('fasts') force the goddess to intervene and fulfil her personal desires.[83]

The songs of *Jai Santoshi Maa* were a great success among college kids, for whom it became something of a cult film. The music by C. Arjun and lyrics by Kavi Pradeep made Usha Mangeshkar a star and even now many who were teenagers at the time of the release remember learning the songs and the dances for the *artis* (worship with lights). When I mention this book, many people launch into '*Main to aarti utaaru, Santoshi Maa ki*' ('I raise the lamps to Santoshi Maa'),[84] and this song is often sung in rituals today.

The film is still shown on television for festivals, such as the last day of Shravana (a month of the rainy season), so it is surprising that there were not more successful copycat films made after it. There were many attempts, often with the same cast (Ashish Kumar, Anita Guha), or with more glamorous stars (Padma Khanna) or even the veterans of the old mythologicals (Shahu Modak, Bharat Bhushan, Trilok Kapoor) but none of these worked. Vijay Sharma, the director of *Jai Santoshi Maa*, who had earlier directed *Rocky mera naam* ('I'm called Rocky'), described as 'most vulgar ... amateur and gross' (Dogra 1977), tried to repeat his success with *Mahapawan teerth yatra* (1975), *Jai Mahalaxmi Maa* (1976) and *Mahasati Naina Sundari* (1979), but none was a success.

Mythologicals as folktales

One genre which produced some popular films was that of the new folktale, whose story may have been made up for a film, featuring magic and popular religious belief rather than big mythologicals. The 1970s and 1980s saw some totally extraordinary horror films.[85] These were often (bad) copies of western films and had very basic special effects (certainly nothing as sophisticated as Phalke's). They copied films such as *The exorcist* (1973, dir. William Friedkin) or films about 'the living dead' (such as *The night of the living dead*, 1968, dir. George A. Romero) with some concessions made to Indian religion such as brandishing an 'Om' symbol rather than a cross, but the religious imagery is highly eclectic at best. The great figures were the Ramsay brothers, Tulsi and Shyam, whose films such as *Bandh darwaza* (1990) have become cult classics. Others such as Mohan Bhakhri added a lot more sex to the horror, in films such as *Khooni mahel* (1987). Although few horror films were made during the 1990s, the last few years have seen A-movie makers such as Ram Gopal Varma experimenting with the genre in a more sophisticated manner, blending it with the ghost story (2002, *Bhoot*; 2004, *Vaastu Shastra*). These are less gothic than the ghost stories of Kamal Amrohi (*Mahal*, 1949) or Bimal Roy (*Madhumati*, 1958) – the latter having a reincarnation theme.

One popular group among these films was 'snake films' in which the hero and/or the heroine is a snake who takes on human form.[86] Snakes are not evil figures in Indian mythology but are auspicious and must be worshipped, especially on festivals such as Naag Panchami. The worship of snakes is a long-established part of forms of Hindu practices. Although these would seem to be B-movies, appealing to unsophisticated audiences, the star casts and financial success suggest a more diverse audience. However, the low status of these popular films is underlined by the fact that *An encyclopaedia of Indian cinema* (Rajadhyaksha and Willemen 1999) lists over fifty films with '*naag*' and related 'snake' words in their titles but discusses only two, the Kannada film *Nagakannika* (1949, dir. G. Vishwanathan), only because it is a folklore film on the lines of the Telugu *Patala Bhairavi* (see below), and *Nagin* (1954, dir. Nandlal Jaswantlal).

Filmistan's *Nagin* was southern superstar Vyjayanthimala's debut in Hindi films, in which she went on to become a major heroine. This film set the style for the erotic, slithery snake dance, with her hit song, '*Tan dole, mere man dole*' ('My mind and body sway'). Another south Indian star, Sri Devi, played a Nagin in *Nagina* (1986, dir. Harmesh Malhotra), which launched her into superstardom in the north. Although Amrish Puri puts in a strong performance as a villainous Yogi and snake-charmer who fights with a trident, the film is best remembered for the moments when Sri Devi becomes a semi-Nagin (she also turns into a snake at other times). The transformation is marked by her blue-green contact lenses and her wiggling dances, especially that of the hit song '*Main teri dushman*' ('I'm your enemy').[87]

Rajkumar Kohli's *Nagin* (1976), which was a box office success, has an all-star cast (Sunil Dutt, Feroz Khan, Jeetendra, Vinod Mehra, Kabir Bedi, Sanjay Khan, Reena Roy and Rekha) and music by composers, Laxmikant-Pyarelal, which takes it into the top class of movies despite the B-movie theme. The film combines the supernatural theme of snakes who come out on *amavas* (new moon nights) with revenge. The Nag (Jeetendra) is killed, which means that his wife (Reena Roy), the Nagin, will kill all involved in his murder. Most of this cast got together again for *Jaani Dushman* (1979, Rajkumar Kohli), in which one of Hindi cinema's great actors, Sanjeev Kumar, played a werewolf, not a creature to have featured previously in the Indian imagination.

Mythological films beyond Bombay

Although I made it clear in the introduction that I make no claims to being encyclopaedic in my discussions of the Hindi film, let alone any other cinemas, I must mention some other traditions in passing. I begin with two language traditions I know before touching on two of the largest cinema industries in India.

Early Bombay cinema was very much dominated by a Gujarati ethos in that many of its makers were Gujarati-speakers (Hindus, Parsis and Muslims), as were many stars and others involved in the process. Further- more, the intertitles were usually in Gujarati alongside other languages and the look was often Gujarati (Mehta 1993). However, the coming of sound meant that Gujarati cinema largely came to be produced and consumed in what is now Gujarat state, with few Gujarati films screened in Bombay where Gujarati-speakers formed the second largest minority after the Marathi-speakers. It appears that Gujarati audiences in Bombay switched to Hindi films as soon as sound came, although Gujarati urban theatre continues to thrive until the present.[88] Gujarati films are mostly regarded as B-movies,[89] so it is not surprising that the dominant genres are those which are regarded as belonging to this circuit, notably folk-tales, in particular, versions of Jesal and Toral, and stories of local gods and goddesses (Tripathi 1985). This group would include *Ranak Devi* (1946, dir. V.M. Vyas), Nirupa Roy's first film, a semi-historical based on the life of a queen of Junagadh who became a *sati* and has a temple in Wadhvan. Following the massive success of *Jai Santoshi Maa* and other goddess mythologicals in the late 1970s, a Gujarati film was made about the Gujarati goddess, *Jai Bahuchar Maa* (1980, dir. Ramkumar Bohra), the patron goddess of hijras. *Har Har Mahadev* (1983, dir. Girish Manukant) is one of the most popular and famous mythologicals, based on the story of the *Kumarasambhava* ('The birth of the war god'), which was made several times in Hindi. The gods, needing a warrior to fight the demons, decide Parvati and Shiva should have a son, but Shiva is a celibate ascetic. When they send Kama, the god of love, to fire his flowery arrows at Shiva, he is burnt to ashes by Shiva's third eye and Parvati has to perform *tapas* (penance) to seduce Shiva. Riding on the wave of video distribution in the early to mid 1980s, this film was widely seen amongst the British-Gujarati community.[90] These films combine elements of the Hindi film, Gujarati urban theatre and folk traditions as well as several particularly Gujarati dance forms such as the *garba* (a round dance) and *dandia* (a stick dance).

The only Sanskrit film I have seen is *Adi Shankaracharya* (1984, dir. G.V. Iyer), a government-sponsored film (by the National Film Development Corporation) that won the President's Gold Medal and many other national awards. The film is a biography of the founder of Advaita philosophy, Shankaracharya, who travels around India conducting debates as is traditional for *acharyas* (teachers, founders of religious sects). He is accompanied by two characters, Prajnana ('knowledge') and Mrityu ('death'). There are many Sanskrit quotes from the ancient sacred texts, notably the *Upanishads*, the *Brahma Sutras* and the *Bhagavad Gita*, on which, as is required for *acharyas*,[91] Shankaracharya wrote commentaries to found his school of Advaita.

One of the most memorable sequences is the opening shot of five performing the *sandhyavandanam* (twilight prayers), reciting what becomes the theme of the film: *akaashaat patitam toyam, sagaram prati gacchati* ('Water fallen from the sky returns to the ocean'), a metaphor for

Shankaracharya's philosophy of the relationship between the *atman* (individual soul) and Brahman. I also enjoyed the play within the film based on one of the chief *Upanishads*, the *Kathopanishad*, in which Nachiketa debates the meaning of death with Yama, the god of death. The classical music by the great Balamuralikrishna contributes much to the film.

This film is not quite a mythological, in that Shankaracharya is a historical figure, but it is not a devotional as it is about philosophy. However, it deserves mention not least as a film about an early form of Indian religion but also because Iyer's achievement is remarkable in that he managed to make an engaging film about philosophy and in Sanskrit, a seeming impossibility.

Even the ICC mentions that mythologicals are more popular in south India than they are in any other region (see above), so it is not surprising that the mythologicals dominated the Tamil film industry in the 1930s (although it is reported that socials such as those with Gohar and Sulochana were also successful),[92] with some companies, such as the East India Film Company, focusing on mythological productions.[93] However, the number drops rapidly during the 1940s and is said to almost disappear by the 1950s.[94] This may be due to the rise of the DMK (Dravida Munnettra Kazhagam – a Tamil nationalist political party), anti-religious, anti-Brahminical and anti-north India. Many movie personnel were associated with the DMK (and indeed went on to be Chief Ministers of Tamil Nadu), which influenced films such as *Parasakthi* (1952, dir. Krishnan-Panju),[95] a film which met severe censorship for its temple scene. An anti-religious stance has never been followed in north India.

It seems that this view, like that of the history of the mythological in Hindi cinema, is somewhat distorted. Even during the height of the DMK's involvement with cinema, religious films continued to have some success, with many viewers reading DMK films as being about Tamil identity rather than as anti-religion (Baskaran 1996: 33). Mother goddess films have remained popular, though again perhaps not on the A-circuit, as can be seen in any music shop selling Tamil DVDs and VCDs.

The Telugu film industry has made many hugely successful mythologicals (Arudra 1984). It had a one-man mythological industry based around the actor, Nandamuri Taraka Rama Rao (1923–96),[96] better known as NTR, who acted in so many mythologicals (forty-two in total, of which twenty-three were stories from the *Mahabharata* and eight from the *Ramayana*) that it seems that these were the only roles he played; he became imbued with a god-like status. However, he also played emperors, kings and folkloric heroes, making a film every six weeks on average. He was already a star when he took his first divine role in his thirtieth film, namely that of Krishna in *Maya bazaar* (1957, dir. K.V. Reddy). This became one of his more famous roles, along with Rama, which he played first in the *Sampoorna Ramanayanam* (1958, dir. K. Somu), made in

Tamil then dubbed into Telugu. However, his biggest role was as Lord Venkateshwar of Tirupati[97] in *Sri Venkateswara Mahatmyam*, Lord of Seven Hills (1960, dir. P. Pulliah), in which as an incarnation of the deity, he emerges from the idol and walks towards the audience. He played this role and other incarnations of Krishna/Vishnu in seventeen films.

As in Tamil Nadu, the film industry is very closely associated with politics, and NTR founded the Telugu Desam Party in 1982 and was later Chief Minister of Andhra Pradesh. From the 1940s to the 1960s, Telugu also had a popular genre of folklore films, which are perhaps regarded as localised mythologicals (Srinivas 2001). NTR was also a star of this genre, and indeed this genre helped make him a star, as Srinivas (2001) shows in his discussion of *Patala Bhairavi* (1951, dir. K.V. Reddy).

Mother goddess films have always been popular in south India, in both Tamil and Telugu. However, *Ammoru* (1995, dir. Kodi Ramakrishna) was the biggest hit of the year in Telugu. It seems its success was largely due to its special effects of morphing and so on, on which a British company, Digitalia, worked for two years. These are much more sophisticated than the flying tridents of traditional goddess movies (though there is one here too), showing instead the monolithic image of the goddess turning into a human astride a tiger, then sending out fire and other forces from her body. However, the film also has a strong story, which is similar in some ways to *Jai Santoshi Maa*, in that it is about a village woman's conflict with her in-laws. She is helped by the mother goddess (Ammoru), and the film has the feeling of a *vratkatha* and social drama. Here, however, the in-laws are involved in tantric magic and the goddess appears as a child servant to help the heroine, Bhawani. The film was dubbed into Tamil as *Amman*, where it was also a major box office success.

Mythologicals as television soap operas

In the late 1980s, when the Indian government relaxed its restrictions on the depiction of religion on television, the mythological had a phenomenal success in the new form of religious soaps. The first major epic, Ramanand Sagar's *Ramayana*, was broadcast in January 1987 and ran for seventy-four episodes. It was soon followed by B.R. Chopra's *Mahabharata*, which had ninety-four episodes and broke all viewing statistics with its audience penetration. Anecdotes abound about national shutdown during the screenings of these programmes; I have my own recollections of waiting at Baroda railway station for almost an hour after a thirty-six hour train journey as all the *ricksha-walas* were watching the *Mahabharata*.

Without wishing to enter debates over the comparisons of film and television and the interaction between the two, the striking difference that is relevant for the present analysis is that these television serials, although they drew on many film conventions (indeed Sagar and Chopra were both famous film directors for many decades), were received by their audiences in a very different way than cinema audiences had ever viewed the mythological film. Among the striking new features was the national viewing at a particular time in the week that created a different audience. The viewing practices themselves were highly disparate – from the private or family viewing in domestic rather than public space, to the public screenings held in areas such as villages where televisions were unaffordable commodities. The transformation of the viewing space into a sacred space was widely noted, as religious ceremonies were performed around the television sets as if the deities themselves were present on screen. In many ways, one may say that the television mythologicals, through the very nature of their medium and the popularity of the programmes across social and even religious groups,[98] succeeded in achieving what the film mythologicals had been trying to accomplish for eighty years with only a limited degree of success.

The simultaneous viewing meant that audiences discussed the meanings of the epics again, creating new interpretative communities, and the simultaneous viewing of the national epics also created a sense of a shared historical (more accurately, mythological) past at a time when the nation was undergoing some of the most rapid and dramatic changes in its history. However, the serials' conflations of existing beliefs about Hindus, and India, history and myth, had enormous political implications, as did the screening of visions of political and familial discussions in the context of Hindu utopias or moral universes, sponsored by state television.

While not many would hold that the screening of the *Ramayana* was the cause of the rise of Hindutva and the destruction of the Babri Masjid, a mosque said to be built on the *Ramjanmabhumi* (birth place of Rama), many people regard these serials as Hindutva (Hindu nationalist) propaganda. Even this is an exaggeration, as there is nothing inherently Hindutva in these series[99] and Rama does not belong to the BJP (Bharatiya Janta Party) or any political or cultural group. A more balanced view is that the Hindutva forces, already rising on the tide of liberalisation and who had made a canny assessment of the media and its power, drew on the symbols that were circulated in this series for their campaign.[100] B.R. Chopra's *Mahabharata* has aroused less controversy as it was presented as much more of a historical epic than a devotional film and was never directly associated with any political campaigns.[101]

Little has been said about the creation of a new Hindu visual regime in terms of religious practice and belief following these serials, and the spate of subsequent television soaps and growth of religious channels, but perhaps this requires a longer time frame.

Mythological films today

It may be expected that the arrival of VHS in the 1980s and the decline of cinema-going may have encouraged the making of more specialised B-movies which could have only a video release, as exemplified by Peter Manuel's research (Manuel 1993) on the impact of the cassette culture of the 1980s on music genres, when technology allowed the new medium to change the way music was marketed, consumed, etc. Similar changes might be expected with the mushrooming of cable and satellite television in the 1990s and then the relatively inexpensive VCD in recent years.

Even with the advent of television mythological soaps, the genre survives on the B-movie circuit. Suketu Mehta's book on Bombay sensitively tells the story of Eishaan, an aspiring actor who finally found work in *Jay Shakumbhari Maa*, a film about the Vegetable Goddess, one of the incarnations of Durga (Mehta 2005: 393–406). This goddess appears when there is famine to provide food, and her tears water the land. At the time of the film, there was a vegetable shortage causing political upheaval but even this was not enough to make the film, another family conflict in the style of *Jai Santoshi Maa*, appeal to a wider audience.

The film was made on a low budget (Rs 40 lakhs, or approximately £50,000) in appalling working conditions – the crew and actors were half-starved, and ironically had no vegetables to eat except potatoes. Dara Singh, who is a great star of the B-movies, came on the sets for a day to play a saint who worships the goddess. The film was shot on 16 mm and blown-up, and the producers expected to release it only in villages. They had some religious motivation in making the film in that they were involved with an ashram, but the director was more used to shooting sex films.

Mehta attended a preview screening where he found the film hilarious and high camp but was taken aback that he was the only one in the audience to have this response. When he told others about this experience, they too expressed their reverence for a religious film, even if it is a 'mythological sex comedy'.

The Hindi film has not produced any blockbuster mythologicals in recent years, certainly nothing on the lines of *Ammoru*, but discussions I have had with some senior producers suggest that following the success of historicals in the west it is time for a new Indian epic.

The mythological film as a much-maligned genre

Many people look down on mythological films and despair of the audiences' taste, such as Satish Bahadur, a well-known film critic and professor at the Film and Television Institute of India, Pune:

> [beginning with Ravi Varma] who conceived the Hindu pantheon in the lowest sentimental values of Victorian painting and popularised

it in cheap reproductions through another mass medium, the colour printing press. For dramatics, Phalke drew upon the crude elements of the 'Company Natak' not the glories of classical Sanskrit drama or the vital forms of the folk theatre. For story material, Phalke did not delve deep into the spiritual meaning underlying the Hindu epics. Rather he used their most obvious ritualistic and superficial level, viz. the magical, the miraculous and the spectacular in the exploits of the Hindu Gods and goddesses (Bahadur 1976: 91–2).

Some of these films, notably the variety that opt for the cultural heritage and historical style, such as the films made by Vijay Bhatt and Prakash Studios, are praised by film critics:

> Rambaan, Vijay Bhatt's latest creation: The golden pages from the epic of Valmiki's Ramayan form the basis of Mr Vijay Bhatt's another great hit, Rambaan. In these days of cheap trading of religious productions, it is indeed a difficult task to offer a picture which faithfully portrays the events and scenes of the immortal works of Valmiki. It is however confidently prognosticated that the picture under the hall mark of Prakash Pictures will prove worthy of its past achievements. The story of Rambaan centres around the episodes originally based on Aranyakand to Lankakand of Ramayana. Art director Kanu Desai is responsible for the outstanding highlights.[102]
>
> Rambaan, Vijay Bhatt's fine mythological: One more picture based on the immortal epic of Ramayan which has been a perennial source of inspiration to all mankind for noble living ... The film includes incidents like Rama's and Seeta's exile in Panchvati, the kidnapping of Seeta by Ravan, the march on Lanka (Ceylon), the death of Ravan and the triumphal return of Rama, Seeta and Lakshman to Ayodhya.[103]
>
> Premiere of Rambaan ... Prakash appears to have spared neither pains nor money to translate to the silver screen, in all the exquisite emotional contents underlying the incidents, the glorious episodes related in Valmiki's epic poem. Director Vijay Bhatt has very delicately handled the scenes so as to emphasise the full significance of the film. Big mob scenes, huge armies marching and fighting, serve as a foil to the delightful sylvan atmosphere of Panchvati. Ashok Vatika and Golden Lanka are a treat to the eyes. Prem Adib as Rama, Shobhana Samarth as Seeta and Umakant as Lakshman give excellent performances.[104]

Other films come in for criticism for their low aesthetics, such as *Valmiki* (1947, dir. Bhalji Pendharkar):

> For Valmiki, Prabhakar Pictures, have ransacked the ever-obliging pages of mythology to conjure up a fitting co-starring vehicle for

Shanta Apte and Prithviraj, both a little past their prime. The film is of course encumbered with all the trappings of mythology including paper crowns and false trinkets. Raj Kapoor, Pratima Devi, Leela and Baburao Pendharkar frolic through this carnival under the pilotship of Bhal Pendharkar. For escapists![105]

(Other critics enjoyed this film more, praising it for its human viewpoint and the presentation of the whole *Ramayana* in about 400 feet of film.[106])

Gokarn (n.d.) discusses the social stratification of the audiences for the mythological film, although this seems to be based on her general observations and 'common sense' rather than any ethnographic research. Gokarn argues that mythologicals are 'Not taken seriously by elite intelligentsia of upper middle class society and the youngsters of school and college going age, especially the western educated' (Gokarn n.d.: 102). Many of these films have cult status, such as *Jai Santoshi Maa*. I have noticed that many British Asians have grown up watching these films, often regarding them as kitsch or camp, but nevertheless enjoying them and learning about their 'religious heritage' through them.

Gokarn then says that these films are aimed at the lower middle class of smaller townships and rural masses:

> who are still overshadowed by the dark veil of ignorance and illiteracy. Thus they fall an easy prey to the film-makers' cinematic gimmicks of titillating glamour and thrilling spectacles. Moreover, these masses have still not been able to shake off the strong stamp of blind faith, orthodoxy and superstition. They have yet to be awakened from their traditional mode of thinking and their God-fearing attitude towards an unknown and unfathomable Divinity. They are further misguided by fraudulent gurus and god-men. The latter are more concerned with self-aggrandisement than the enlightenment of the gullible masses (Gokarn n.d.: 102).

No doubt part of the reason these films are held in low regard is their popularity among women:

> DRAUPADI DRAWS UNENDING CROWDS AT ROXY AND IMPERIAL, BY TVP – An easily noticeable feature of the crowds thronging to see Draupadi is the presence of women of all classes. They seem to think that Draupadi is their special subject. It so happened the other day that my seat was practically surrounded by lady witnesses on all sides and I could notice their reactions to various scenes with peculiar advantage. Their admiration of Sushila Rani in her various moods in the different scenes of Draupadi was obvious. But what impressed me most was their frank remarks in condemnation of courtiers of the

durbar of Dhritarashtra when Draupadi appeals to Gandhari, the mother of the Kauravas, for justice. Draupadi has a special reason to do so. Because in an earlier scene she had laid her heart bare to Gandhari and told her that she saw a dark future as a result of the gambling which was advertised by Shakuni as merely for amusement and Gandhari had assured her that she would protect her all through and that she should make her completely at home in her Hastinapur sojourn. Gandhari is helpless and in a rage she throws up her bangles and asks all her warrior courtiers to wear them if they cannot give the protection that Draupadi demanded. The pathos and drama in this incident in the picture is most impressive.[107]

The enduring popularity of the mythological

Myth itself has enduring popularity. As Wendy Doniger has reminded us throughout her work, film is also a creator of myth itself. These myths survive not because they are historically true or false but because they are held to be true in popular traditions. The cinema may not present the orthodox versions of the myths but it presents popularly held beliefs, the episodes people like to turn to for fundamental stories which can be applied to their daily lives, in a manner which is easy to follow as it may be in the style of other popular genres such as television serials. Thus many family problems are likened to the *Ramayana*, a motif which appears frequently in the social film in an allegorical form, but which is shown directly in the mythological film. These myths answer life's major questions and give us stories to live by as much as stories we spin ourselves through psychoanalysis or whatever other means we choose. One does not have to believe in the stories any more than Freud believed in the Greek myths (Oedipus and others) he used to tell his own stories for our times, or we may not believe in Spiderman, though we may believe that there is a hero inside us who can fight against injustice.

These myths also contain deep-seated and spiritual ideals of golden ages which many people hope they can bring about again, whether a Jerusalem in England or a *Ram Rajya* in India. Many of these myths are regarded as not only religious in value but also as part of India's cultural heritage. This would certainly be true of the *Mahabharata*, which is a foundational text of the Indian nation, its stories known to non-Hindus. However, mythological films are loved also because they are religious – and the pleasures of religion can be mapped.

There are clearly many parallels between cinema-going and religious experiences (see Introduction). The mythological film directly combines entertainment with religious purpose. While the medium of cinema requires the mythological characters to be presented as rounded human characters and their actions need to be explained logically, there is no problem for many people in seeing things that defy rationality, such as miracles. Many people (not just in India but also in the west) believe in miracles, but this has always been a stick with which to beat the Indian religious film. When religion tries to explain miracles scientifically, it risks losing its sense of awe and mystery at the divine. Many viewers enjoy the awe and astonishment created by these special effects (see J.B.H. Wadia on *Lanka dahan* above) and technology has always had a great appeal in attracting cinema audiences.

The relation of the audience to the screen gods and goddesses may be explained through *darshan* and corpothetics (see above) but one must add to the usual mechanisms of character involvement and the love that one may develop for screen characters, the *bhakti* or devotional love (see Chapter 2), that the viewer already brings to the viewing. Indeed, one of the great pleasures of mythologicals is seeing one's imagined myths and gods on screen. One may have seen them on chromolithographs but there they are two-dimensional and static, or one may have seen them enacted in popular performances but perhaps amateurishly or from a distance and only from one angle. However, film brings the characters to life, projecting them onto a screen and allowing us close-ups and different angles. Film also allows idealisation in that the makers can choose beautiful people and shoot them to look more beautiful; locations can be elaborate or exquisite; and the songs by major composers are sung by the country's best singers.

While it seems that the majority of the audiences for the mythological films were Hindus, the films have been watched by members of other religious communities. Mankekar (2002) notes that the television version of the *Mahabharata* attracted many Muslim and Sikh viewers. These audiences may have been attracted initially by curiosity about the serial's immense popularity but they continued to watch it as they formed their own interpretations of the stories, often drawn from their readings of other television serials.

Another of the great pleasures of the mythological film is closely allied to that of the Indian film's melodramatic mode, namely that we are in a moral universe, where the world is ultimately a safe place, righteousness rewarded and wickedness punished. One can enjoy the pleasures of the cinema, and the mythological in particular, without giving up – indeed by reinforcing – orthodox moral principles such as devotion to gods, respect for elders, love for your country, a wife's devotion to her husband. One can also enjoy the otherwise taboo in the guise of the mythological:

> Ironically the only nude sequence in an Indian film was filmed on Sakinabai in a mythological film 'Sati Anasuya' way back in the twenties. Recently, a widely published still from 'Har Har Mahadev' showed Padma Khanna and Gopi Krishna performing some kind of a sexual

circus. The secular deeds of our gods, like making away with the clothes of bathing women, can provide profitable material for Indian mythological film-makers. In fact, it was this particular episode which inspired Raj Kapoor to film that super-hit number of 'Sangam' 'Bol Radha bol'.[108]

As noted above, I have long felt that nationalism has been overdetermined as part of the viewing of Indian cinema, perhaps to give the film some kind of validity, to take it seriously. I am not denying that films are in part about nationalism[109] and 'Indian-ness', and that in recent years they have incorporated the issue of the diasporic Indian (see Chapter 4), but this is just one of many themes that run through these films. There is no doubt that the mythological, in particular during the colonial period, fits in neatly as an allegory of the present, often with a view to avoiding colonial censorship:

> MYTHOLOGICAL ALLEGORY, BY SARDI – Unity Production's Kuruk-shetra is a purely intellectual approach to mythology. It presents a modern allegory, in mythological guise by depicting the similarity between present times when our country is in the throes of political change, faced with famine and sunk in lethargy, and the days of the Pandavas and Kauravas when the cousins fought against one another but in the face of a common foe united together. The treatment of this allegory is novel. The actress becomes so engrossed in her role that following a sad event which opens her eyes to Bengal's starving peasantry, she is inspired with the spirit of Draupadi to serve suffering humanity.[110]

Many thought the popularity of mythologicals could be explained largely as strategies for avoiding censors' cuts, and that they would no longer be popular in independent India:

> SENSE AND CENSORSHIP, FREEDOM OPENS NEW ERA FOR OUR FILMS, BY SARDI.
> With the dawn of freedom, our films enter a new era of which sense-less political censorship will not, we hope, be a part. There was a time, not so long ago, when the uneasy conscience of the foreign government led it to cut out even harmless scenes which merely showed portraits of our political leaders such as GANDHIJI and NEHRU!!!! It must be said to the credit of our producers that despite the hand-icap of censorship, many of them still managed to infuse into their pictures the idea of freedom and its worth. Historical and mytho-logical screen figures particularly were made eloquent mouthpieces for delivering the message of freedom, albeit in a veiled manner. Today

there is no need for us to gloss over facts. While I do not advocate the digging up of old grievances, it is only right that the freedom struggle just ended should find its due place on the screen, not so as to exacerbate the feelings of those who till yesterday were on the other side of the fence, but merely to present facts as they occurred, not necessarily by themselves but woven into the fabric of a film story ... For a time, let us permit the gods and goddesses of mythology to take a well-deserved rest from the screen, and let us pay homage to the valiant men who only recently fought each in his own way to keep the fires of freedom aglow.[111]

This turned out not to be the case, in that the mythological did not disappear, nor did censorship. Mythologicals remained important as ways of interpreting the world. A review of the mythological *Gokul* (1946, dir. Vasant Painter) points out, 'What is really admirable in "Gokul" is the parallel which the producers have drawn between a mythological story, and the current Indian situation.'[112] While:

A MYTHOLOGICAL FILM WITH A TOPICAL THEME, KAMALA KOTNIS LEADS IN AHALYA – This film is a mythological picture but with a theme that is topical even today, namely the plight of abducted women and their rejection by society. The film is not a mere catalogue of miraculous events, but also gives Kamala Kotnis a fine chance for acting in the title role.[113]

The mythological has a more important role in nationalism: to create sacred myths for the new nation, to incorporate mythological and ancient time as well as non-modern worldviews into this new nation, and to define the culture and the cultural heritage of India,[114] albeit in ways that often sat uncomfortably with Nehruvian secular ideals. The mythological supports the widely held view that Indian history began 5,000 years ago in the time of Rama, and that this is a 'sacred history' (Eliade 1959: 95). The serials conflate Indian history with Hindu mythology and culture; they were not the first to do this, but perhaps they intensified and gave it a modern visual form and narrative, which has been open to various political uses, notably the increasing popularity of a Hindutva ideology during the 1990s.

Myths tell us about realities, what really happened at the beginning of time, as myth is more 'real' than the everyday. They move the human into the realm of the gods, making us the gods' contemporaries, living in an eternal present (or an eternal past) rather than in historical time, a time. The gods join us on earth, bringing their divine presence into our world, making that world new and allowing us to refuse the modern. We can enjoy a 'religious nostalgia' (Eliade 1959: 92) and find meaning in a world that can be resanctified by re-enacting – or re-viewing – the deeds of the gods (Eliade 1959: 99), keeping us in their divine time and sacred realm.

The beginnings of a pan-Indian non-regional style in cinema may be traced back to the mythological, which drew on the pan-Indian imagery of Ravi Varma, the touring Parsi theatre and Sanskrit versions of mythology. Many of these mythologicals, as the television mythologicals, found national audiences despite language issues. With the coming of sound, the Hindi cinema, largely through the social film, created a generic, north Indian-ness, largely centred around Punjab/Uttar Pradesh; even if the city which is most represented, Bombay, is far away from these centres, its population is largely from those regions. With the coming of sound, some more localised and regional mythologicals were made, although it is the devotional film that is strongly regional. While pan-Indian mythologicals (notably from the two great epics) continued to be produced, many non-Hindi film industries in India have also produced films about local deities and this is discussed in the next chapter.

Mythologicals also produce a 'neo-traditionalism'. A clear example is *Jai Santoshi Maa*, which spread a cult of a 'new' deity. However, it is not clear how much the mythological film is influencing practice and belief, although there is some evidence from the television serials, as described by Rajagopal (2001). It seems that India may also have produced 'secular' myths of the nation in films like *Mother India*, but there are no Islamic mythologicals, although there are Islamicate myths of the nation, especially stories of Akbar. These genres are discussed in Chapters 3 and 4 below.

The mythologicals are now enjoying a new life as they are transferred to the relatively cheap VCD, and shops in the lower-class locales have an enormous range of these films. Most of my personal collection is from Video Plaza on Lamington Road (Bombay), where these are kept to the fore, the back shelves stocking a variety of (soft?) porn. The religious films are shown on television monitors during festivals.

Although it is not possible to predict the future of the mythological film, there seems to me immense potential for the genre at present, even in the A-circuit. Religion is being talked about more in the world, and is certainly not fading away. The mythological and religious are productive in different media – stories, plays, poems, chromos, painting – but it seems that they cannot shake off their folk image and hence their downmarket element to re-emerge in cinema, although the religious is becoming more present in the social film. If they could do that and draw on new computer-generated imagery, there might be potential in the genre again, not least for the overseas market where the B-grade mythological has remained popular.

Two films from Hollywood may make the Indian producers think again. One was Mel Gibson's *The Passion of the Christ* (2004), whose spectacular success may make producers think about a 'Hindu' equivalent. The other was *Troy* (2004, dir. Wolfgang Petersen), which failed for many reasons but in my opinion the major fault was the absence of the gods. Without the gods playing with humans, as they do in Homer's *Iliad*, it is the story of a selfish romance that destroys a city and many people's lives. It seems unlikely that an overtly devotional film would be the starting point for a revival of the mythological film, but a historical type, such as a retelling of the *Mahabharata*, which some major figures in Bombay are already discussing, may well be a move in this direction.

Chapter 2

The devotional film

Although it is widely accepted that India's first entirely Indian-made film was *Raja Harischandra*, some sources, such as Rajadhyaksha and Willemen (1999) give precedence to R.G. Torney and N.G. Chitre's *Pundalik* (1912), a devotional film about a saint from Maharashtra. A contemporary advertisement from Coronation Cinematograph, Sandhurst Road, Girgaum, says, 'Almost half the Bombay Hindu population has seen it last week and we want the other half to do so before a change of programme takes place.'[1] Gokarn (n.d.: 8) cites a review from the *Times of India*, 25 May 1912 – 'Pundalik has the power to arrest the attention of the Hindus. As a religious drama, it has few equals.' (The Coronation advertisement's mention of the accompanying programme 'New screaming comics' suggests devotion was not the only object of the evening.)

Whichever of the two films was made first, it is not disputed that the mythological (see Chapter 1) and the devotional are the founding genres of Indian cinema. This chapter discusses the devotional genre, films about spiritual devotees (*bhaktas* and *sants*), drawing on India's rich premodern *bhakti* traditions.

Gokarn (n.d.: 3) notes that the generic definition of the devotional is not clear. Like other cinematic genres in India, the mixing or hybridity factor makes it hard to ascribe a film firmly to one category or another. Some may class mythologicals as devotionals as there is some overlap, especially with later films. (See discussion in Chapter 1.) While the generic categories may be leaky (see Neale 2000), my division here allows us to look at very different kinds of films from those in Chapter 1 and I have also mentioned films about 'godmen' in this chapter as they are very much in the spirit of the earlier devotional films.

As well as the mythological, the devotional genre is also closely aligned with the historical (see Mukhopadhyay 2004) in its presentation of historical figures rather than mythological, heroic or divine characters. Within historical, I include legendary or hagiographical figures as well as those from actual history. So while the life of the devotee may be hagiographical

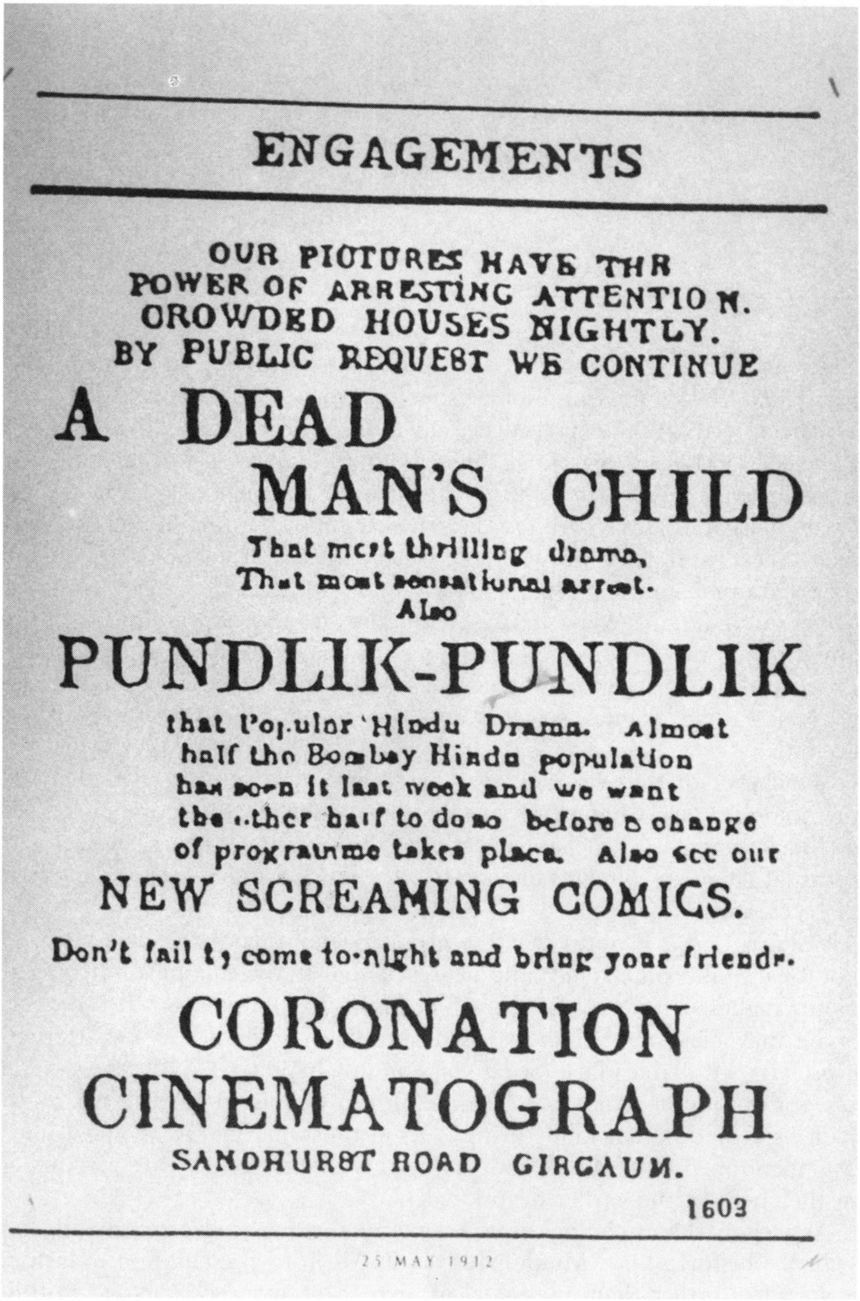

Figure 2.1 Pundalik (1912, dir. N.G. Chitre and P.R. Tipnis). Advertisement for the devotional film that some reckon the first all-Indian film.

or the gods appear, a king or some other figure locates the film in historical rather than mythological or past time.

The devotee, usually a *sant* (see below), is a person whose devotion makes them celebrated by a community of worshippers even though they are often drawn from the margins of society. The devotionals mostly narrate the often miraculous lives of India's many medieval singer-saints, who are associated with the traditions of *bhakti* or 'loving devotion' (see below). Gokarn (n.d.: 3) points out that the films follow a biographical narration from the saint's usually mysterious birth, through a childhood marked by otherworldiness and maturity before finding superhuman and miraculous powers as an adult which mark him or her apart from other people. The saint is often from a marginal social group or is harassed by a dominant class. Much of the story of the saint's life is about conflict with society and religious orthodoxy in which he or she triumphs, whether by argument or by miracles and other divine intervention. The saint is then acclaimed or even worshipped, at which point, his or her mission complete, he or she chooses to leave the mortal world. Some presentations of mythological stories are as devotionals and the films seem to be labelled as both (as Prakash's production, *Bhakta Dhruv*)[2].

These films differ from the mythologicals as they show new visual relays of looks between the audience, the devotee and the divine, allowing the audience to relate to the film very differently from the audience of the mythological film, which demands more awe on the part of the spectator, who has to watch from something of a distance.

The devotional films are often set outside Brahminical religion or question some aspects of it, and celebrate the introduction of vernacular languages into worship. Nearly every 'regional' language of India has a strong *bhakti* tradition, and this means that even though these films were closely associated with the nationalist movement (see below), they often present a much more regional nationalism than the mythological, which is often pan-Indian. The future national language, Hindi, also has key texts in its variants such as Braj Bhasha (many of the Krishnaite songs) and Avadhi (in particular the work of Tulsidas).

Most of the *sants* were famous poets of medieval India whose work is valued not only for its religious content but also for its poetic expression. Their compositions were songs (different genres in different languages) that expressed the devotee's deeply personal and emotional relation to the deity, so providing the film makers with ready-made songs. Although devotionals were made during the silent period (Phalke made *Sant Namdev* 1922, *Sant Meerabai* and it seems a *Sant Tukaram*[3]), they flourished with the coming of sound, often serving as showpieces for singers, such as K.L. Saigal in *Bhakta Surdas* (1942, dir. Chaturbhuj Doshi, prod. Ranjit).[4]

The *sant* films are nearly all set in the pre-British period, often during the so-called 'Muslim period' of medieval Indian history, although they do not refer to this directly. For example, Tukaram, the most celebrated of all the Maharashtrian *sants* is shown to have been visited by the Maratha leader, Shivaji (1630–80), regarded by many as one of the great leaders in Indian history. This background may well have been important for the original audiences of these films, who watched them under British rule. Some of the *sants* are claimed by more than one religious tradition, notably Kabir, who even during his lifetime had Muslim and Hindu followers, and later Sikhs, so it is not surprising that his work is often celebrated for its anti-communal messages.[5]

The *bhakti* movement

The *Bhagavad Gita*, composed around the second century BC or later, is regarded as one of the most sacred texts from ancient India. As part of his instruction to Arjuna, Krishna says there are three ways of approaching God: action (*karmamarga*), knowledge (*jnanamarga*) and the path of devotion (*bhaktimarga*). The first path appeals to the Brahmin, but it is hard to follow since it requires one to act but with detachment, and the second is not open to all. *Bhakti*, the path which all can follow, here means a way of sacrifice, discipline and duty. It later comes to mean a religious attitude to the divine, often in the form of a personal relationship. There are not one but many types of *bhakti* and in this chapter we look at this form of personal devotion.

The impact of *bhakti* on the formation of the religion we call 'Hinduism' was enormous and extended over the whole sub-continent. The most important change was the shift towards theism or the worship of a single deity (god or goddess), or one of his avatars (incarnations), usually Krishna or Rama (incarnations of Vishnu). There were religious differences in doctrine (notably in attitude and the centrality of emotion) and practice (forms of public worship), new popular forms of devotional songs (such as the *bhajan* and the *kirtan*; hagiographies of the new gurus and saints) in the vernacular languages, alongside or instead of Sanskrit. Bhakti was also a social movement in its (at least initial) rejection of Brahminical authority and its critique of views of caste, gender and so on.

The beginnings of this devotional worship, which marked a break from the earlier Vedic or Brahminical ritual (*karmamarga*) and Upanishadic and later philosophies (*jnanamarga*), are clearly seen at the start of the second millennium AD, in south Indian temple cities such as the Nataraja temple at Chidambaram and the Rajarajeshwara temple in Tanjore, where Puranic deities are worshipped in temples which are the focal point of these cities. This new theism tends to focus on Shiva, Shakti and on Vishnu and his ten incarnations, especially as Rama and Krishna but also other orthodox (*smarta*) deities. The king is often identified with the deity in the temple and Brahminical rituals are associated with these temples that are not only religious but are also the focus of the arts, such as dance (in particular the cult of the *devadasis* female servants of the gods), music and so on.

All *bhakti* cults focus on a personal approach to an *ishtadevata* ('a chosen deity'), often a localised deity who has many human attributes, where devotion is the focus. Many *bhaktas* surrender to grace of Vishnu although approaches to Shiva are often more complex, emphasising teaching, action, knowledge and ascetic practices. However, all forms of *bhakti* emphasise the importance of emotions as a way for the human body to connect to the (usually) embodied deity.

I mention this form of *bhakti* in order to counterbalance the presentation of *bhakti* as an entirely popular and reformist movement, associated with low castes, women and the spread of vernacular languages. It is more accurate to see *bhakti* as belonging to both elite and popular forms of religion, which are not necessarily contradictory.

The *sants* are *bhaktas* who compose poems, songs and sayings that spread among their followers.[6] Their devotion to their god (whether a personal form, his name or the guru) is particularly strong, and so they themselves become venerated (though not usually considered divine) by their followers; their lives, the miracles within them and their encounters with god often become the subject of hagiographies. Many of the *sants* of north India were Vaishnava, but most of them are associated with specific regions and are not widely known beyond these areas. This would include Chaitanya in Bengal, Orissa and around Mathura; and Narsi Mehta of Gujarat whose fame was spread somewhat by his inclusion in Gandhi's ashram prayers. *Bhakti* in Gujarat was dominated by the followers of Vallabha, the Pushtimarg, who were set apart from other groups and demanded total devotion (*ananya bhakti*) to their particular form of Krishna, Shrinathji; they were too distinctive and too Brahminical to be of more general interest to a film-going public. However, some of the poets of their sect, notably Surdas (see below), have emerged as *sants*.

This dynamic between elite and popular forms is seen clearly through language. The early *bhaktas*, those who practise *bhakti*, composed songs in vernacular languages, expressing their emotional and personal love of god. The first *bhaktas* emerged in what is now Tamil Nadu in the sixth century, the first long *bhakti* poem, dated from 550 AD, being to the god, Murugan, a southern god who is later identified as Shiva's son, Skanda.[7] This is followed by poems to gods such as Shiva and Krishna, previously associated with the north, from the seventh century, composed by the sixty-three Shaiva Nayanmars and twelve Vaishnavite Alvars. Tamil already had an established literary culture, namely the Tamil 'secular' literature, called *Sangam* (Ta. *Cankam*) literature. This literature belonged to the learned assemblies of Brahmins, dating from the first century BC, which was in two main forms, poems of war (*puram*) and love (*akam*) (Ramanujan 1985), which had created an emotional and erotic language that was taken up by the *bhaktas*. Before this, all religious composition was in Sanskrit forms of middle Indian languages (Pali, Prakrits), and was composed by and circulated mostly among educated, high-caste men. Tamil was the only mother tongue at this time with a literary tradition, while the other languages had only oral literature. *Bhakti* compositions appear next in Kannada, in the tenth century, then in Marathi and Hindi, but the process of transmission and the spread of *bhakti* is not known.

However, Sanskrit remained important within *bhakti*, being the language of key texts of this new religion, in particular those associated with Krishnaism, such as its foundational text, the *Bhagavata Purana* (a Sanskrit composition from south India dated to the ninth or tenth century). Many of the great Vedantic thinkers also incorporated *bhakti* into Sanskritic practices, and writing in Sanskrit notably were Ramanuja (d.1137); Madhva (1197–1276), Nimbarka (thirteenth century) and Vallabha (1479–1531).

The early Tamil *bhaktas* were from diverse backgrounds – Brahmins, traders, peasants and low castes such as washermen and fishermen, and even included a woman (Ramanujan 1973, 1981). In Maharashtra, some were high caste, including Jnaneshwara (Dynaneshwar) (*c.* 1290) – although he and his family are outcaste by the other Brahmins – while there were many lower-class writers such as Namdev (*c.* 1270–1350), Eknath (1533–99) and Tukaram (early seventeenth century). Yet Ramanujan (1999) reminds us that the majority of *bhaktas* were male and upper caste rather than low caste. However, *bhakti* does pose panditry, maleness and pride as obstacles to approaching the divine. The gender issues raised by *bhakti* are very much part of its radical nature. Every regional movement has at least one female *bhakta*, often from upper classes, who rebelled against their background. Being male is not a privilege; indeed male saints have to overcome maleness, perhaps needing a third gender, suggests Ramanujan (1999: 291). One of the ideal roles in *bhakti* is often that of women in love with god whom they recognise as their husbands. This brings them into conflict with their families, and their defiant gestures often include throwing away their clothes and their shame, most famously Mira (see below) tying on the *ghunghroos* (ankle bells) of the common dancer. However, Sangari (1990) reminds us that in *bhakti*, women still have to relate to men, whether a male god or a male guru, and she contrasts the roles of ordinary women and female *sants*.

Bhakti historically exists in a dynamic hybrid form between high and low. Its opposition to orthodoxy – views of caste, gender and ideas of god – often marks it as radical but the glorification of its revolutionary nature and its power as a social movement have often been overplayed (see Fuller 1992, Ch. 7) and, I argue, this is true of much of what we see in the devotional film. However, during the freedom struggle, religion, in particular the approach of *bhakti*, was regarded as part of Indian history and culture in ways that had a powerful impact on the devotional film. M.K. 'Mahatma' Gandhi (1869–1948), regarded as the father of the nation, practised his 'experiments with truth', which are closely aligned to *bhakti*, in his everyday life and politics. This connection between Gandhi and his politics was an essential part of the popularity of the devotional film during the pre-independence period (see Mukhopadhyay 2004).

The *sant* film's rise in popularity in the 1930s was greater than that of the historical and mythological, which had previously been more popular. It is no coincidence that the devotional rose to such prominence during the 1930s when nationalism was one of the dominant public concerns in India and Gandhian nationalism was at its height.[8] It was certainly clear that the Prabhat film makers had Gandhi in mind when making their films, as seen in Shantaram's choice of the name *Mahatma* for what was later to be *Dharmatma*, and in the kind of *bhakti* that these films depicted, which was clearly recognised by the audience. At a meeting of the Indian Motion Pictures Congress in Bombay 1939, K.M. Munshi praised *Sant Tukaram*, linking its concerns with nationalism, Gandhi and *bhakti*.[9]

Although Gandhi was a member of the Indian National Congress, his deep religious beliefs informed his key views[10] and he was regarded by many people as a living *sant*. Gandhi's father was a Vaishnava Pushtimargi while his mother was a Pranami, a sect that combined Hindu and Muslim beliefs, giving reverence to Vaishnava and Islamic texts. Gandhi had no learned knowledge of Hindu texts but he evolved his own form of ethical Hinduism with little interest in ritual and deities, drawing in a selective and eclectic manner on texts such as the *Bhagavad Gita*[11] and the *Ramcharitmanas*, and was heavily influenced by the *sants* and *bhaktas* who sought social justice, notably caste reforms. However, he also had an interest in theosophy and other religious traditions which formed part of his bricolage of ethics, such as Christian pacifism, salvation and redemption[12] and Jain non-violence alongside Hindu traditions of renunciation, notably celibacy. Gandhi followed a moral path, on which *satya*, truth, was the highest principle; he practised *ahimsa*, non-violence, *satyagraha*, passive resistance and so on. He thought that politics required the same moral force as his private life and he sought to find a way to incorporate these views into his politics and his view of an ideal society, based on a rejection of modern civilisation.

Although he tried to avoid sectarianism, and often challenged orthodoxy, in particular by his emphasis on caste reform, Gandhi was so highly regarded in part for his own morality and religiosity which could only identify him as a Hindu (see Hardiman 2003, Ch. 7). Given his espousal of morality and religion, it is not surprising that he became regarded as a Mahatma himself (see Amin 1984). Although other political leaders, such as Bhagat Singh, were associated with religious imagery, and were honoured as 'Shaheeds' or martyrs, they were not regarded as saints.[13]

While Gandhi understood the use of symbols, notably *khadi*, homespun cloth, and the spinning wheel, for his campaigns, and he was a prolific writer, he did not use the modern media, as we saw in Chapter 7, and was largely hostile to cinema.[14] An article in *Mauj Majah* implores Gandhi to see a film,[15] but he did not change his mind until he saw *Ram Rajya* in 1945 (see Chapter 1). When asked to write for *The Mirror*, Gandhi's office replied: As a rule Gandhiji gives messages only on rare occasions and these only for causes whose virtue is ever undoubtful. As for the Cinema Industry, he has the least interest in it.[16] K.A. Abbas published a letter addressed to Gandhi in response to the latter's criticism of cinema.[17] In particular he took issue with Gandhi's likening it to 'evils like gambling, sutta, horse-racing, etc., which you leave alone "for fear of losing caste"'. He suggests the benefits cinema might bring. It is not thought that Gandhi responded to this letter.

Gandhi was filmed and after his assassination in 1948, film reviews were suspended for a while until reviewing two films about him:

SARDI REVIEWS OUR SCREEN
Film documentary of Mahatma's last journey: the preview of The Light That Shone was given this morning at the Metro Cinema which was attended by HE Raja Sit Maharaj Singh, the hon'ble Mr B.G. Kher and other distinguished citizens. The Light That Shone shows how the nation mourned the death and paid its homage to the mortal remains of its beloved leader Gandhiji. There is a moving commentary by Mr D.F. Karaka. The film also shows thousands of people paying their respectful homage to the sacred ashes in the Town Hall and the vast concourse of men and women which followed the urn on its last journey to Chowpati. Not the least impressive feature of the film is the song, Lead Kindly Light. As H.E. said, it is the most moving and impressive documentary film conveying the nation's grief at the loss of its beloved leader.[18]

SARDI REVIEWS OUR SCREEN
Interesting short on Gandhi: Mr Tarachand Barjatya has produced an interesting three-reeler depicting various phases in the life of Gandhi. The title Vishwadeep Bapu or Light of the World, Bapu, is singularly appropriate. Directed by Dwarka Khosla several of the scenes have been shot on the actual spots that have become landmarks in the history of the nation due to Gandhi's association with them. After a glimpse of Porbunder where the Mahatma was born, we follow him to England at the time of his early student days, to South Africa where he forged his unique weapon of civil disobedience, to his Sabarmati Ashram, thence along the route of the famous Dandee March, to the Quit-India movement, to Noakhali Bihar and Delhi,

where he breathed his last. The commentary, written by Nilkanth Tiwari, is moving. It is well delivered by Raj Mehra.[19]

There have been a few films about Gandhi since his death, the most widely seen being Richard Attenborough's *Gandhi* (1982), which won a popular audience, Oscars and was acclaimed by some historians, such as Francis Robinson:

> As a film specifically about the man, *Gandhi* succeeds brilliantly. Many sides of his character are revealed as we follow the Mahatma's path from his early struggles against the pass laws in South Africa to his final crusade against communal violence as India won independence: there is courage, determination, compassion, humanity, humour, faddishness, his shrewdness in the world of politics . . .[20]

The *sant* films

Although *bhakti* started in south India and, although south India has produced many devotional films,[21] my focus is on north India, from as far south as Maharashtra to the 'Hindi' north. Within that area, I concentrate on the *sant* tradition as most of the devotional films in Hindi, Marathi and Gujarati are about these devotees. I have included Maharashtra because the films of Prabhat Films during the 1930s are some of the best examples of the genre and together constitute almost an entire group of *sants* associated with a particular cult. These films are also significant for their presentation and their audience reception of the nationalist movement of the time, and *Tukaram* is perhaps one of the greatest films ever made in India.

Early devotionals

Unlike the mythological, there has been little discussion on the roots of devotional films in urban theatre in the nineteenth century. Perhaps this is because the songs of the *sants* and *bhaktas* flourished in the *satsang* or community of followers and were less associated with performance genres than the mythological, which was linked to *Ramlilas* and other types of theatre. However, some actors were renowned for their performances of *sants* and *bhaktas*,[22] and the actors who played these roles in the films often spent much of their later careers re-enacting them in live performances, in particular Vishnupant Pagnis in his role of Tukaram.[23] The songs are clearly a major attraction of the devotional, along with the possibility of raising social issues, of showing an exemplary life and allowing for the spectacle of showing miracles.

After *Pundalik*, several silent *sant* films were made, including the Madans' *Bilwamangal/Bhakta Surdas* (1932), in which the star Gauhar acted as

Chintamani, the beloved of the blind poet saint. This was a hit in Calcutta and Bombay. Others included S.N. Patankar's *Kabir Kamal* (1919) and Oriental's *Narsinha Mehta* (1920).

Two silent devotionals ran into problems because of their overt references to Gandhi, the first of which was Kohinoor's *Bhakta Vidur* (1921), produced by and starring Dwarkadas Sampat. The film drew so many parallels to Gandhi's freedom struggle, and Vidur's Gandhi-cap and spinning of the *charkha* (the spinning wheel Gandhi used for making homespun *khadi* cloth), that it was banned in some provinces of India. It also had a music score that was performed live with every show, including a song in praise of the spinning wheel (Rajadhyaksha and Willemen 1999: 244). The Hindustan Company's *Bhakta Prahlad*, directed by Phalke in 1926, was famous for its special effects showing the trials and tribulations of Prahlad, who was presented as a *satyagrahi* or follower of Gandhi's plan of passive resistance. After these films, references to Gandhi (and the nationalist struggle) were more carefully planned to avoid censorship.

The coming of sound in 1931 gave great impetus to the devotional film as it had a ready-made stock of popular songs and well-known stories of revered and loved figures who had often performed miracles, and the devotional became a popular genre during the 1930s.

Devotional films of New Theatres

Some of the first sound films that Calcutta's elite New Theatres made were devotionals. Their first major sound release was *Chandidas* (1932), the story of a fifteenth-century Bengali Vaishnavite poet, adapted from a Star Theatre play. The director, Debaki Bose, himself a Gandhian and a Vaishnava, emphasised the priest Chandidas' love for Rami though he was a Brahmin, she a washerwoman. The landlord tries to seduce her and burns her house down when she refuses him but Chandidas rescues her and follows Vaishnavism rather than Brahminical orthodoxy. This film was an enormous success, running for over a year in Calcutta. It had short dialogues and used background music effectively, as well as foregrounding Chandidas' verse. The generic category of this film may be disputed as the songs are all love songs by Chandidas to Rami rather than in praise of god.

New Theatres then remade *Chandidas* in Hindi (1934, the only version I have seen), directed by Nitin Bose, starring K.L. Saigal whose songs, composed by Boral, were a huge hit. The other stars were Uma Shashi, Pahari Sanyal and Nawab. This time, the script, by Agha Kashmiri, gave great emphasis to caste injustice and romantic love. Although this was a very Bengali film in its subject and many of its features, such as the clothing and some of the speech, as well as the style of music, the film reached a non-Bengali audience and after this New Theatres made all their films in Bengali and Hindi (Mukhopadhyay 2004: 87).

New Theatres then turned to some non-Bengali devotionals. Debaki Bose directed *Puran Bhagat* (1933), again with music by R.C. Boral. It seems surprising that this very Bengali studio chose a popular Punjabi story, retold in many *kissas* (narrative forms).[24] Prince Puran of Punjab, cursed before birth by King Silwan of Sialkot, is unjustly sentenced to death but is rescued by Gorakhnath of whom he becomes a disciple. New Theatres found it hard to find a distributor in Bombay but Gokarn (n.d.: 48) notes that it was a great success all over India, largely because of the music, especially K.C. De's songs.

New Theatres then made a film about the Rajasthani *bhakta* Mira – *Rajrani Meera/Meerabai* (1931, dir. Debaki Bose), again with music by R.C. Boral in a Hindi version with Prabhat's Durga Khote and Prithviraj Kapoor as well as a Bengali version. However, Debaki Bose then turned back to a more local figure when he directed *Vidyapati* (1937), the story of the Maithili poet and Vaishnava saint who lived in the fourth/fifth century in what is now Bihar. Although the film, with the script written by Qazi Nazrul Islam, is concerned with a romantic love triangle, it builds the film around Vidyapati's poetry as a devotee of Krishna, concentrating on music and song rather than miracles.

Perhaps it was the decision of the personnel of New Theatres that they chose to make historical or cultural films about devotees rather than more religious films about devotees. The links to politics in their films were also less obvious than those of other contemporary studios. It may have been for this reason rather than the one a critic suggests for the inability of the New Theatres' devotionals to find a non-Bengali audience: 'Tragedy is bred in the bones and marrow of Bengal and unfortunately or fortunately for the rest of India it has no poetic charm.'[25]

Prabhat Film Company

Prabhat Film Company was founded in 1929 by a group that broke away from the Painter brothers' (Anantrao and Baburao) Maharashtra Film Company in Kolhapur, and then moved to Pune in 1933. Vishupant Govind Damle (1919–45) was a middle-class, educated Brahmin, while Sheikh Fattelal (1919–56), a painter, was from a Muslim family of masons who lived in Kolhapur. V. Shantaram (1901–90), who had previously been in Bal Gandharva's theatre group, is best remembered as one of the country's most acclaimed directors from the 1930s for his social films such as *Amar Jyoti* (1936), *Kunku/Duniya na mane* (1937), *Manoos/Admi* (1938) and *Shejari/Padosi* (1941). He is also well known for later work, such as *Do aankhen barah haath* (1957), which he made for his own production company (Rajkamal Kala Mandir) formed when he left Prabhat in 1942. After his departure, the studio never recovered and soon closed down, its premises now home to the Film and Television Institute of India.[26]

Prabhat produced a number of mythologicals (see Chapter 1) and famous socials, but was also well known for its devotional films in the 1930s and 1940s. While some staff worked as technicians on each other's films, Prabhat's most famous directors were V. Shantaram, who had made several mythologicals, but made only one devotional (*Dharmatma*, 1935) before switching entirely to social films, while Damle and Fattelal made four films of which one was a mythological (*Gopal Krishna*, 1938) and three were devotionals (*Sant Tukaram*, 1936; *Sant Dnyaneshwar*, 1940; and *Sant Sakhu*, 1941).

Prabhat's devotionals were concerned with Maharashtrian *sants*. Maharashtra's *sants* were mostly Vaishnava, often called the Varkari Panth (Pilgrim's Path) (see Fuller 1992: 210–14), associated particularly with the cult of Vithoba at Pandharpur, one of the largest pilgrimage sites in India, and which defines the geography of Maharashtra.[27] Vithoba is a form of Krishna, standing on a brick, with his consort Rukmini at his side. His cult focuses less on the erotic devotion of some of the Krishna cults and more on parental love towards the deity. The Varkari *sants* include Jnaneshwara/Dnyaneshwar, who wrote a Marathi commentary on the *Bhagavad Gita*; Namdev, who is known in the Punjab because his verses also appear in the Sikh *Adi Granth*; Eknath; Janabai; and the most revered of all, Tukaram. While Jnaneshwara was a Brahmin, Namdev was a tailor, and Tukaram a *shudra*; Janabai and Sant Sakhu were women and have come to be associated with anti-Brahminism and caste reform.

Mahadev Govind Ranade (1842–1901), a lawyer, journalist and social reformer, notably of the caste system, interpreted *bhakti*, in particular that of the Varkari Panth, as a key part of the history of Maharashtra and indeed of India in its creation of a 'national' unity, not least for its anti-Brahminical roles in promoting 'vernacular' languages and criticising the caste system. Ranade even incorporated Shivaji, the leader of the Maharashtrians, into his scheme of reform and national unity by associating him with the Maharashtrian *bhakti* movement, which is Vaishnava, although as a devotee of his family's deity, Bhavani, he was a Shaivite. 'Lokmanya' Bal Gangadhar Tilak (1856–1920), one of the heroes of India's freedom movement, interpreted Shivaji's role in Maharashtrian history as legitimising a violent struggle, thus making Shivaji an anti-Muslim as well as anti-British figure. It is interesting that it is Ranade's views, in conjunction with Gandhi's, that prevail in the movies of Prabhat Films.

Dharmatma, 1935, dir. V. Shantaram, Hindi and Marathi

Sant Eknath was a Brahmin who opposed caste distinctions and fed 'untouchables' at his house before he fed the Brahmins, and he went to eat at one of their houses. He wrote a commentary on a chapter of the *Bhagavata Purana*, called the *Eknathi Bhagavat*, and he wrote many independent verses, *abhangas*. It is said that god lived with Eknath as his disciple without Eknath knowing it.

Shantaram made this as a political film rather than concentrating on miracles. Shantaram had previously made a film on Shivaji as a parallel to the national movement, *Swarajya Toran* ('The banner of self-rule'), which was banned until he made cuts and renamed it *Uday kal*, (Thunder in the hills). Shantaram later said that he chose the topic of Eknath so he could draw parallels between Eknath's criticism of the caste system and Gandhi's campaigns in the 1930s to abolish untouchability.[28] He tried to make this link explicit in the original choice of title, *Mahatma*, which was refused by the Bombay Censor Board.

Shantaram does not aim at a traditional form of iconography but instead he shows early signs of direct expressionism, which he learnt in Germany and which was to characterise his later work in the film; for example when 'good thoughts' are mentioned he cuts to flowers and lamps (Shahani 1985: 199).

The famous actor Bal Gandharva starred in the role of Eknath, the only male role in his career. This was something of a gamble as it was unclear if the audience would accept him in a male role, even though the *bhakti* movement valorises the feminine. He was also not easy to work with, as Shantaram Athavale writes:

> [Shantaram's] persistence and confidence as well as tireless effort, good humour, and understanding were all tested when he cast the famous

Figure 2.2 Sant Tukaram (1936, dir. V.G. Damle and Sheikh Fattelal). Tukaram (Vishnupant Pagnis) sings the praises of Vithoba.

> Bal Gandharva as Saint Eknath .... Shantaram's magic direction
> made many stars to blossom .... In contact with his touchstone,
> their talent became pure gold.' (Gokarn n.d.: 40)

The *Bombay Chronicle* had an advertisement for the film:

> He loves them who love all ... to know it smartly, fail not to see
> Dharmatma, Bal Gandharva Prabhat Picture, the noblest subject ever
> filmed. Krishna Talkies.[29]

Then it featured it as Film Fare for the Week:

> Dharmatma ... the theme is woven around the life and personality
> of the great and venerable Hindu saint 'Eknath' whose great humani-
> tarianism was the wounded in India in the 16th century.[30]

The film was well reviewed:

> CINEMA USHERS IN CHRISTMAS.
> Dharmatma at the Krishna ... the story of this picture is based on
> the life of Saint Eknath, a great man who was the very spirit of
> equality and fraternity and who sacrificed his very life in the cause
> of humanity. The incidents are so linked that they form a homoge-
> nous whole, leaving upon the mind of the spectator an impression of
> complete unity among all irrespective of caste and creed, till at last
> it reaches the climax. One incident leads to another.[31]

Sant Tukaram, *dir. Damle and Fattelal, Marathi*

Prabhat's most famous and acclaimed film tells the story of Maharashtra's
most loved poet and saint.[32] Tukaram was born in 1608 and vanished in
1650. He was a low-caste *shudra*, who lived in a village called Dehu,
about thirty miles from Pune, on the banks of the River Indrayani. He
wrote in colloquial Marathi using rich imagery of the everyday. (The songs
in the film are Tukaram's own verses apart from one new one by Shantaram
Athavale composed for when Tukaram is guarding the field. Apparently
it was so like one of Tukaram's own verses that scholars contacted Prabhat
to find out the source! [33])

It is not surprising that Tukaram was taken up by nationalists such as
Ranade, who sought to counteract reformist Hinduism in the nineteenth
century that turned towards Brahminical texts. Tukaram's popularity was
such that after the coming of sound, two versions of his life were made
in 1932 by the Sharda Film Company and by Master and Company, but
these were not very well received (Watve 1985: 18). These films focused

on the miraculous in Tukaram's life story, but Damle and Fattelal gave more emphasis to his saintliness among the ordinary and everyday, with miracles depicted in the midst of strikingly realistic settings and performances, which makes them seem part of life.

Tukaram had lost his first wife and child in a famine and dedicated himself to god to the neglect of his second wife, Jijai, and their two children. A Brahmin, Salomalo, was no scholar, preferring to spend his time with a courtesan. However, he was jealous of Tukaram's following so stole Tukaram's poems and presented them as his own, accusing Tukaram of stealing his poems and questioning a *shudra*'s right to interpret the Vedas. Salomalo invited Pandit Rameshwar Shastri to Dehu to examine the claim that Tukaram had defiled the Vedas. Salomalo presented false evidence and Shastri ordered Tukaram to throw his poems into the river and never to discuss religion in public. Tukaram did this and sat by the river for thirteen days with his family, all fasting, until god returned his poems. During this time Shastri fell ill, and, realising this was punishment for his injustice, became Tukaram's disciple. Salomalo then appealed to temporal power, inviting Shivaji to the village. Shivaji tested Tukaram by giving him jewellery and clothes. When Tukaram returned these, Shivaji too became his disciple. Salomalo then informed the Mughals that Shivaji was in the village and they came to seize him while he was listening to Tukaram preaching in the temple. Tukaram invoked god who protected Shivaji. Tukaram was ready to leave this world and god came to take him to heaven. Tukaram invited his wife but she decided her responsibilities were to her home and family so Tukaram went to heaven alone.

The film shows different styles, often associated with specific characters and cuts in between them. Tukaram was played by Vishnupant Pagnis, who, like Bal Gandharva, usually played female roles in theatre (his troupe was called Swadesh Hitinchak Mandali). He was cast at Shantaram's suggestion and initially Damle and Fattelal were very unhappy with his 'feminine mannerisms'.[34] However, they worked with him to modify his performance and it is in part this 'femininity' that makes him so appropriate to the role of a *bhakta*, with its emphasis on the feminine as an approach to the divine (see above).

Pagnis was also a famous singer of devotional songs, and before beginning his role in the film he went to pray at Tukaram's *samadhi* ('memorial') at Dehu.[35] Shahani (1985) points out that the pace of the film is Pagnis' songs and reverie, as he barely moves in film, swaying only his torso, his face often shot in close-up. Kapur argues that the *sant* is iconic as symbolic meanings converge on him and that the style of representation and performance of Pagnis as Tukaram is such that his face is privileged as sign, allowing it to be not only iconic but also indexical, of both actor and character (Kapur 2000: 240–1). This may further allow the possibility of the audience forming part of the *satsang* or community of worshippers, not so much by the presence of the deity, but through the devotee himself. Kapur argues that religious iconicity is mediated to secular effect through shots of the devotee mediating between god and the viewer, and the direct address of the saint. She draws attention to the shots of the god from over the shoulder to Tukaram and then in reverse with Tukaram so the viewer adores the saint as well as the god. She argues that the reciprocity of the gaze through the cinematic medium makes for 'an intersubjective truth-effect that is ultimately secular'.[36]

Tukaram's otherworldliness is contrasted with his wife's down-to-earth style. Jijai (Gauri), his wife, is shown as a village woman, earthy, practical, unglamorous, devoted to her husband and family, working hard at her housework and looking after her beloved buffalo. In a very touching scene, she follows Tukaram when he goes to the forest to praise god, insisting that he eat properly, and she shows her simple love and devotion to her husband who infuriates her in so many ways. In a famous scene, she is washing her buffalo when she loses her temper with her husband for his lack of concern for her children's welfare, and she drags the child to the temple, armed with a stick to beat the deity. Gauri was not a professional actress but a sweeper at Prabhat who took some roles, starting as an extra before ending up as one of their 'stars'.

Shastri, a learned Brahmin, is contrasted with the village Brahmin, Salomalo, who represents orthodox, Brahminical religion in its worst light. He speaks a formal language and composes elaborate verse, which is contrasted with Tukaram's. When he sings Tukaram's verses, he converts them to a 'pop' style, as is seen at the beginning of the film when there is a cut from Tukaram singing his own verse to Salomalo singing a vulgar version.[37] He is not out to compete with Tukaram's religious devotion but wants to destroy what he perceives to be a threat to his own status. Salomalo visits a dancing girl, thus showing his spiritual bankruptcy, while allowing the audience to enjoy a different kind of music and dance, and some cinematic glamour. Shahini (1985: 249) points out that the dancing girl is often shown in tableaux of a Ravi Varma style. Shahani mentions that Salomalo moves with the jerky, askew movements of the *tamasha* (popular Marathi theatre) actor (Shahani 1985: 249), very different from the serene Tukaram.

When Shivaji visits Tukaram's house as his disciple after hearing of his devotion, Jijai, who is infuriated with her husband's lack of practicality, is finally impressed. Shivaji represents worldly power but of a good and benevolent kind, which contrasts with Tukaram's spiritual power and Salomalo's corruption. This incident supports Ranade's view of the coming together of Shivaji and the Varkari Panth, although such stories are dated from the eighteenth century.

The realism of the acting and the settings does not make the miracles (the arrival of God in the village, the creation of an army from the body of Vithoba and so on) jar, but rather makes them part of everyday life, in a way that they are commonly regarded to be.

The film has a timeless quality, seeming to be set in any Maharashtrian village, and it is made with a great honesty and simplicity, or, as Shahini puts it, there is a 'total and integrated conjunction of belief, social action, and the lack of deception, which gives it such dignity' (Shahani 1985: 202).

Sant Tukaram was screened at the Fifth International Exhibition of Cinematograph Art in Venice where it was chosen as one of the three best films in 1937. It ran for over a year continuously in Bombay and its popularity in Maharashtra was such that whenever it was screened it drew enormous crowds from miles around (*Filmindia*, January 1941, reports when it was shown in a village of barely 300 people, the audience was 1,500).

Sant Dnyaneshwar, 1940, dir. Damle and Fattelal, Hindi and Marathi

Dnyaneshwar, the Marathi spelling of Jnaneshwar, was from a family of Brahmins of Alandi, who had been excommunicated after their father took *sannyas* (religious withdrawal from the world) although married, then returned to his wife under his guru's orders. After their parents commit suicide, Dnyaneshwar and the other children are excommunicated. As a child-preacher, he wants to learn the *shastras* (scholarly texts) but no one will let him until he gets a buffalo to recite the Vedas. They were eventually allowed back into the Brahmin fold on the condition that they observed celibacy. Dnyaneshwar wrote a commentary in colloquial

Figure 2.3 Sant Dnyaneshwar (1940, dir. V.G. Damle and Sheikh Fattelal). Dnyaneshwar (Shadu Modak), in a pious pose, leads his family and other followers.

Marathi, the *Dnyaneshwari*, on the *Bhagavad Gita*, when he was still a teenager. It seemed he joined the Varkari group, perhaps under influence of Namdev, another *sant*. However, the film does not have references to him or to the other *sants* he met such as Gora Kumbhar, Kabir or Janabai, or to his older brother whom he took as a guru.

The script was again by Washikar who had written the script for *Tukaram*. Again the reviews and comments showed that the film was trying to make some anti-communal stance in difficult times, and justified the use of miracles to attract the audience, but not detracting from its value as a social document, valuing it for its human emotions and ennobled sentiments.[38] Prabhat films are not just to entertain, but also to explain one religion to another, and this film was made during difficult times. The first part of the film concentrates on the struggle of young Dnyaneshwar (Yeshwant) and his three young siblings – ostracised by the Brahmins for the mistakes of their parents, and treated as badly as the low castes, even though they were Brahmins by birth – which evokes great sympathy from the audience. The second part of the film has many more miracles and devotional songs and led to much of the criticism of the film, such as that by K.A. Abbas:

> Any ventriloquist can make a buffalo recite the Vedic scriptures, any aviator can fly in the air. But only a Tukaram could give away the last sugar-cane to the neighbour's children while his own were hungry; only Dnyaneshwar could preach equality of mankind in defiance of the might of orthodoxy, only Gandhi can give a message of peace and non-violence that makes a man into a saint. Both from an intellectual and from a sociological view-point we would wish progressive producers like Prabhat to depict these 'human' qualities of the saints rather than their super-human miracles.[39]

Another critic in the *Bombay Chronicle* responds that Abbas is too intellectual and that miracles are part of the widely accepted view of his life:

> The 'miracles' of Dnyaneshwar constitute his spiritual personality embalmed in popular symbolism ... Who, with an aesthetic heart, will think of exposing this legendary beauty to the mechanical process of the slicing machine of intellectualism?[40]

The debate continues as another writer quotes passages from the film itself to show that miracles are not at the heart of the film nor of Dnyaneshwar's teaching, which is not just about debates:

> 'Learned and intellectual people', says Nivritti [Dnyaneshwar's brother] in the picture, 'are encrusted by the rust of their own knowledge. You

should therefore begin with the masses, whose emotions and instincts are yet to be corrupted.'

In the film Dnyaneshwar refutes miracles, telling the villagers not to believe in ghosts, and the villain, Visoba, says: 'If we recognize purification certificates obtained by magic and miracle, the low-caste snake charmer may as well claim to become a Brahmin.'

To remove the miracles would be wrong because:

> The miracles associated with him are . . . an organic part of his personality . . . . Is not Mahatma Gandhi, in our own times, regarded as an incarnation of God by the very masses for whose enlightenment he lives and strives? . . . In another age . . . the Dandi march and the moral victory over the White Man in South Africa would be moulded into the shape of miracles.[41]

An editorial in *The Mirror* points out '"Dnyaneshwar" without miracles would not have been Dnyaneshwar at all . . . . It has been argued that a ventriloquist can make a buffalow [sic] talk. Well, he might. But that does not make him a saint.'[42] Dnyaneshwar and his siblings also travel on a flying wall, and visitors to Alandi are now always shown this wall as an object of devotion.[43] Although the buffalo episode is rather comical, the Yogi riding on a tiger is actually quite spectacular.[44]

The older Dnyaneshwar was played by Shahu Modak, who took many roles in devotionals and mythologicals, even though he was a Christian.[45] A protégé of Bhal Pendharkar, he acted as a boy in the first Marathi talkie, *Shyamsundar* (dir. Bhalji Pendharkar, 1932), and acted in Prabhat's *Aadmi* and many other films. His acting in the film is superb and his devotion and saintliness are not at all cloying.

The film's advertisements promoted it as a religious experience: 'Alandi in Bombay! Thousands rush to take "darshan" of Dnyaneshwar' (*The Mirror*, 21 July 1940), and:

> To the world torn between the forces of destruction
> Dnyaneshwar
> Brings the timely message
> 'Equality among men'
> Prabhat's
> Proud picturization
> Of
> The life-story of the
> Greatest philosopher-poet
> Which inspired a nation
> Shows running in Central, Hindi and Marathi at 4.45 to 9.45 with
>   a 1.30 show on Sat and Sun.[46]

While the film had a great success in India, running for almost ten months, it was also shown overseas, and is said to have been the first Indian film screened in the USA (Watve 1985: 43). This film was shown in New York at the Little Carnegie Theatre as *Gyandev*. It was reviewed in the *Herald Tribune*, where it was acclaimed for its faith in God and the struggle against religious bigotry. Its technical qualities were also appreciated, both its sound and photography. The *New York Times* described it as being like a story of the prophets, with 'piety and a love for camera tricks', while *PM* said it was 'the first film ever generally shown in this country from India's little-known but brisk film industry'.[47] It is said to have been praised by Frank Capra in *American Cinematographer* for its technical qualities (Watve 1985: 43).

Sant Sakhu, 1941, dir. Fattelal, Damle and Nene, Hindi and Marathi

There is no recorded source for the story of Sant Sakhu, played by Hansa Wadkar. The first half is a family drama of the ordeal of a saintly daughter-in-law in an orthodox home, where the husband is torn between his wife and his mother. In the second half, God comes to help her and win over her mother-in-law. Sakhu is desperate to go on the pilgrimage to

Figure 2.4 Sant Sakhu (1941, dir. V.G. Damle and Sheikh Fattelal). Vithoba blesses Sakhu (Hansa Wadkar) and her husband.

Pandharpur but her mother-in-law ties her to a post. When she finally gets there, the pilgrims witness her death at Vithoba's feet and they cremate her. However, she returns from the dead and as there is yet another divine Sakhu, no one knows which is which. This film concentrates on the astonishment of the miracles rather than on *darshan* of Vithoba, and on the appeal of the *saas-bahu* ('mother-in-law and daughter-in-law') story.

Some reviews thought the acting was poor,[48] while the *Bombay Chronicle* was more favourable:

PRABHAT'S FILM BECOMES CITY'S RAGE

In depicting the biographies of saints, there is one great advantage for any producing company. These biographies are already well-known to the masses of people and they love to see their representation on the screen in a life-like manner. Sant Sakhu is so much like an actual slice of life itself as Prabhat's earlier productions, Dharmatma, Tukaram, Dnyaneshwar.[49]

And:

SAKHU'S LIFE ON SCREEN

Prabhat's biographical feature now in the third week at the Central Cinema brings to artistic life one of the best loved saints in that brilliant array of saints who enriched the life of regenerate Maharashtra. Sakhu was not like the other saints, Tukaram, Dnyaneshwar, Ramdas, Eknath, left as a treasure of devotional literature. Sakhu's was a simple life of a frail woman, yet richly dramatic and the Prabhat directors have exploited all the drama while adhering courageously to the facts of the biography.[50]

Prabhat are said to have made two more devotionals to complete the group of Varkari Panth devotees, but these seem to have attracted little attention. *Sant Janabai*,[51] (1949, dir. Govind Ghanekar, starring Hansa Wadkar, in Marathi and Hindi) was produced by Prabhat but it seems that Keshav Talpade's *Sant Namdev*, 1950,[52] was not a Prabhat film.

Gokarn discusses another devotional, *Bhakticha Mala*, (1944), which she lists by V. Shantaram, but it seems to be a production of Shantaram's later company, Rajkamal Kala Mandir Studio, directed by Keshavrao Date. A peasant, Savtamali, follows the path of *karma* or action, but he says he is too busy with his work in the fields to go on a pilgrimage to the temple of Vithoba in Pandharpur; the other villagers think he is an atheist and attack his fields. Vithoba refuses to give the others *darshan* but comes to the village to visit Savta, even though the other *sants* are aghast.

The reviews were not kind to the film. Gokarn (n.d.: 42) reports: 'The roly-poly Master Krishnarao also does not fit into the role of a brawny field labourer. It is obvious that he is chosen by the director more for his singing than for his acting talent ... and Amirbai's acting and singing are stagy and theatrical in typical traditional trend of Maharashtrian theatre companies.'

This film is interesting as it challenges the followers of *bhakti* who are setting up their own new orthodoxy to question and regulate the worship of others, showing that devotion remains at the heart of *bhakti* rather than other practices that have grown up around it such as pilgrimage.

Prabhat's films are superb, not only as religious films but also as world cinema of its time. Their mythologicals, devotionals and social-reform films all included masterpieces and the recent appearance of these films on VCDs and planned translations of some Marathi writings on the studio and its personnel are eagerly anticipated. Even though they are religious ('Hindu') films and made in Marathi, they are crucial in the study of Maharashtrian and Indian nationalism, as they show a much closer connection with Ranade's reformism and Gandhi's quest for national unity than any forms of Hindu nationalism, several of which have their roots in Maharashtra at this period. The Prabhat films undermine simplistic arguments about media and Hindutva, which are often made following the television mythologicals and the increasing presence of religion and religiosity in the social film of the 1990s.

Narsi Mehta – Gujarati Sant

Although Gujarat had a rich *bhakti* and *sant* tradition (Dwyer 2001), the Gujarati film industry never created a wider Indian audience as Prabhat and it made relatively few devotional films, with Gujarati-speakers such as Vijay Bhatt preferring to work in Hindi and sometimes even Marathi rather than Gujarati. However, Bhatt made a devotional about Narsi Mehta who is regarded as the greatest poet of Gujarat.

Narsi's dates are uncertain; the traditional dates of 1414–80, are largely discredited in favour of 1500–80. He tells many of his life events in his poems but he has also been the subject of numerous hagiographies. A Nagar Brahmin, he was said to be mute as a child until Krishna granted him the power of speech and so he became a devotee of Krishna. Married with a son and a daughter, he had a difficult family life, largely because of disputes with his brother's wife. Thrown out of home, he prayed to Shiva, and falls into a trance. Shiva takes Narsi to Gokul to see Krishna's *raslila* dance. Narsi is so absorbed in the dance that he does not notice when the torch he is carrying burns his arm. When Krishna puts out the fire, Narsi wakes up and gives his family the gifts that Radha and Krishna gave him. He then leaves his brother's house and sets up on his own in Junagadh. He sings his devotional verses to Rama and Krishna, and his philosophical and ethical verses, while playing small cymbals. Many mythical stories surround his life, the most famous of which is the account of his daughter's *mameru* – the ritual giving of gifts by parents in the seventh month of a daughter's first pregnancy. When Narsi could not afford to do the necessary, Krishna appeared and gave them himself. Equally famous is the story about the time when he was excommunicated by the Nagars for eating with the low-caste Dheds, which resulted in a Dhed appearing between every Brahmin at a Nagar feast.

The following *pada Vaishnava jana* is the most loved of all his verses. It draws on Jain traditions in the description of the true religious person, and has become widely known outside Gujarat through having been a personal favourite of Gandhi. It is probably the best-known Gujarati lyric and, since it is non-sectarian, being a description of a Vaishnava, it is used by all Vaishnava groups in Gujarat including the followers of Swaminarayan:

> *The true Vaishnava is the one who feels another's sufferings as his own.*
> Even when he helps the sufferer, he does not feel proud.
> He praises everything in the whole world, he does not speak ill of anything,
> In speech, action and thought he is steady, his mother is extremely blessed.
> He looks on everything dispassionately, he has abandoned desire, another's wife is like his mother.
> He does not speak any untruth, he does not lay his hand on another's wealth.
> Delusion and ignorance do not enter him, detachment is firm in his mind.
> He sings along with God's name, all holy places are in his body.
> He is without greed, and bereft of deceit, he has turned away from lust and anger.
> Narasaiyo says at the sight of him, the family is saved for seventy-on generations.

The first film on Narsi was Sagar Movietone's *Narasinh Mehta*, (1932), in Gujarati, directed by Nanubhai Vakil. It was an overtly Gandhian film with emphasis on Narsi's *bhajans* and faith rather than his miracles. In contrast, Vijay Bhatt's film *Narsi Bhagat*(Hindi)/*Narsi Mehta*(Gujarati) (1940) (see Chapter 1 for more on Vijay Bhatt) concentrates on miracles, rather than devotion as did *Sant Tukaram*, even though he cast Vishnupant Pagnis after his performance as Tukaram and Prabhat's Durga Khote as Narsi's wife. Bhatt shows at length nearly all the miracles associated with Narsi's life (see above), and the gods themselves appear several times in the film.

Narsi's songs are used to good effect in the film, as they are worked into the narrative to illustrate episodes of his life, and the film ends with the great *bhajan*, *Vaishnava jana*, summing up the film's narrative, which concerns what it means to be a Vaishnava.

Bhatt's film was successful, running to silver jubilees in many parts of India, but not on the scale of *Tukaram*. The *Filmshow Annual* 1941 (published from Karachi and Lahore) says, 'Narsi Bhagat has proved a veritable gold mine; it is doing topping business in every station.'

Hindi sant films

There are three main types of *sant* who are important for cinema in north India. Two are Vaishnava, one based around Rama and one around Krishna, and the third is non-Vaishnava, *nirgun* ('formless') *bhakti*.

The *Ramcharitmanas* of Tulsidas (1532–1623), a telling of the *Ramayana* in Avadhi, an eastern variant of Hindi, based on several versions of the *Ramayana*, has become the dominant telling of the story of Rama in north India. Many versions and sections of his *Ramayana* are the basis of mythologicals (see Chapter 1) but there are many fewer films about the life of Tulsidas himself. None of the versions of the *Ramcharitmanas* has met with great success at the box office. The first was a flop, with N.G. Devare of Kohinoor in 1934; then Jayant Desai of Ranjit Movietone in 1939 made one with Pagnis, who had played Tukaram, and a script by Washikar, who had written *Sant Tukaram* in Hindi and Marathi. The film is the story of a young pleasure-loving type who becomes ascetic and 'translates' the *Ramayana*, opposed by Brahmins but helped by many miracles. Another version directed by Balchander Shukla and Harsukh Bhatt in 1954 was critically acclaimed.[53] Again, the film is about the young man's scholarship and devotion to Rama, with episodes about his romance and marriage, which breaks down due to malicious gossip, leading Tulsidas to the path of renunciation. It shows in detail his search for Rama and his decision to 'translate' the *Ramayana* into the vernacular language.

Krishna *bhakti* in north India has been mostly sectarian, and such films are felt to appeal only to restricted audiences, so films about Chaitanya would not be expected to meet any success in western India.[54] The dominant Vaishnava sect in western India is the Pushtimarg, the followers of Vallabha, a highly Sanskritising and exclusive group. However, part of their *seva* (worship) of Krishna involves the songs of some of north India's most loved poets, including Surdas, whose vast popularity extends beyond the sect.

Although versions of the Surdas story go back to the silent period (I mentioned the Madans' 1932 production, *Bilwamangal/Bhakta Surdas*) above, there are surprisingly few films about him and no major release.

The most famous would be the K.L. Saigal version (dir. Chaturbhuj Doshi, 1942).

> Saigal and Khurshid in Bhakta Surdas – Ranjit released their sublime devotional Bhakta Surdas. During the first week this picture has won unprecedented popularity everywhere and had the most coveted honour of breaking all previous box office records. Bhakta Surdas brings to the screen Saigal and Khurshid, the singing idols of millions, together for the first time and so, picturegoers were looking forward to them for having the joy of hearing the sweetest songs.[55]

> Bhakta Surdas, 6th week at Opera House
> A sinner turned a saint – that is the great story of Bhakta Surdas, now in the 6th week at Opera House. Drawn by desire he goes to the house of a singing girl and drawn by pious devotion he ends at the feet of Lord Krishna. Surdas is directed by Chaturbhuj Doshi and has a grand cast of Saigal (etc).[56]

And little is remembered of Vijay Bhatt's film:

> SARDI REVIEWS OUR SCREEN
> The Blind Saint: The Gujerati photoplay, Bhakta Surdas, from the Prakash Studios presents a lofty tale. Bilwamangal is a man in love with life; but for him life stands for the gratification of every lustful desire. No excuse is too low if he can get near to Chintamani, a singer who first opens his eyes to the evil of his carnal ways. He decides to turn over a new leaf and along with Chintamani becomes a wandering devotee. When, however, he one day sees a beautiful woman, the flesh calls once more. It is from this character that the name Surdas, as applied to the blind, originates, for when the mendicant realises that his eyes are windows through which temptation finds welcome, he shuts them for ever by blinding himself.[57]

One of the most popular *bhakti* poets is Meera or Meerabai (*c.* 1500–47). There are conflicting versions of her biography (see Dwyer 2001: 63) but she was a Rajput queen who refused to live with her husband, saying that she was married to Krishna. She claims that attempts were made on her life, so she fled to Dwarka. Meera imagines herself as a *gopi* (milkmaid) in her songs of her erotic devotion to Krishna with whom she eventually merged. Versions of Meera's songs are found in the literary traditions of Gujarat, Rajasthan and Braj.

As a great woman devotee, it is not surprising to find several films about her (such as Sagar's *Meera Bai*, dir. Chaturbhuj Doshi, 1932, and one by Shalimar, dir. W.Z. Ahmad, 1947[58]), but it seems that the version of the film made in 1945 with Subbalaxmi was so successful that it eclipsed all others. Gulzar's version (1979) was not a great success, although critically acclaimed. It had a star cast with Hema Malini and Vinod Khanna and music by Ravi Shankar, but the singing of the *bhajans* was a little disappointing after the Subbalaxmi and Lata Mangeshkar versions. The film avoids presenting any miracles and Meera comes across as rather selfish and strange, while King Bhoj is something of a martyr.

The 1945 version was directed by an American, Ellis Duncan, who made several Tamil films, despite never learning the language.[59] The original version of this film was made in Tamil with M.S. Subbalaxmi, who was to become the most celebrated female singer in Carnatic (south Indian) music. The Hindi version is introduced by the poet and freedom fighter, Sarojini Naidu. The film follows the stories of Meera's life well known from her legends, and the eighteen *bhajans* that Subbalaxmi sang have become standard versions of the songs. However, it was not so well received; as *Picturpost* (15 Nov. 1945: 47–50) pointed out, it lacked miracles, showing 'just a woman who sings bhajans which are also none too pleasing to hear'. It also accuses the film of lacking conviction and realism and not being emotional enough. It then says that Subbalaxmi is wrongly cast as she is a Carnatic singer, not a Hindustani singer. It then says she is not physically pleasing, even saying that she is scary when she shows her teeth, ugly and unemotional. The director does not get off lightly either, his direction being called 'bungling'. However, other reviews were more favourable:

Figure 2.5 Meera (1945, dir. Elis Duncan). Meera (M.S. Subbalaxmi), the devotee of Krishna Giridhar Gopal.

SARDI REVIEWS OUR SCREEN
Resurrecting Meera: It is in the fitness of things that the South Indian singer Subbulakshmi's first Hindi film should depict her as the immortal Meera the singing saint who was a profound devotee of the Lord Krishna. More than the story of the Queen of Mewar who preferred a heavenly to an earthly diadem it is the voice of the star singing her bhajans and padas that is the picture's chief attraction. Strangely enough it is a foreigner Ellis R. Duncan who has wielded the megaphone for this film. Narendra Sharma's lyrics embellish this photoplay, the story of which is from the pen of Amritlal Nagar. Subbulakshmi's admirers will find this film highly entertaining.[60]

The third and last group of *sants* includes Kabir, Nanak and others. These *sants* are not Vaishnava but they mix Vaishnava *bhakti*, Sufism and Nath yoga. They follow *nirgun bhakti*, which is sometimes taken to mean 'where god has no form', but Gold (1987: 204) points out that this does not mean God is literally formless but rather that there is less emphasis on the image.

Of these, Kabir (1398–1448)[61] a weaver of Benares, is one of the best-known and loved for his strong images, folk wisdom and his critical and cutting words (see Vaudeville 1974). His name is Muslim but he was born into a low-caste group of weavers (*julaha*) who had converted to Islam. He is claimed by both Hindus and Muslims and many of his verses are found in the Sikh scriptures as he was influenced by many sources.[62] He uses Rama and Hari as names for God, along with Allah and impersonal names such as *shunya* ('emptiness') and *shabda* ('word', 'sound'). When he died, the Hindus wanted to cremate him, the Muslims to bury him. Kabir's ghost told them to lift the shroud. All they found was a heap of flowers. The Hindus took half and cremated them at Varanasi, the Muslims buried the other half at Maghar.

His followers are known as the Kabirpanthi, a sect of Hinduised *sadhus*. He was much referred to by Gandhi and Tagore and became a symbol of Hindu–Muslim synthesis, the position which most of the films show. However, if one reads Kabir's works, he is scathing about Hindu, Muslim and Nath practices, and it is clear that the films' image of him is sanitised and glosses over his trenchant criticism of institutionalised religions. Reviews of *Bhakta Kabir* (1942, dir. Rameshwar Sharma) present this view:

BHAKTA KABIR, BY A CORRESPONDENT: Last Saturday, I went to see the 6:30 show of the film Bhakta Kabir. It was delightful and thought-provoking. After seeing it one can say with certainty that most of the differences between the Hindus and the Mussalmans are artificial. Such pictures capture the imagination and inculcate unity which is the need of the hour. Although I saw the picture four days ago the impression it left on my mind is still fresh. The Unity Productions have done a real service in presenting Kabir who to say the least must be regarded as the symbol of Hindu–Muslim unity for all times to come. The way in which his dohas have been woven into the story is simply remarkable. The picture must be seen by all who want to have a realistic grip of religion and what it ought to teach.[63]

KABIR IN 6TH WEEK AT MINERVA
Never before in the history of film exhibition such a high tribute as to exempt a picture from entertainment Tax has been paid as in the case of Unity Production's screen epic Bhakta Kabir which is specially exempted from entertainment tax of the Punjab government. While commenting over this picture, they said that Kabir was not an ordinary type of picture which caters for public taste as usual. It is a unique screen epic which has wonderful significance and power to move the people towards National Unity. Hence Bhakta Kabir deserves all the credit to go as landmark of purposeful production.[64]

An advertisement proclaims: 'Kabir kills communal bogey! They stoned Jesus Christ, a son of a carpenter. They stoned Kabirjee a sun [sic] of a weaver. Its [sic] a challenge to all those high-brow anti-nationalists.'[65]

Guru Nanak (1469–1539) was the founder of the religion known as Sikhism or Gurumat.[66] The status of guru passed to nine more human gurus, then the last guru, Guru Gobind Singh, made the scripture (the *Guru Granth Sahib*) the guru, entrusting the spirit to it and to the community of followers (the *panth*). The *Guru Granth Sahib* (the final version of the *Adi Granth*) is in verse and contains writings by Hindus (such as Namdev) and Muslims (such as Kabir) as well as the *shabads* (devotional songs) of the gurus.

The last of the *sant* films is said to be *Nanak naam jahaz hai* (1969, dir. Ram Maheshwari), a Sikh devotional in Punjabi. Made for the five-hundreth anniversary of Guru Nanak's birth, it is not about the *sant* himself but is a family drama. Two close friends quarrel and one's wife accidentally blinds the other's son. After the aunt, the niece and the man have travelled to various *gurdwaras*, allowing scope for us to see holy places and to hear *shabads*, the young couple get married. Finally, as the wife sings in praise of Nanak at the Golden Temple in Amritsar, a light moves seemingly from a lamp in the Akal Takht (although lights are forbidden there) to the husband's eyes, restoring his sight. This film was the first big Punjabi hit in post-independence cinema and is still shown on television on Sikh religious festivals, notably Guru Nanak's birthday, in India and in the diaspora.

Appeal of sant films

Some of the appeal of *sant* films is the same as that of the mythologicals, in the familiar stories and in the manifestation of the divine in the everyday:

> SARDI REVIEWS OUR SCREEN
> Familiar mythological subject: In this land where on men is quickly bestowed the halo of sainthood, it is not surprising to find our screen inundated with stories of mythological saints. Usually they are very poor men or royal personages who toss aside their crowns for heavenly diadems. Bhakta Dhruva belongs to the latter variety.[67]

The films, as contemporary retellings of tradition, reinvigorate the traditions themselves, making stories visible, questioning the role of tradition and making the experience of devotion available through this new and accessible medium. However, the writer was aware of the sensitive issues involved here, as Shivram Washikar, who wrote *Sant Tukaram* among other Prabhat films, talks about this:

> [The writer] must be in between believer and researcher – have to remember much of the audience will be devout believers and don't want the story to deviate, however sophisticated they may seem. They insist even on things like Draupadi and five husbands though these don't fit current views. I tried to keep something of value to present – so here a Maratha family's ordinary life.[68]

One very popular element of the devotional are the much-loved songs of the devotees, which are given new music, performed by some of the best singers and given new meanings by adding visuals and placing them within the narrative of the devotees' lives. It is hard to explain the position that these songs have in India, but they are among some of the best-known lyrics and poems (see Hawley and Juergensmayer 1988). Some of these effects are part of the attractions of Indian cinema (see Dwyer and Patel 2002, Ch. 1), and the devotional film brings together key elements of the Indian cinema, notably song, music, image and emotion.

Like the mythological, there seems to be some religious experience in the viewing of the films but this is not well documented. It seems that the devotional produces some particular personal contact with the deity and with the devotee, as noted above in the discussion of *Sant Tukaram*. Perhaps an analogy may be drawn with the viewing of films that show *tirthyatras* (places of pilgrimage), where the viewer benefits from the sight of the holy place. This is clearly one of the pleasures of *Nanak naam jahaz hai*, which shows the couple visiting key *gurdwaras* not only to their own benefit but also to that of the viewer.

All the major devotees created communities of followers (the Kabir-panthis, the Sikhs), and it seems that the films may well produce a feeling of community, of being part of an audience rather than a spectator, bound to the film by the songs and the emotions. The relationship of the viewer to the devotee is complicated as the reverence and devotion for the figure are tied into film-viewing practices and emotional relationships to characters within films.

The devotional film is much more regional than the mythological film. Even though films about the devotees have been made in languages other than their own (so dual-language versions of most of Prabhat films, Ellis Duncan's *Meera* and Vijay Bhatt's *Narsi Mehta*; while some original–language films were made in other language areas such as *Tukaram* in Tamil by Balkrishna Narayan Rao (1938), and M.L. Tandon's Telugu version in 1937[69]), their appeal has largely been in the areas where they are already familiar figures.

In many ways the devotional is allied more closely to the social film and the historical than is the mythological film. All the figures presented were not just devotees, mystics and poets but also social reformers. For example, Guru Nanak's *shabads* show his profound mysticism and poetic skills but his founding of a new religion shows his philosophical and his organisational skills as well. Kabir is presented as synthesising the beliefs of different groups (Muslims, Hindus and Nath yogis) and thus as some-thing of a social reformer, although, as noted above, he was actually a bitter critic of all their institutionalised practices and shallow beliefs. The films all raise major social concerns, which it sets in the context of the rural, eternal, symbolic and political. This kind of social questioning that was popular in Indian cinema from the 1930s to the 1950s has largely moved outside the commercial cinema into its own genres of the 'middle' or parallel cinema, exemplified by makers such as Shyam Benegal.

Unlike the mythological, which is set in other *yugas* (aeons) and 'non-historical' time, the devotional is set in actual historical time where the devotees meet rulers and other attested figures. Although in a film like *Sant Tukaram* the historical attractions (costume, language and so on) are played down to such an extent that the film has the feel of the 'time-less' village, the presence of Shivaji and the reference to battles ground it in a historical framework. The devotees are presented as figures of their time, who created an impact on history by reforming society and reli-gious practices and beliefs. As the historical film (see Mukhopadhyay 2004), the devotional themes and issues had resonances with the present. It is clear that many of the devotionals were linked to the independence movement, and more explicitly to Gandhi's beliefs and actions (see below), and with the rise of the social genre after independence, the devotional genre fell from favour as the themes no longer seemed appropriate to, indeed were in opposition to, the concerns of this-worldliness, of love and romance and the family in the new nation.

Gokarn divides devotional films into good and bad. Among the former she lists the following: *Rajranee Meera* 1933, *Sant Dnyaneshwar* 1940, *Sant Sakhu* 1941, *Bhakticha Mali* 1944, *Sant Tukaram* 1936, *Sant Tulsidas* 1954, *Mahatma Kabir* 1954, *Shirdi ke Saibaba* 1977, *Meera* 1979 for their character, dignity, authenticity, devotional fervour of songs, spiritual atmosphere (Gokarn n.d.: 100), while she accuses the bad films of being shallow, superficial, crude and ignorant; they distort the biography and deify the *sant*.[70]

> Such films are utterly degrading in taste and stigmatise the sublime characters that they attempt to delineate. Hence such films do not deserve to be categorised under the genre of 'Devotionals'. It is on account of such sub-standard films that spectators have lost interest and belief in Devotional subjects ... playing upon the baser human instincts of sensuality and sentiment of the spectators, without any thought for uplifting their rational thinking or ennobling their emotional sensibilities and spiritual capacities. Thus, the true import of Devotional Films is lost in the illusory name of spectacle and fantasmagoria (Gokarn n.d.: 97).

Like the mythological (see Chapter 1), she blames these faults on the devotional's appeal as a lower-class and rural film, popular among the masses (see Gokarn n.d.: 102, quoted above).

There was certainly an ongoing debate about the audience and the appeal of these films throughout the time they were made. The elite preferred the films which were 'authentic' and focused on the social and historical aspects of the film, whereas the lower classes enjoyed the miracles. The latter were unabashed, rejecting this criticism of their pleasures as an example of leftist 'intellectualism' and they preferred the miracles.[71]

All directors feel that they need to strike a compromise between the social aspects of the film and the miracles, as mentioned above in the critics' analysis of *Dnyaneshwar*.

Godmen

There are several films about new gurus, who are unusual in that they claim no lineage from other gurus but are new figures and are often regarded as divine. Some claim their lineage from recent godmen as Sathya Sai Baba claims to be a reincarnation of Sai Baba of Shirdi.

Some have claimed only the status of teachers and scholars. This would include Swami Vivekananda who has been the subject of several films (e.g. *Swami Vivekanand*, dir. Amar Mallick, 1955) but none has made a major impact. In recent years, he has become a figure claimed by the left (mostly secular) and the right (Hindutva) in Indian politics,[72] so it would have been fascinating to have his life presented in very different ways by these groups.

One of the most popular saints of modern India is Sai Baba of Shirdi, who has a strong following all over the country, in the global South Asian diaspora and among many in the Bombay film industry. The life and works of Sai Baba of Shirdi (1836–1918, although some say b. 1856) are detailed and entangled. Rigopoulos (1993) is an academic monograph on Sai, while the standard work among the faithful is Dabholkar (1999). In summary, Sai Baba appeared in Shirdi (now in central Maharashtra) in 1872, aged about sixteen and dressed as a Muslim fakir in a *kafni* robe and headdress (although older images show it as white, it is now usually saffron, the sacred colour of Hinduism). He said he did not remember his origins and is claimed as both a Hindu and a Muslim. His name suggests both are possible as *Sai* is a Persian word meaning approximately 'saint', used for Muslim ascetics, while *Baba*, a term used for some Sufi *pirs*, is also a Hindu and Sikh term meaning 'father', used for parents and gurus. The standard story is that he was born a Brahmin but brought up by Sufis, which is supported by his request to be with Brahmins at his death (White 1972: 868). He had a Hindu guru he called Venkusa.

When he arrived in Shirdi, he wanted to stay in a temple but the priest was not sure of his Hindu-ness, so he lived in a disused mosque for the rest of his life. He worshipped in the style of an *aarti* with lamps and incense (still performed today at his shrine by Brahmins) and also kept a constant fire, *dhuni*, a practice associated with the Nath yogi, as well as performing the Islamic *namaz* (prayers).

Sai Baba performed many miracles in his life and continues to do so now by using yogic *siddhis* (powers). His shrine at Shirdi shows clear Muslim origins, as it is built around his grave in the manner of a *dargah* (grave of a Muslim *pir*).

Sai Baba is something of a patron saint to the film industry. Raj Kapoor and his family were among the first devotees, and he now has a widespread following among the industry. As many directors like to take the first reel of their film to Shirdi to have his blessings, there is even a helicopter service from Juhu (the centre of the industry in Bombay) to Shirdi for Rs 80,000 or so (about £1,000).

It is hard to locate Sai Baba's particular popularity in the film industry without knowing more about his wider popularity. Certainly his syncretism has great appeal, for, unlike Kabir's criticisms of both traditions, Sai Baba really does blend different religious traditions, although the Hindu side seems to be dominant now.[73] Muslims such as Sheikh Fattelal's son regard him as an important holy man, though not a Muslim as such.[74] There is also the nearness of the shrine to Bombay and perhaps also because some of the most successful members of the film industry (Raj Kapoor and Yash Chopra among others) are devotees. However, it seems that in part his appeal is that he is an easy figure to approach, not requiring study or fasts, but simply devotion. His giving of miracles is a major part of his popularity, as with Sathya Sai Baba (1926–) (see Swallow 1982 and Babb 1987). This magical side of his grace appeals to members of the industry who seem to be struggling with impossible odds to find success with their films – this comforts their anxieties and they can have instant blessings for their enterprises.

A film made on Sai Baba in 1977 (*Shirdi ke Sai Baba*, dir. Ashok Bhushan) is often regarded as one of the last great religious films made in India (see Gokarn n.d.). With a cast of top stars supporting Sudhir Dalvi as Sai Baba, it is produced by the superstar Manoj Kumar and the Sarla Charities Trust. A young boy is dying of blood cancer, his mother (Hema Malini) hears a devotee (Manoj Kumar) singing to Sai Baba. He gives her the *vibhuti* ('ashes'), which produce a miracle (with a lot of zoom shots showing the miracle as cuts between the song, images of Sai Baba, the boy and the parents). The boy wakes up and demands to go to Shirdi. The boy's father, a doctor (Rajendra Kumar), has a long dialogue with the devotee whose sight was restored by Sai Baba. The film then tells the life story of Sai Baba, based on Dabholkar (1999), showing him as a Muslim, calling himself a fakir and reciting from the Quran, but also as a Hindu who recited from the *Bhagavad Gita*. Greedy, scheming Brahmins are mocked but others are shown to be good; untouchability is attacked; and people are reformed. The central performance of Dalvi is very strong, the film has a sincere feel and the miracles are often moving, despite their technical simplicity and the tableau-style presentation of the scenes.

Concluding remarks

Many groups of organised Hinduism which follow gurus and other leaders use privately circulated media, such as weekly blessings, DVDs, VHS and CDs that are available at community centres/places of worship or through the Internet. The Swaminarayan movement (see Dwyer 2004b) was quick to use these as part of structuring itself as a global movement. Although the Swaminarayan temples show pictorial stories of Swaminarayan's life in narrative form and I have seen a television serial about the miracles of Swaminarayan, the only film on his life is the 40-minute *Mystic India* (dir. Keith Melton, 2004). The sect has long produced books in Gujarati and English, have used VHS messages from the leaders for several years and now have active and informative websites.

Although there have been very few devotional films in the last few years, it is too soon to say that the genre will not be revived. Given the popularity of devotional songs available in other media (cassettes, CDs, radio, television), there is no reason that issues of morality, religion and other spiritual questions may not reappear on film, in particular with the computer-generated images of recent years, which could allow for spectacular miracles and historical reconstructions. However, in the last few years, Indian cinema has had other concerns which are broader and remain rooted in the omnibus social film. But before I discuss some of these in Chapter 4, I first look at the other major religious tradition in India, Islam, which has produced films that may be said to belong to an Islamicate tradition or a Muslim imagination rather than being concerned directly with religion.

Chapter 3

The Islamicate film

Given Islamic restrictions on the depiction of God and his Prophets, there is no equivalent 'Islamic' film to parallel the mythological and devotional films and so it may be said that there is no 'Filming the gods'. However, since there is at least one genre which mentions the religion by name, that is the 'Muslim social', and there are several other styles of films (perhaps sub-genres) often ascribed to this genre, there is a clearly identifiable group of films which are concerned particularly with Muslims though not with Islam itself. As these films are concerned with religion as part of everyday social and cultural life among Muslims, rather than with religion and religious belief per se, and are in no way Islamic, these films may be described as 'Islamicate',[1] which 'would refer not directly to the religion, Islam, itself, but to the social and cultural complex historically associated with Islam and the Muslims, both among Muslims themselves and even when found among non-Muslims' (Kesavan 1994: 246).

(There is no genre called the 'Hindu social' as Hindu practices and beliefs are the 'norm' in Hindi cinema. See Chapter 4.) This discussion of Indian Muslim culture and society also shows how much religion in India is part of culture and society in all communities and how much Indian Islamicate culture is rooted in India itself as few films show the wider Muslim community. Very few films link Indian Islam to West Asia/The Middle East and the Arabic world, although specific (sub-) genres refer to the fantasy world of the Arabian Nights and ancient Persia, to the Ottoman Empire and to India's Other, Pakistan after it was created by the Partition of India in 1947.

In this chapter, I look at the relationship between cinema and Muslim culture, beginning with the issue of Muslims working in the film industry. I then move on to the roots of the cinematic Islamicate culture in the Muslim culture of north India, in particular the connections Hindi cinema has with its language, literature, music and clothing. I draw particular attention to Urdu, which emerges as a cosmopolitan language in Bombay theatre and cinema, while retaining its Islamicate associations. I then turn to the Islamicate genres of Hindi cinema before looking at the representation of Muslims in other genres, tracing their historical changes.

Cinema and Muslim culture

Indian cinema has deep roots in the culture of north India, in particular the new public culture that emerged in the nineteenth century, itself in part a product of many changes in Indian culture that began as part of the colonial encounter and other social shifts of the time.

Although Muslims live all over India, it is rarely remembered now that the majority urban population of north India before Partition was Muslim. It was spread across the whole social spectrum from royalty and aristocracy, a landowning (*zamindari*) class as well as the beginnings of an educated middle class, a petty bourgeoisie and to lower classes. Bombay, as a Presidency city, had its own peculiar demography, with a very diverse population. Most of its Muslim population was formed of a petty bourgeoisie of Gujarati trading castes (see Dwyer 2000a, Chapter 3), such as the Khojas and Memons. It is hard to say why there were few Muslims in Indian cinema in the early days (RICC: 83). Perhaps this was because most of the Muslims in Bombay at the time were small traders and saw the industry as an unknown financial risk. In Bengal, most of the early cinema makers were from elite, *bhadralok* ('gentry') or aristocratic backgrounds as were several of the Bombay film makers. Although the pioneers of early Bombay cinema came from diverse backgrounds – Phalke was Maharashtrian, actresses were often Jewish (Sulochana or Ruby Meyers), or Anglo-Indian (Patience Cooper) – it could be said that early Bombay cinema was very Gujarati, with major figures including Chandulal Shah, the personnel of Kohinoor Film Company (1919–32), the Krishna Film Company (1924–35), and many Parsis, such as Ardeshir Irani who co-founded Star Films Limited, then Majestic Films and the Imperial Films Company (1929–38),[2] and the Wadia brothers' Wadia Movietone (1933–) and so on.[3]

The new visual regime which evolved in late nineteenth-century Indian public culture was a new visual field, where an interocularity was established between forms such as chromolithography, theatre and so on. Interestingly, although there is no historical study of Islamicate chromolithographs,[4] there are many images which are kept in Muslim homes, mostly images of Mecca and calligraphy of verses from the Quran.[5] Although the production of images was anathema to orthodox Muslim culture, India has a long tradition of the production of images among Muslims, most famously in Mughal miniatures and illustrated books. Although Muslim painters had abounded in the courts where they painted human images, the human image (at least of adults) is mostly absent in the production of chromolithographs, which were perhaps too closely associated with images of the gods. All images are still somewhat restricted, although images of Mecca and other shrines are permitted, with Shi'ites allowing a wider range of subjects (see Pinault 2001). Islamicate culture is also associated with music, singing and dancing, which are also frowned on by the orthodox, but these can be viewed under the sign of Indian culture.

It was only with the coming of sound, that is to say post-1931, that larger numbers of Muslims entered the industry. The perception that the industry has a disproportionate number of Muslim stars, producers, directors, stunts, in fact at all levels, is only true of the Indian cinema after this point. Even with the coming of sound the big studios of Bombay Talkies, Prabhat and New Theatres, had few Muslims in the production side but included significant persons such as Sheikh Fattelal at Prabhat, who co-directed *Sant Tukaram* (see Chapter 2).

Among the many Muslim directors is A.R. Kardar (1904–89), originally a painter and photographer (so a possible contradiction to the suggestion of the absence of Muslims in early cinema in the paragraph above). He worked as a director in Lahore, Calcutta, then in Bombay, where he founded his own studio. However, the greatest Muslim director was undoubtedly Mehboob Khan (1906–64). Mehboob's story is a classic rags-to-riches as he came to Bombay to work as an extra and founded a major studio, which is still in the hands of his family.[6]

It seems Mehboob often worked with other Muslims: his actors included Sardar Akhtar (his wife), Yaqub, Madhubala, Nargis, Nimmi, Noorjehan, Dilip Kumar (as well as non-Muslims such as Ashok Kumar and Nadira); his favourite music director Naushad and singers Rafi and Shamshad Begum (as well as non-Muslims Lata Mangeshkar and Mukesh).

One of Mehboob's early films is *Al Hilal* or the *Judgment of Allah* (1935). It is a Muslim popular historical set in the Ottoman Empire showing the struggle between Muslims and the Romans.[7] Ziyad, the son of the sultan, is captured by the Romans. A Roman princess, Rahil, falls in love with him and sets Leila (Sitara) to guard him. Leila and Rahil help him escape. This film shows curious features which are residues of silent cinema as sound was unfamiliar and new, such as scenes with no dialogue, just music. There are many court scenes and grand dialogues. The use of terms such as *azad*, *qaidi* and *ghulam*, about slavery and freedom, which are used frequently to criticise the Romans, could easily be interpreted as references to the British. One rallying cry of '*Al Hilal zindabad*' could easily have been taken as an audience-rousing moment against the British.

Mehboob made a Muslim historical, *Humayun* (1945), about the Mughal emperor, written by Agha Jani Kashmiri, with music by Ghulam Haider, starring Nargis and Ashok Kumar. The film's line is that Muslims gave India freedom but it also emphasises the good relations between the Mughals and the Rajputs, and shows 'Islamic' miracles – when a father prays that he may take on his son's illness, he is hit by a lightning bolt and dies.

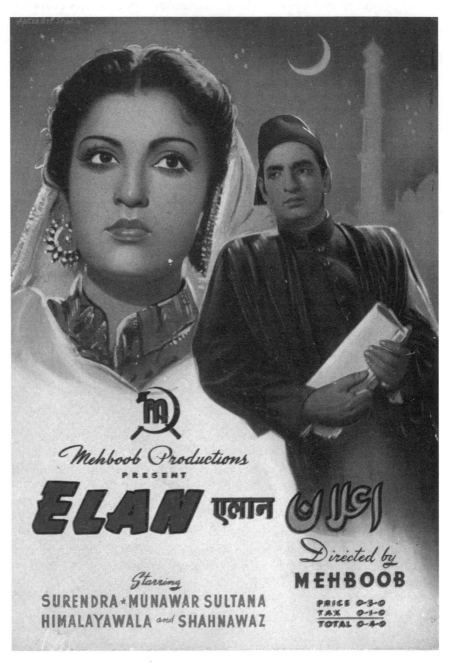

Figure 3.1 Elaan (1947, dir. Mehboob Khan). Song booklet of this Muslim social.

Mehboob also made Muslim socials such as *Najma* (1943), set in early twentieth-century Lucknow, with a wedding refused because the princely family will not accept a bourgeois (doctor) son-in-law, and *Elaan* (1947), where good and bad half-brothers are rivals for a woman who has to marry the richer bad brother. After his death, the good brother wants to marry her but she commits her life to education and sings a stirring song from within *purdah*.

However, nowadays Mehboob is best known for his social films, in particular *Anmol ghadi* (1946), which has some of the best songs of Hindi cinema sung by Noorjehan and Suraiya, the two great singing stars, and most importantly, *Mother India* (1957). These films do not have any Muslims, most strikingly absent in the latter, which is regarded as the national epic (see more in Chapter 4).

Several of the great music directors of Hindi film are Muslims, such as Ghulam Haider, who is said to have discovered Noorjehan and Lata Mangeshkar, the two greatest female singers of India (later Pakistan and India). Haider wrote the hit music for *Khazanchi* (1941), where he introduced Punjabi music that later became a dominant part of Hindi film's hybrid style. He migrated to Pakistan after Partition as did Noorjehan. Many other top musicians of Hindi cinema have been Muslims, including Naushad Ali (see below), one of the greatest music directors, and there have been many popular Muslim female singers in addition to Noorjehan such as Suraiya and Shamshad Begum, although their style was eclipsed by Lata Mangeshkar and then her sister Asha Bhosle, along with Geeta Roy (later Dutt). Mohammad Rafi dominated male playback singing in the 1950s and 1960s, until Kishore Kumar became more popular, but now nearly all playback singers are Hindus.

Many of the writers of Hindi cinema were Muslims including Agha Kashmiri, Akhtar Mirza, Saadat Manto and the first superstar writers Salim (Khan)–Javed (Akhtar). Most of the lyricists of cinema have been Muslims with a background in Urdu poetry, including Majrooh Sultanpuri and Sahir Ludhianvi, until the 1970s when Anand Bakshi dominated, although Javed Akhtar is currently one of the most critically acclaimed.

The coming of sound to Indian cinema meant that Hindi cinema needed stars with the right accents. Therefore, vaguely north Indian so Urdu-speakers, who were mostly Muslims or Punjabis educated in Urdu, were popular choices, although there were many from other areas (Ashok Kumar from Calcutta and many from Bombay). Many of the top female stars were Muslim, including 'Glorious' Gohar (one of the few stars to be successful in silent films and talkies), Noorjehan, Suraiya (both singing stars), Nargis, Madhubala, Meena Kumari and Waheeda Rehman. The 1960s saw Saira Bano and Mumtaz, with Zeenat Aman and Parveen Babi in the 1970s (and Shabana Azmi, although she is more associated with 'middle' cinema), but there have been no major female Muslim stars in recent years. The reasons for this shift are not clear but are perhaps to do with changes in class and performative traditions. There have been fewer major Muslim male stars, although Dilip Kumar was one of the top stars of the 1950s and 1960s. There were few Muslim stars in the next decades but in the 1990s, the three Khans (no relation), Aamir, Salman and Shahrukh, dominated the box office with Shahrukh still the top star in 2005 (despite strong competition from the revival of the career of the greatest superstar of Hindi cinema, Amitabh Bachchan). (For a discussion of name changes among Muslim and other stars, see Chapter 4.)

The reasons for the change in the industry in the 1930s are not clear but it seems that they may be due in part to the shift in cinema from being just a visual (silent) medium to the addition of sound, in particular the creation of a musical cinema where songs and melodramatic dialogues soon established themselves as a major 'attraction' (see Dwyer and Patel 2002, Ch. 1). This was one of many features taken in part from the Parsi theatre, which had been popular since the mid-nineteenth century, when it had created new audiences and a new public for the theatre (Kapur 1993a and Hansen 2000, 2004). This theatre drew on a rich repertoire of fantasy and historical romances from the Persian *Shahnameh* and the Indo-Islamic romances as well as Shakespeare and Hindu mythologies (see Chapter 1). It seems no coincidence that Parsi theatre went into decline in the 1930s, when sound came to the cinema, as the pleasures the talkies offered were greater than those of the silent cinema (Hansen 2000: 89). With the decline of the Parsi theatre, many of its personnel migrated to the cinema industry, in particular those whose skills lay in the newly required specialisms of the Urdu language (lyricists, dialogue writers and actors) and in music, where Muslims had long worked alongside Hindus, and these were the areas in which the Muslim personnel dominated. Many of these people may have formed a major part in the creation of an Islamicate cinema, although the role of people from other religious communities should not be overlooked.

Before looking at the Islamicate genres, I discuss some of the features of this cinema that are most closely associated with Muslim culture, namely language, literature (in particular the lyric), musical genres and clothing.

Urdu and Hindi cinema

The majority language of India's northern cities before independence was a lingua franca that could be variously described as Hindi, Urdu or Hindustani. Much has been written about the intricate and entwined emergence of these languages and their separation in north India.[8] The terms are used differently over time but in short, Hindi and Urdu, though almost identical at some levels, have very different scripts (Hindi being Devanagari; Urdu, Perso-Arabic) and diverge considerably at higher registers, where

Hindi draws on Sanskrit and Urdu on Persian and Arabic. The separation of Hindi and Urdu from the mid nineteenth century on is due in part to political reasons, with Urdu becoming seen as a 'Muslim language' due to its association with Muslim courts and its close ties with Persian language and literature. While this may have been true for parts of north India, Urdu was also the language for Hindus and Sikhs in the Punjab until 1947.

One of the major differences between the languages is the literary traditions with which they are associated. Urdu emerged as a literary language in the Deccan courts of the sixteenth century before appearing in the Mughal court of Delhi and the Avadhi court of Lucknow, and hence it is associated with courtly culture and a refined literature of which the lyric tradition is the most celebrated (see Matthews *et al.* 1985, Pritchett 1994). Although courtly culture declined in north India after 1857 with the establishment of British rule, literature thrived in the new print and public cultures and the new reading publics were formed. Modern literature, such as the novel and the short story, as well as newspaper and journal culture, in Urdu emerged in the late nineteenth century and flourished in the twentieth century. There was also a significant market for popular literature in Urdu, such as the *dastans* and *qissas*, which had previously circulated mostly as oral stories.

The 'Hindi film' is made in a colloquial form of Hindi, which at some registers is identical to colloquial Urdu, and given the general visual absence of writing in the film (the title is given in Roman, Devanagari and Perso-Arabic with subsequent titles in Roman and occasionally Hindi), it can be disputed whether the film is in Hindi or in Urdu. Some films were censored as being in Hindi and others in Urdu, even through the 1960s, often for no apparent reason,[9] although now they are almost exclusively listed as Hindi. This is for complex political reasons, largely to do with Hindi's status as the national language of India and Urdu's as that of Pakistan, and the increasing association of Urdu with India's minority Muslim population, rather than anything to do with the form of the language itself.

Alongside Hindi language and cultures, all these Urdu cultures, increasingly associated with the Islamic, are found in Hindi cinema. Although the culture of the courts may seem far away from cinema, the place it has held in the imagination has remained, as can be seen in the many films that are located within this world, albeit filtered through the popular imagination, or, more precisely, the culture of the bazaar. However, in at least three areas the cinema has kept closer to courtly culture, namely language, song lyrics and music and the association of these with a Muslim world.

However, there is little written about Urdu's emergence as a 'popular' language or lingua franca, as research has focused on the Hindi–Urdu split in what was formerly United Provinces, in British India, and is now Uttar Pradesh (UP), rather than looking at the history of Urdu in other

Indian cities. Even cities like Calcutta, which are popularly held to be strongholds of Bengali, had many Hindustani-speakers in the census of 1911, and the history of this emergence of Urdu beyond its traditional areas (Ahmadabad, Hyderabad) in the Presidential cities of Bombay and Calcutta remains to be written. Urdu newspapers were published in these cities where Urdu seems to have become important as the lingua franca. This would begin to explain the Urdu dominance of 'Hindi' cinema and the location of the Hindi cinema outside the Hindi-belt of north India.[10]

Kathryn Hansen (2004) traces the shift in the Parsi theatre, based in Bombay, from Gujarati to Urdu in the late nineteenth century. The writer, Dadi Patel, encouraged its use, not as a first language, but as a lingua franca suitable for poetry and song. From the 1880s, Parsi theatre recruited Urdu writers from north India in particular Delhi and Lucknow so there was an association with the courtly tradition.

Urdu was not necessarily regarded in Bombay as a Muslim language, though it was associated with UP Muslims, while other Muslim groups such as Gujarati Muslims, Iranis as well as non-Muslims such as Parsis, Punjabis, Jews and other minority communities of Bombay learnt Urdu as their second language and it begins to be something of a lingua franca. So when sound came to cinema in the 1930s, the language chosen for cinema was a form of Urdu that would be the most widely understood. The film makers were not interested in the politics of language but in reaching the maximum audience while using a form of language appropriate to their subjects and style. Islamicate genres had a particularly Persianised Urdu in the 1930s and 1940s. Iqbal Masud (n.d.) writes:

> In this matrix of music and dialogue, 'high' and 'popular' Muslim cultures come together. As late as the 1960s, a film 'Villain' traps a heroine by using a disguise and quoting Ghalib: *Badal kar faqiron ka hum bhes Ghalib/Tamashai-I-ahl-I-karam dekhte hain.* (We put on the garb of a beggar to test the generosity of the rich). The audience understood and applauded the quote.[11]

This tension between Urdu as courtly, literary language and as a language of the bazaar has always energised it culturally, and later cinematically. After the decline of Persian in north India (Alam 2004), north Indian Muslims could be said to be provincials rather than cosmopolitans. Even their Persian was mocked as it became archaic; Sir Syed Ahmad Khan's Persian was reported to sound outmoded in comparison with the Agha Khan's modern Persian in Aligarh in 1897.[12] However, Parsi theatre and, from the 1930s, the cinema returned Urdu to a non-provincial status. Whatever it is called nowadays, some registers of the language Hindi-Urdu-Hindustani remain India's lingua franca, which, it is generally accepted, cinema has actually created.

The language of Hindi cinema has received relatively little attention, in particular in English publications, although there is at least one book-length Hindi publication (Vasvani 1998). Mukul Kesavan (1994) argues that Urdu is the bedrock of Bombay cinema whereas Harish Trivedi (2006) makes a convincing case for Hindi. While historically the roots of Hindi cinema are deep in a cosmopolitan world of Urdu, the Hindi cinema uses both Hindi and Urdu, as well as other forms of this lingua franca and a mixture of other Indian languages (Punjabi and English in particular) as it is interested in creating a language that is suitable for its purposes, which can reach as wide an audience as possible. Sometimes Hindi cinema wants a resonant and quotable language in a high register for a sonorous effect, whereas at other times it wants an everyday language of the bazaar. These languages can be hybrid, sometimes 'pure', but they are always carefully selected, while the song lyric may contain specific languages: for love and romance (see the discussion of the *ghazal* below and also Chapter 4), for humour, for style and so on. For example, regionalisms are used to mock provinciality and a lack of sophistication, so Punjabi Sikhs provide comedy as do notorious Gujarati shibboleths in *Kal ho na ho* (2003, dir. Nikhil Advani). English is used to show education and sophistication and its misuse provides hilarious moments for the audience. Street slang is very popular to mark out lower-class characters, and Bambaiyaa (Bombay dialect) is particularly popular with streetwise *tapori* characters, notably in *Munnabhai MBBS* (2004). The languages used for expressing love or emotions can be quoted for dramatic effect or in real life, whatever language they use. The Hindi/Urdu divide is brought out in Yash Chopra's *Veer-Zaara* (2004), in which the Pakistani (Muslim) characters speak Urdu, the Punjabi villagers speak a mixture of Punjabi and Hindi, while the hero, an Indian Air Force helicopter pilot, speaks Hindi. All educated characters use English occasionally, as they would in real life. While 'pure' Hindi is often mocked (in films such as *Chupke chupke*, 1975, dir. Hrishikesh Mukherjee) and the Hindi teacher is a frump whose classes are a waste of time in *Main hoon na* (2004, dir. Farah Khan), Urdu usually evokes romance and exoticism.

It is hard enough to keep up with the changes in the language of Hindi cinema over the last few years. In the last decade, there are now mixed-language films, such as *Hyderabad Blues* (1998, dir. Nagesh Kukunoor), which mixes English, Hindi/Urdu and Telugu, and although films in English have been made since the beginning of sound, it seems likely that more will be made in coming years. Hindi cinema continues to use a broad spectrum of variants of Urdu and Hindi, whose roots in Islamicate culture are mostly now hidden. However, Hindi films, though banned, are understood in Pakistan[13] and Urdu, however 'Hindified', is still learnt by new generations of South Asians living in the diaspora and is understood in areas of India where Hindi and Urdu are not indigenous or learned.

Literary influences: story and dialogue writers in Urdu traditions

Literary and popular traditions of Urdu entered the cinema with Urdu writers. Several of these were writers from Parsi theatre who moved to cinema, such as Agha Hashr Kashmiri (1879–1935), whose range included Hindustani versions of Shakespeare, original plays and (Hindu) mythologicals. Other important figures include K.A. Abbas (1914–87), the grandson of the great Urdu poet Hali, who was educated at Aligarh Muslim University. An influential person at several levels, he was a journalist, a novelist, a film reviewer for *Bombay Chronicle* (1935–47) as well as a scriptwriter, and he began his career with Bombay Talkies. Although he directed his own films he is best remembered for his work with Raj Kapoor, writing his *Awaara* (1951) and *Shri 420* (1955) (co-written with V.P. Sathe) and *Bobby* (1973). The famous Urdu writer, Saadat Hasan Manto (1912–55), wrote scripts for several studios (Imperial, Filmistan and Bombay Talkies). He wrote a modern, 'secular' Urdu, far from the *nawabi*, Lucknawi style. The relationship between this realist style of writing for film and literature has not been analysed. The most famous scriptwriters of Hindi cinema, Salim–Javed, have also been neglected, although there are two books of interviews with Javed Akhtar, one about cinema (Kabir 1999) and one about his lyrics (Kabir 2005) in which Akhtar presents his own views on the history of writing and Indian cinema.

This area of scriptwriting, again discussed in Hindi though not in English (Joshi 2002), is deserving of scholarly and critical attention, a little more of which has been given to the film song.

Literary influences: the film song

The area in which Urdu and Islamicate traditions have had their greatest impact is in the lyric traditions which flourished in the nineteenth century in the Muslim courts. Hindi cinema is one of the few places that provides a space in the twentieth century for Urdu culture, especially poetry, but nowadays, only a few in the audience have a very scanty knowledge of Urdu poetic vocabulary, which draws heavily on Persian. The Urdu language has long been simplified for cinema, presumably to bring it as near as possible to the lingua franca without losing its poetic quality.

The major literary form that has been used in Hindi cinema is one of Urdu literature's major genres, the *ghazal*, which has become popular in many north Indian languages (Matthews *et al.* 1985, Sadiq 1995). It is a much-loved literary form, used by most of the great Urdu poets, although many critics of Urdu literature disdain it.[14] The *ghazal* is derived from a Persian literary form, consisting of simple, rhymed couplets mostly using stock imagery of passionate but unrequited love, full of misery and woe. An extreme example of this is Ghalib's[15] address 'To a dead mistress':

Dard se mere hai tujh ko bekarari hay hay . . .
At last you are affected by my pain . . . (Matthews 1997: 34–5)

The *ghazal* often draws on Sufi influences, allowing it to be read as both profane and divine: the *'ashiq* ('the lover' can be the poet and/or a mystic), the *ma'ashooq* ('the beloved' can be human or God), concealed behind the veil. Love often overthrows the bounds of religion, the poet claiming that love has made him an unbeliever. The imagery is that of Persian poetry: the formal garden, the tulip and the rose, and the nightingale (*bulbul*), quite distinct from the imagery of traditional Hindu classical (Sanskrit) and devotional (*bhakti*) poetry with which it is sometimes, erroneously, compared. A striking feature of the *ghazal* is that the love portrayed is illicit desire, which is always unrequited, the beloved being cruel and unkind to the lover. The gender of the beloved is often unclear, or may be male or female. Other forbidden pleasures form key elements of the *ghazal*, namely the celebration of the delights of wine and intoxication:

Yeh masael-e-tasavuf, yeh tara byan, Ghalib!
Tujhe ham vali samajhte, jo na bada xvar hota.
These questions of mysticism and your discussions, Ghalib!
We would have thought you a saint, if you weren't such a drunkard!
(Ghalib from Ahmad 1971: 33)

The *ghazal* is a performative genre, usually recited in the poetry gathering (*mushaira*), whether in *tarannum* (semi-melodic chanting), or sung, in *qawwali* or semi-classical style. The performed *ghazal* was an aristocratic genre which became popular in Lucknow in the late 1700s as declining court and feudal landowners (*zamindars*) were replaced by new landlords (*taluqdars*) who favoured light classical forms over traditional classical music. It was sung in a wide range of styles by courtesans, who were trained singers and dancers. Even when they began to give public performances, as concert halls and other venues opened and traditional patronage declined in the twentieth century, the *ghazal* remained an exclusive genre.

This use of the *ghazal* is seen in other forms of Urdu writing, such as in the famous letters of Ghalib, where verses in Urdu or Persian, by Ghalib himself or by others, intersperse his prose.

This use of the *ghazal* in a kind of counterpoint to prose is ideally suited to the popular film, where it serves similar functions, as it highlights or summarises the diegesis of the film's narrative. In the film this is heightened further by the fact that the *ghazals* are in Urdu, whereas the surrounding dialogues are in a more colloquial Hindi. The use of music removes the *ghazal* even further from the spoken word of the film, and with its themes of loss, nostalgia and sadness it remains one of the great pleasures of the film.

Given these elements, it is not surprising that the *ghazal* was taken up by film composers from the earliest days of cinema, while connoisseurs deplored the popularised style and hybrid music of the cinematic *ghazal*. It fell out of favour in film by the end of the 1950s and seemed to be a dying genre, until it was reborn on the audio cassette, whose cheap technology introduced it to a mass market. The first wave of *ghazal* superstars emerged – the Pakistanis, Mehdi Hasan and Ghulam Ali – who sang in a new semi-classical, gentle and sweet style, accompanied by the harmonium, and tabla. They were followed in the 1980s by a new generation of popular singers (Anup Jalota, Pankaj Udhas, Jagjit and Chitra Singh, Roop Kumar and Sonali Rathod – all non-Muslims), who used an even more simplified style, a kind of easy listening that was soothing and sweet but had a classy air. The language was simplified and made more colloquial, to be comprehensible to an audience which knew only Hindi. Cassette and CD sleeves often glossed the Persian and Urdu words into English. This form of the *ghazal* became very popular, its soothing, gentle poetry appealing mostly to the middle classes and urban elites.[16] One of the reasons for its success is undoubtedly its refined, easy-listening effect but the poetry itself remains important as a major medium for sad, romantic love songs, which have been largely squeezed out of cinema by upbeat dance numbers.

This *ghazal* is important because it provides one of the few public spaces left for Urdu literature in modern India, its aural nature bypassing the script for those who can understand but not read the language. Its influence on the Hindi film lyric is immense, with the whole lyrical language of love being derived from the *ghazal*.

While a distinctive form of the *ghazal* itself is not found so frequently nowadays in Hindi film songs, its influence is huge, with its language permeating the Hindi film lyric, albeit in a diluted form. Even a film song with no religious context (though on religion and the language of love see Chapter 4) will use terms from the *ghazal* and the Islamicate tradition: for example, as in '*Maar daala*'. In part this is because of the tradition of Muslim poets – Majrooh, Sahir, Shakeel Badayuni – but more because the major lyricists, including Hindus such as Shailendra and Anand Bakshi, were all educated in Urdu and use its language of love with Islamic references rather than expressing any particular belief. (NB Sahir writes a '*Mirabhajan*' – '*Aaj sajan more ang laga lo*' in Pyaasa, using the Hindu language of love – see Chapter 4).

Music and performance

Indian classical music was centred around the courts and thus often associated with Islamicate culture; though being, again, in no way 'Islamic'.

Iqbal Masud (n.d.) says that Naushad Ali brought Uttar Pradesh's folk music and the elegance of its courts to film music. Naushad Ali (1919–) had trained with orchestras who played in cinema, and was no musical purist. Yet even though he brought in western instruments and large orchestras, he was always the composer that producers sought for films which required a more classical feel. Among his most famous compositions were films set in Mughal times such as *Baiju Bawra* (1952, dir. Vijay Bhatt) and *Mughal-e Azam* (1961, Mr. K. Asif) as well as socials such as *Anmol ghadi* (1946, dir. Mehboob Khan) and *Mother India* (1957, dir. Mehboob Khan).

There is no such thing in India as 'Muslim' music, although there are genres associated with Muslims, notably *qawwali* (see below). I do not think one can say there is anything 'Muslim' about Naushad's music, which draws on classical Hindustani *ragas* and UP folk music as well as various western influences. However, he certainly knew how to evoke a feeling of the Muslim courts where appropriate (in *Baiju Bawra* or *Mughal-e Azam*), but his use of UP folk music in *Mother India* has no Islamicate reference.

Some composers use a song with Muslim or at least Islamicate associations in their films. The *qawwali*, a song associated with Sufism, is often sung by two opposing teams in a *muqabla* ('contest'), often taking themes

Figure 3.2 Anarkali (Madhubala) in *Mughal-e Azam* (1961, dir. K. Asif). One of the key films for reminding viewers that the part-Hindu Mughal rulers were not invaders.

such as love versus beauty. It is distinguished by its rhythmic clapping and light melodies which often create a feeling of ecstasy in the audiences. Traditionally performed on Thursday nights at *durgahs* ('shrines') of Sufi *pirs*, the *qawwali* achieved a phenomenal popularity largely through the non-film *qawwalis* of Nusrat Fateh Ali Khan who became one of the giants of the world music scene. Nusrat's repertoire was mostly songs in Urdu and Punjabi, which were dedicated to holy men (Mast Qalandar, Shams-e Tabriz) and composed by famous poets (Bulleh Shah, 1680–1758) but could also be interpreted as referring to earthly love. He recorded a few popular songs and even made an excursion into film making but the Sufi-inspired *qawwali* remained his favourite. Several film makers have been inspired by Nusrat's *qawwalis* to copy the tunes and modify the lyrics to remove any spiritual meaning, although some echo of a higher love remains for some listeners: '*Kinne sona*' becoming '*Kitna sona*' in *Raja Hindustani* (1996, dir. Dharmesh Darshan); '*Mast mast*' being definitively turned into an 'item' song in *Mohra* (1994, dir. Rajiv Rai) and '*Mere piya ghar aaya*' in *Yaraana* (1995, dir. David Dhawan), with the chorus adding '*O Ramji*', to remove any Sufi sentiment. Others have composed original *qawwalis*, such as those of A.R. Rehman, which are also spiritual ('*Piya Haji Ali*' in *Fiza* 2000, dir. Khalid Mohamed), whereas some are just to celebrate love (the fusion *qawwali*, lyrics by Javed Akhtar, music by Anu Malik, '*Tumse milke dil ka jo haal*' in *Main hoon na*, 2004, dir. Farah Khan). The *qawwali* provides a general cultural reference, perhaps a link to a world of divine passion, with a 'classy' cultural association and good, 'cool' form of world music.

'Islamicate' clothing

The different genres of Islamicate films (see below) show a variety of clothing that is regarded as appropriate for Muslims to wear in the Mughal court, in the courtesans' *kotah* and on the streets of modern Bombay. The fantasy films incorporated the Oriental style of Hollywood, seen in the films of Valentino and of Douglas Fairbanks Jr and the Cecil B. deMille Biblical epics (themselves all drawing on the contemporary Middle East and other popular images for their depiction of the 'Orient'), while the historicals drew on historical documents, and both drew on art, chromolithography and theatre.

In the Muslim social and other films, Muslim men often wear unremarkable clothes such as western-style outfits or *kurta-pyjamas*, but may be shown wearing clothing that marks them as Muslims. Some Muslim men, like Hindu holy men, intellectuals, baddies, and Sikhs, wear beards and they may wear small Muslim caps as one of the friends in *Salim langde pe mat ro* (1989, dir. Saeed Mirza), who wears a cap and a *kurta* while the other Muslims wear western clothes. For formal occasions, in particular in historical films, Muslim men wear *sherwanis* (a kind of frock-coat) and loose or tight pyjamas. This was the dress adopted by Nehru and is often regarded as the most formal dress in India, as it is adapted from court dress, although the Nehru-cap is not a Muslim item. Pathans (Afghani Muslims) wear a particular style of turban and embroidered waistcoats, as Pran in *Zanjeer* (1973, dir. Prakash Mehra), while Punjabi Muslims wear a type of *salwar khameez*. Sometimes clothing is specifically Muslim, even though it would not be realistic. For example, the students wear fezzes in *Phool* (1942, dir. K. Asif), which may have been worn by supporters of the Caliphate, but which now are mostly for comedy as worn by Shammi Kapoor in *Dil deke dekho* (1958, dir. Nasir Husain) or Rishi Kapoor in *Amar, Akbar, Anthony* (1977, dir. Manmohan Desai) as these are no longer worn but mark Muslim-ness (Amin 2004). Other exaggerated items of clothing regarded as marking Muslims are worn for *qawwali* performances, which often include a whole range of gesture and language which verges on the camp.

Muslim women's clothing is somewhat more realistic as they are shown wearing Muslim garments such as the *salwar khameez* or Punjabi suit, originally a Muslim dress which became popular in north-west India, and has also become a national and even international dress. The suit comprises trousers (loose *salwars* or tight *churidars*), a long shirt and a scarf. The stylistic variations are endless, the scarf alone carrying a range of meanings according to whether it is used to cover the head, the breasts or worn like a western scarf. In some films, Muslim women wear the *sherara* (a long culotte-type skirt), usually now for weddings, though for everyday in older films.

While many Hindu women veil themselves in the presence of older men, by covering their heads and sometimes their faces, the veil is largely associated with Islam. This is also true in the films, and it plays important roles in some genres, such as the Muslim social and in the courtesan films. In the Muslim social, the hero catches a glimpse of the heroine, but her veil (the full *burqa*) often leads to a tragedy of mistaken identity in films such as *Chaudhvin ka chand* (1960, dir. M. Sadiq). The removal of the *burqa* can be a sign of transition in films such as *Bombay* (1995, dir. Mani Ratnam) when Shaila Bano's *burqa* flies off in the wind as she runs to meet Shekhar, signifying that she has abandoned her traditional modesty. In the courtesan film (see below), the heroine may wear a veil, but her honour is not that of wider society. In *Pakeezah* (1971, dir. Kamal Amrohi), the heroine clings onto her honour (hence the name her beloved gives her, Pakeezah, Pure), and accuses men of trying to rob her of it by removing her veil in her famous song '*Inhe logon ko*' ('Ask these people'). The veil is erotically charged by the idea of concealing and revealing, and numerous songs in Hindi films are about veils, even if the heroine no longer wears one herself.

To sum up, traditions of language, literature, music and clothing which have their roots in the north Indian Muslim world are transformed into a cosmopolitan, Islamicate aesthetic, in Bombay, initially in theatre and then in cinema, that pervades the whole of Indian public culture throughout the twentieth century and into the present. I now turn to the particular genres of films that are closely associated with Muslims and which can be loosely described as 'Islamicate' genres.

Some call all films with strong Islamicate content 'Muslim social', e.g. Iqbal Masud (n.d.) would include a category I would separate as the historical. I am going to use an umbrella term, the Islamicate film, and then list several (sub-)genres which also include non-Islamicate films, e.g. the historical or the courtesan film; these also have 'Hindu' or 'secular' variants (see Chapter 4) but I shall not discuss these in any detail here.

These films have a visual aesthetic that ranges from the exquisite (*Umrao Jaan*, 1981, dir. Muzaffar Ali and *Pakeezah*, 1971, dir. Kamal Amrohi) to high kitsch (*Nikaah*, 1982, dir. B.R. Chopra), in their use of Islamicate costumes, and their use of *mise-en-scène* of both indoors and sets, their language, gesture and expression.

The fantasy film

Although from its beginnings Hollywood developed the genre of the fantasy film, often set in the exotic Orient, the Indian cinema also drew on this

Figure 3.3 Rekha as *Umrao Jaan* (1981, dir. Muzaffar Ali).

genre, which was popular in the Parsi theatre. It was loved for its theatricality and the opportunity it gave for display with its music, stunts, costumes, language, gesture and excitement. This is one of the few Islamicate genres which is set outside India, in magical, imagined places or in exoticised Islamic countries. *The thief of Baghdad* (1924, dir. Raoul Walsh, starring Douglas Fairbanks, Jr.) was the most popular film of its decade in India (RICC: 21), and the Wadias, who had copied Fairbanks' costume in *The mark of Zorro* (1920, dir. Fred Niblo) for 'Fearless' Nadia's customary outfit, were delighted to show him around their studio on his visit to India in 1934 (Wenner 2005: 49).

The genre was variously called the fantasy film, the adventure film or the Arabian Nights film, but was most commonly called 'Mahomedan pictures'.[17] The genre had nothing to do with anything Islamic but was set in the Muslim world, which was seen as a location for spectacle, adventure and exoticism. It drew on rich story traditions from the Arab world, such as those of the '1001 nights' or the 'Arabian Nights', as well as Persian stories from ancient Iran, such as the Persian *Shahnahmeh*. Mukhopadhyay (2004) points out that these were differentiated from the Hindu ancient world, and the world of the *sants*. These genres drew on a visual culture that had been enriched by chromolithographs, whereas the fantasy film genre drew on a display of pageantry and spectacle associated with Islamicate courts, in a historical jumble, where the modern and the old mixed in clothing sets and so on.

The Persian stories were shared by the Parsis and the Muslims and brought them together in a shared heritage of a Persian culture that was exaggerated by deliberately archaic language, exotic costumes and usually very 'Oriental' sets.

In the silent days the genre relied on its visual exoticism, stunts and racy narrative. Early examples include *Bulbul-e paristan* (1926, dir. Fatima Begum; probably the first woman director in India[18]). Sound gave the genre a huge impetus with song and dance. The first talkies in India belonged to this genre, including *Alam ara* (1931, dir. Ardeshir Irani) and *Shirin Farhad* (1931, dir. J.J. Madan), and perennial favourites such as the *Indersabha* ('Indra's court', its Hindu theme shown in the Islamicate style) (see Hansen 2000), *Yahudi ki ladki* ('The Jewish girl', set in the world of ancient Rome, again shown in an Islamicate style) and *Hatim Tai* (the name of a character from the Arabian Nights) have been remade several times.

The historical film

One of the oldest genres in India is that of the historical film, whose popularity is often associated with the rise of the nationalist movement.[19] Some were set in the glorious past of ancient India, often in the great Mauryan

Empire and hence included Buddhist stories. The Maratha Empire was one of the most popular historical settings for early films, especially, of course, for those of Marathi cinema. Tilak had previously popularised the cult of Shivaji, as the hero and emblem of Maharashtrian nationalism, as the Marathas had fought against the Mughals and against the British. The Hindu nature of this empire was central to the films, as they promoted *dev-desh-dharam* ('God-country-religion') in films such as *Poona raided* (1924, dir. Mama Warekar), which showed the Marathas repulsing Aurangzeb's attack on Poona. Many films about Rajputs showed images of Muslims as cruel conquerors with Hindu women becoming *satis*, such as Dhirendranath Ganguly's *Kamaner Agun – Flames of the Flesh* (1930), where the queen of Chittor kills herself to escape Sultan Alauddin Khalji of Delhi.

One of the early historicals was the silent *Shiraz/Das Grabmal einer groszen Liebe* (1928, dir. Franz Osten), made as an Indo-German collaboration during the colonial period, which displayed similar *mise-en-scène* to the Oriental fantasies that were typical of Hollywood at the time.[20] Princess Selima loses her parents when their caravan is attacked and she is raised by the potter Shiraz. She is abducted and sold as a slave to Prince Khurram, later Shah Jehan. The jealous Dalia schemes for her to be caught talking to Shiraz who is condemned to be trampled to death by an elephant. A pendant reveals Selima's royal background, she saves Shiraz and becomes Mumtaz Mahal. When she dies, the emperor seeks a design for her tomb. From the hundreds of models presented to him, he selects a design by the old, blind Shiraz so the tomb is a monument to both men's love. A contemporary advertisement says: 'Slave Markets and Savagery, Purdah Intrigue and Harem Jealousy, Life and Sudden Death of a Love that Flowered in the Flames of Desire' in a 'wonderful setting of eastern glamour and gorgeousness'.[21]

In the 1930s communal representations became very sensitive during times of tension between religious communities, and Muslim historicals were popular only among Muslim communities of northern and western areas.[22] In August 1933, Shaikh Sadiq of the Muslim League raised a question in the Legislative Assembly regarding the 'censorship of cinematograph films calculated to offend Muslim sentiments'. He questioned the intentions of non-Islamic directors such as Ezra Mir in his *Noor Jahan* (1931) in presenting Muslim themes.[23]

A few films show the Islamic world outside India as Muslims became aware of pan-Islamism through the Khilafat movement, which aimed to restore the Caliph to Turkey after defeat by the British in the First World War. Gandhi combined support for this movement with his non-cooperation movement. This world was seen in films such as *Al Hilal* (1935, dir. Mehboob Khan) discussed above, whose name *Al Hilal*, was also the name of a radical Urdu journal edited by the Khilafatist and Congress leader Maulana Abul Kalam Azad (Mukhopadhyay 2004: 95) and *Phool* (1944, dir. K. Asif), which is a mixture of the historical, the Muslim social and the fantasy film (discussed below as a Muslim social).

However, historicals set in the Mughal court were made to promote national unity. They presented the 'Muslim period' as integral to Indian history, often presenting a composite religious culture as an ideal to be emulated. One of the most popular of these films was Sohrab Modi's *Pukar* (1939). The Emperor Jehangir imposes the death sentence on a Rajput, Mangal Singh, who killed his beloved Kanwar's brother and father in self-defence. Kanwar pleads for his life to the Empress, Nur Jehan. When Nur Jehan accidentally kills a washerman with an arrow, she is faced with a demand for retributive justice by the widow. The Emperor cannot condemn her and offers his own life. The washerwoman forgives him and he then pardons Mangal.

The film's success rested on its depiction of the sumptuous court. It opens with a shot of the Taj Mahal and a written slogan 'The glory that was Ind'. It then shows the beautiful settings of the court and the elaborate costumes, including the famous human chessboard, and the elaborate language which Iqbal Masud (n.d.) says set the style for later films. The writer, Kamal Amrohi, uses different styles for the various characters, so the Emperor and his wife (acclaimed performances by Chandramohan and Naseem Bano) speak Persianised Urdu, the Rajputs pure Hindi and the lower castes use varieties of colloquial Hindi. The film is remembered for its idealisation of just government, as the fair rule shows that Hindus and Muslims are equal before the law, but in its time it was its call to end the death penalty, which alluded to the death sentence passed on Shaheed ('Martyr') Bhagat Singh in 1939 (Mukhopadhyay 2004: 101).

One of the favourite stories of the historical film was that of Anarkali, and her love for Prince Salim (later Jehangir), son of the Great Mughal, Akbar. It is not clear whether she was a historical figure, but she was certainly a person of legend. Hers was a favourite story for Indian theatre, the first film being a silent in 1928, made by the Great Eastern Corporation of Lahore: *The loves of a Mogul prince* based on Syed Imtiaz Ali Taj's play, *Anarkali*. The Imperial Film Company of Bombay made its own version of the film with Sulochana, and in 1952 Filmistan made *Anarkali* with Bina Rai and Pradeep Kumar but K. Asif's *Mughal-e Azam* outshone them all.

Mughal-e Azam tells the story of the Great Mughal, Akbar (r. 1556–1605). The film's making was itself something of an epic as it was made over fifteen years, with a complete change of cast (the original included Chandramohan, who played Jehangir in *Pukar*, Nargis and Sapru), several writers and so on. It had the largest budget of any film of its day, Rs 15m, which was spent on costumes, sets and extras. The film has superb cinematography, mostly in black and white, though some songs were shot in colour, including Anarkali's most defiant song, '*Pyar kiya to darna kya?*', shot in the Sheesh Mahal or Mirror Palace. The film has recently been coloured by computer to attract a new audience but has been critically panned even though its initial opening drew the curious to see it.

The story is of Anarkali (Madhubala), a dancing girl in the Mughal court. Prince Salim (later Emperor Jehangir) (Dilip Kumar) falls in love with Anarkali but, his father, Emperor Akbar (Prithviraj Kapoor) forbids him to continue this affair. Salim leads a campaign against his father, is defeated and sentenced to death. Anarkali offers to sacrifice her life to save Salim and is buried alive, although Akbar allows her to escape through a tunnel unknown to Salim.

Mughal-e Azam tells Mughal history in the context of the new nation, emphasised by the voiceover at the beginning and the showing of the Muslim sites of India, yet it tells family history rather than social history. The film brings out themes that are popular in Hindi film, notably the struggle between father and son, and between public duty and private desires, and the self-sacrificing woman. The film evades issues of Hindu–Muslim relations even though it featured the Mughal famed for his fairness. However, it suggests religious tolerance in the court as Queen Jodhabai (Durga Khote) was a Hindu and Anarkali sings a Hindu devotional song on the occasion of the Janmashtami festival (the birth of Krishna), 'Mohe panghat pe', in which Akbar participates in the rocking of the swing in which the child Krishna sits.

Mughal-e Azam has added magnificence from Naushad's music (and Shakeel Badayuni's lyrics) and, in particular, two songs sung by Bade Ghulam Ali Khan ('*Shubh din aayo*' and '*Prem jogan banke sundari piyo chali*').

Most of these historical films always drew on the Congress Party's idea of history, and its heroes were those seen in Nehru's *Discovery of India* (1946), such as Akbar, rather than heroes of the Muslim community, such as Aurangzeb, Changhis Khan and Mahmud of Ghazni.

While recent years have seen a small revival of the historical, some of these have been set in other periods, such as the Mauryan Empire (*Asoka*, 2001, dir. Santosh Sivan, which shows his conversion to Buddhism), or in the colonial period (*Lagaan*, 2001, dir. Ashutosh Gowariker; *Mangal Pandey/The rising*, 2005, dir. Ketan Mehta) or the Partition (see below). While numbers are too small to detect a trend, these do include one film set in the Mughal court, namely *Taj Mahal: an eternal love story*, 2005, dir. Akbar Khan. The historical film shows only the royal and aristocratic Muslim, never the Muslim peasant or worker. This figure is also seen in a variant of the historical, the courtesan film.

The courtesan film

The courtesan appears throughout Indian cultural texts (see Dwyer 2000a: 194f), so it is not surprising that courtesans feature in many films, mostly in minor roles.[24] However, some of the most popular films in Indian cinema may be classed as 'courtesan films', in that their heroines are courtesans, while the usual gender imbalance of the films is reversed in that the heroes have minor roles. In films that have the courtesan in minor roles she is often Hindu but in the major films she is always a Muslim. (Many courtesans in north India took Muslim, often Shi'ite, names even if they were Hindus to associate themselves with Lucknawi culture.) The two great films in which the main heroine is a courtesan are set in nineteenth-century Avadhi Lucknow and Kanpur (*Umrao Jaan*, 1981, dir. Muzaffar Ali) and Delhi/the Punjabi princely state of Patiala in the early years of the twentieth century (*Pakeezah*, 1971, dir. Kamal Amrohi). Lucknow and Delhi were once two of the great centres of courtly Muslim culture.

The courtesan, whose trade flourished in India until the early twentieth century, was more like a geisha or hetaira. The most accomplished courtesans were said to be from Lucknow, the capital of Avadh. This city became north India's major cultural centre after the decline of Delhi and was renowned for the quality of its Urdu language and literature (see Oldenburg 1989). It was annexed by the British in 1856 and was one of the major centres of struggle in the 1857 uprisings. Although landowners from Avadh maintained a courtly culture in Lucknow at least until independence, it never achieved the sophistication of its earlier days, which are still remembered with great nostalgia by its elite. The world of the courtesan also declined during the British period, as other spheres of public culture emerged. The final blow was dealt after independence as the loss of wealthy patrons came about with the abolition of *zamindars* ('landowners'), and salons were banned. [25]

Oldenburg's study of courtesans (*tawa'if*) in Lucknow, drawing on interviews with retired courtesans, shows very close similarities to Umrao Jan's story narrated by Ruswa (Ruswa 1996). Courtesans were either born into the trade or young girls sold into it by their parents or others. Umrao Jan was born in Faizabad, kidnapped as a young girl by her father's enemy and sold to a courtesan in Lucknow. They lived in households (*kotha*) run by a chief courtesan (*choudhrayan*), who had acquired wealth and fame through her beauty, her music and dancing talents, which she used to set up her own house where she would recruit and train younger courtesans. The courtesan had to learn music, Persian and Urdu poetry, Arabic grammar, and to dance the *mujra*, a dance where she pays her respects to the assembly rather than offering an erotic spectacle. The best houses kept skilled male musicians and were important patrons of music. The sons of the gentry were sent to the *kothas* to learn manners and Urdu poetry, and presumably the art of lovemaking. Other women lived in the establishment, including the regular prostitutes (*randi*), who are often euphemistically called courtesans. Although the profession of the courtesan has disappeared, she has remained an important figure in literature and later in film throughout the last century (see Dwyer 2000a: 125).

The courtesan has also been a popular figure in film, where her attractions give rise to a variety of pleasures in the audience. She is portrayed as a victim of men's lust and as an object of the viewer's pity, but also delights the audience in being the object of the male gaze as she dances for his entertainment.[26] The combination of a beautiful actress, and the opportunity for music and dance to be incorporated into the narrative are important, but viewers also enjoy the spectacle of the body, the elaboration of scenery and in particular of clothing, tied to a certain nostalgia arising from the decline and disappearance of courtesan culture.

The courtesan in the film makes her living by her sexual charms, and so is presented as an object of desire to the men in the *mehfil* ('gathering') and to the cinema audience. This usually culminates in the *mujra*, where the film maker emphasises the details of lyrics and all aspects of the *mise-en-scène*. The role of the courtesan in films has been given only to the most beautiful actresses, such as Meena Kumari as the eponymous *Pakeezah*, while the most glamorous actress of her generation, Rekha, has had numerous courtesan roles including that of Umrao Jaan. Although the courtesan displays her sexual allure at all times in the film, she is usually presented as averse to her trade, to which she has been driven by the injustices of society, and calls her body a *zinda lash* ('living corpse'). An accomplished singer and dancer, she also writes *ghazals* in which she expresses her desire for love and marriage, which she knows will be denied her because of her profession. Yet one of her attractions is that she is the woman who is the opposite of the wife; like the beloved of the *ghazal*, she is unattainable, remote and perfect. Her sexuality is not associated with reproduction, nor is she expected to offer any nurture unlike the Hindu heroine – rather she is the essence of female eroticism. (Oldenburg, 1989, argues that most courtesans, like many prostitutes, practised lesbianism (*chapat bazi*), considering heterosexuality to be work, not pleasure.)

In Hindi cinema, the courtesan is pure (*Pakeezah*) and part of this is that she never appears in any way immodestly dressed. In fact one of the pleasures of the courtesan film lies in its elaborate use of clothing and make-up. While Stella Bruzzi has discussed the meaning of clothes in western cinema (Bruzzi 1997), the semiotics of costume in Indian cinema has been little explored, although it is an important source of symbols and signifiers of codes concerning status or class, westernisation and the symbolic use of colour (see Dwyer 2000b). Clothing in cinema is clearly a source of spectacle, sometimes taken to extremes in song sequences where the heroine, and sometimes the hero, has numerous costume changes to present a heady excess of consumption. As Bruzzi has argued, clothing is an important component of eroticism. This is foregrounded in the courtesan film, where the heroine's clothes heighten sexuality by their opulence and rich colours and textures, and their elaboration presents an exaggerated exhibition of gender difference. The veil is used to effect in the film to hide and conceal, in a display of eroticism rather than modesty, seen in the first song in *Pakeezah* ('*Inhen logon ne ...*' 'Those people ...') where the courtesan sings how men have taken her veil or her modesty. The courtesan is the woman who is constantly available for the male gaze, yet she remains concealed within her *kotha*, away from the eye of wider society.

The courtesan film also fetishises the woman's body, usually the feet, which are one of the few uncovered parts of her body, although they are decorated with colour and jewellery. This is very clear in *Pakeezah*, when the lover leaves a note tucked into Pakeezah's toes on the train: '*Aap ke paon bahut haseen hain. Inhen zameen par mat utariyega, maile ho jaayenge!*' ('Your feet are very beautiful. Do not let them touch the ground, they will get dirty!'), and in her dance at her lover's wedding where she lacerates her feet on broken glass to leave symbolically resonant bloody marks on the white sheet of her performance.[27] The only other parts of her body which are usually visible are her hands, hennaed, manicured and bejewelled; and her mask-like face, again elaborated, painted and jewelled, her hair tied back, and covered with a veil and more jewels.

The courtesan is a totally romantic figure: a beautiful but tragic woman, who pours out her grief for the love she is denied in tears, poetry and dance. Yet although denied marriage and respectability, she is also a source of power. The courtesans in the film live in splendid buildings, which are decorated exquisitely. As Veena Oldenburg has pointed out (1989), the courtesan achieved her material and social liberation by reversing constraints on women's chastity and economic rights, succeeding through her combination of talent and education. The courtesans set up their own society within the *kothas*, where they inverted many of society's rituals such as celebrating the birth of a girl like the birth of a boy in mainstream Indian culture. Perhaps women enjoy the pleasures of the courtesan film as they find a figure of masochistic identification, a woman who cannot find the love she wants, yet knows that a woman's sexual attractions can provide her with power, or they may simply enjoy the beauty of the whole image. Men may also enjoy the voyeuristic pleasures of looking at a beautiful, sexually accomplished woman whose status as victim allows for male fantasies of 'saving' her – mostly from other men.

The beauty of the actresses in the courtesan film was not the only reason for their popularity. They were also women who had strong star personas, as the most beautiful, most tragic stars who themselves were never lucky in love.[28] Their off-screen lives were read onto the image of the courtesan in the film, as can be seen most clearly in the taking up of these stars as camp and gay icons, notably in the case of Meena Kumari (1932–72) (see Dwyer 2000a).

Umrao Jan Ada,[29] an Urdu novel by Mirza Mohammad Hadi 'Ruswa', published in 1899, presents the story of Umrao Jan, a courtesan of Lucknow and Kanpur, as supposedly true. It is set at the last moment of Lucknow's glory: the 1857 uprisings occur in the novel when Umrao Jan is at the height of her power. The novel's popularity remains strong, although many know the story of Umrao Jan in the eponymous film of 1981 (see below).

The view of the courtesan presented in the film is very different from that presented in the Urdu novel. Instead of the exquisite Rekha portraying an innocent Umrao Jaan, who falls in love with one of her clients and whose story is told as a failed love story, in the novel Umrao admits she was rather plain and never fell in love although she had a number of significant affairs in addition to her regular clients. Rather than pining for an impossible love affair, she loves her work, her poetry and the pleasure, luxury and respect that this brought her. Aware of the pleasure of nostalgia, the last chapter in the book is the account of Umrao's reading of Ruswa's story of her life, where she sums it up herself in a clear, insightful manner. She was a prostitute, no beauty, but a woman of intelligence and skill:

> 'It was my profession to dance and sing and steal men's hearts. I was happy or unhappy depending on whether I was more or less successful than others in my profession. I was not as pretty as the others, but because of my talent for music and mastery of poetry, I was one of the best.' (Ruswa 1996: 189)

The courtesan film, although hardly made today, remains one of the most popular film genres, in particular the two great films mentioned above. It is loved by Muslim and Hindu film audiences alike and I wish to explore these pleasures in some more detail.

One of the greatest pleasures of the courtesan film is undoubtedly nostalgia, largely for a lost Islamic world. Memory and nostalgia, pain and loss, are themes of the *ghazal* (see above), with an added historical dimension emerging with modern ideas about linear history. This is seen clearly in Ghalib's mourning after 1857 in his exile from Delhi whose great culture is now faded:

> The rose's scent, the tulip's colour,
> > fill the world
> While I lie pinned beneath the heavy
> > rock of care.
> The spring has come, but what have
> > I to greet it with?
> Helpless, I close my door, that none may
> > enter there. (Russell and Islam 1994: 163)

This pain is taken to greater extremes in the Shi'ite mourning for the death of Imam Husain, commemorated every year in the month of Muharram (see Pinault 2001). Lucknow is one of the great centres of Indian Shi'ism, famed for its Muharram processions, when its great *imambaras* (Shi'ite assembly halls) house *taziyas* (replicas of the tomb of Husain). During this time specific Shi'ite genres are performed, notably the *marsiya* ('elegy') on martyrdom of Imam Husain, whose best poets, Mir Anis and Mirza Dabir, were from Lucknow, and *soz* (literally 'grief') songs or dirges about the death of Husain, for which Umrao Jan says she was famous in Lucknow.

Lucknow's rise to fame as a centre for Urdu language and culture was also predicated on a loss, following Nadir Shah's sack of Delhi in 1739 when many nobles abandoned Delhi, moving to Lucknow. Lucknow itself was reduced in status when the British annexed Oudh (Avadh) in 1856, a subtle reading of which is presented in Satyajit Ray's 1977 film *Shatranj ke khiladi/The chessplayers*. The British inflicted further losses on the Muslim elite, banning them from living in Delhi after the 1857 uprisings, for which they were held largely responsible.[30] The British had already 'abolished' Persian in 1835 as the language of administration, replacing it with English, and the new forms of modern literature which they taught in their institutions weakened the hold of Persian, and to some extent, Urdu as *the* elite language of literature.

The two great courtesan films, *Pakeezah* and *Umrao Jaan*, were made by figures who mourned this passing. Kamal Amrohi, who directed the former, was known in the film industry as the great master of Persian and Urdu language, which he used to advantage mostly in historical films such as *Pukar* (1939, dir. Sohrab Modi). Javed Akhtar, perhaps the only Urdu poet who can be said to be 'popular' at the beginning of this millennium, has argued that Amrohi's script for *Mughal-e Azam* should be taught in schools as one of the great works of modern Urdu prose.[31] The film *Umrao Jaan* was made by Muzaffar Ali, himself a member of one of the princely families of Lucknow, and it is a film of great beauty and sadness, without the happy ending usually required of the Hindi film.

The imagery of the *ghazal* is found in both films, which, in addition to this feeling of loss, deploy spectacle in the beauty of the courtesan, her costumes and in interior scenery. The camera plays on the surfaces of her and her surroundings, presenting a totally saturated, excessive and elaborate image of formal and constructed beauty. This is seen in Persian carpets, crystal candelabra, courtyards with fountains, pools, 'Islamic arches' and elaborate 'Muslim' clothes. This is supplemented by the use of word and gesture as the dialogues are written in a particularly flowery form of Urdu, reminding the listener/viewer that Urdu has a glorious history as the language of poetry and indeed of a great high culture and of formal manners (*adab*), whose rules and performance give delight in their elaboration. It is also the language of love in modern India, largely through the association of the *ghazal* with the love lyric of the Hindi film (Dwyer 2000a, Chs 2 and 5). The films also present music and dance in a light classical style rarely seen today but which is still accessible to an untrained audience. Music is an arena where Muslims and Hindus have both performed together, many of the exponents of 'Hindu' lyrics being Muslims such as the most famous singers of the courtly style, *dhrupad*, the Dagar brothers. This is seen clearly in Umrao Jaan's training in the film, where her first song is replete with imagery of Krishna's pastoral idyll.

These Islamicate films give pleasure to Muslims and Hindus but I suggest they are very different pleasures. Clearly a possible reading – perhaps that experienced by many Muslims – suggested by the above is one of nostalgia for the loss of a glorious past, which could be interpreted as being destroyed by the advent of modernity and westernisation. This could be augmented by sorrow at the present low status of Muslims in India, perhaps also a mourning for the genre of the *ghazal*, itself nostalgic with its tales of unrequited love and depictions of beauty, which is being reduced to the *filmi ghazal* and the audio tape rather than the rich poetry of the *mushaira*. There may also be sadness at the loss of the pleasures shown in many elements of performance, which, since they are unacceptable to orthodox Islam, which rejects alcohol, illicit sex and performance of dance and music, are no longer available to those who wish to remain within the Muslim community of India.

I should like to suggest another reading that underlies the pleasure of these films. In these films, Islamic culture is located in a woman who lives outside respectable society. However exotic and desirable, this woman makes her living as a prostitute and represents a socially unacceptable sexual but non-reproductive femininity like the beloved of the *ghazal*. This behaviour marginalises her, positioning her outside the domain of the modern female citizen by creating a powerful image of a decadent femininity, very different from the active sexuality of the Hindu woman within the bounds of marriage and the family, explored by the Hindi film. This marginality is enforced by these films, which locate Muslims in the past, albeit a glamorous and exotic past, meaning that their presence in the modern world is anachronistic, for they are archaic, outmoded and non-modern, even if they are exotic and beguiling. This reading is not exclusive but may underlie other possible readings of this film. However strong its presence, I argue that this pleasure is alarming in that this dominant form of Indian public culture continues to position the Muslim as Other, making it unclear how the Muslim can be a citizen of modern India.

The Muslim social

The term 'Muslim social' is sometimes used in a broad sense to mean all films which refer to the Islamicate world, but I prefer to use it as a counterpart to the 'social' genre (see Chapter 4) as romances set in a roughly contemporary Islamicate world. It is hard to say when the first Muslim social film was made, in part because the genre is quite fuzzy.

The oldest example I have seen is *Phool* (1944, dir. K. Asif), which is fascinating as it mixes several 'Islamicate' genres, being partly a Muslim social, that is a film set in the contemporary (or seemingly contemporary) world, partly an Arabian Nights fantasy with veiled Arab princesses dancing on fabulous stage sets, and also one of the few films to show 'Islamic' miracles.

Safdar (Yakub) has promised to finish building a mosque but he loses his money through his in-laws' scheming. When his daughter Shama (Suraiya) is about to marry Salim (Prithviraj Kapoor), he suddenly realises his duty as a Muslim and rushes off to fight for his *qaum* ('community') of Muslims in Turkey in the Balkan wars, leaving her a flower (*phool*) and a model of the Taj Mahal. He falls under the spell of a dancer, Princess Leila (Sitara Devi), who comes back to India with him where they tour Delhi, Agra, Cawnpore, Allahabad and Lucknow doing an amazing stage show. Leila's magic potion has made him forget Shama and his mother while he thinks he is Farid, not Salim. Even the sight of the flower he has given Shama does not quite jog his memory. Rekha (Veena), their Hindu friend, prays to Krishna and the image comes to life as Shama joins her song. Salim's mother (Durga Khote) is injured in a struggle with Salim and Leila but her blood restores his memory and he picks a flower, which he takes to Shama. In the final resolution of the plot, the son of the wicked in-laws who is trying to marry Shama too is struck down by lightning outside the mosque, the couple are reunited and the film ends with the cry, '*Allah ho akbar!*' ('God is great!').

While singing-star Suraiya is the noble heroine in the film, Sitara Devi plays an Oriental(ist) temptress, with her ring containing magic powder, her veils that do not cover her body and her use of the occasional Arabic word (she calls Salim, 'Habibi' and 'Hindi'). She has a spectacular 'item number' in the film, an extraordinary song where the stage is made of piano keys, she dances on drums and women form a harp which she plays.

The very stylised Urdu dialogues for the Muslims and more Hindi versions for the Hindus were written by Kamal Amrohi, who worked with Asif again on *Mughal-e Azam* before going on to make his own *magnum opus*, *Pakeezah*. The music is by Ghulam Haider, who was one of the most popular music directors after the success of *Khazanchi*.

Although this film is set in the period of the Caliphate (Khilafat) movement (1920s), showing students in India wearing *sherwanis* (long coats such as those worn by Nehru) and fezzes, there are clear resonances with contemporary politics. The Pakistan resolution was made in 1940, and 1942 was the Quit India movement, so it was hardly surprising that censorship reports demand the deletion of the sequence of students marching through the street with the Caliphate flag, which looks almost identical to the Pakistan flag in black and white. (These sequences are on the version I saw in the archives in Pune.) However, the film makes a show of close friendship between the Muslim family and their Hindu friend Rekha, with the first song of the film being a spectacular Diwali song with Busby Berkeley type effects.

Many of the Muslim socials show Muslims living apart from any Hindus, such as with the image of the Muslim woman, beautiful, romantic, yearning and, usually, veiled. The film embodies the essence of the *ghazal*, with its stories of doomed love, the cruelty of the beloved and so on. Like the courtesan film, the Muslim social until recent years presented a historic, fixed version of the Muslim community.

Many of the Muslim socials were great hits on account of their music, notably *Barsaat ki raat* (1960, dir. P.L. Santoshi), where a succession of brilliant *qawwalis* composed by Roshan with lyrics by Sahir Ludhianvi have kept it popular even until today: '*Na to karavan ki talaash hai, na to hum-safar ki talaash hai*' ('I am not searching for a caravan, nor am I searching for a travelling companion'), as well as its *ghazals* such as the title song '*Zindagi bhar nahin bhoolegi voh barsaat ki raat*' ('I shall remember this rainy night all my life'). Another is *Chaudhvin ka chand* (1960, dir. M. Sadiq), whose title song is one of the most popular songs of Hindi film music, which also shows the exoticism of *purdah* and doomed love in this exquisite world, and *Mere Mehboob* (1963, dir. H.S. Rawail) was remembered for its star performances (Sadhana and Rajendra Kumar). *Nikaah* (1982, dir. B.R. Chopra) is also best known now for its songs by Ravi with lyrics by Hasan Kamaal, including the famous *qawwali* ('*Chehra chupa liya hai*'), Salma Agha's own renditions of her song ('*Dil ke armaan aansuon mein beh gaye*'). The film has a wonderful sequence that typifies the ethos of the Muslim social where the weeping Nawab is listening to an old gramophone recording of Ghulam Ali's rendition of Hasrat Mohani's Urdu *ghazal* '*Chupke chupke*'. This song encapsulates the decadence of the film, for he is being punished for his own wilful actions and yet the genuine sorrow is in the images and the words, and the music.

Some are remembered for their poetry and their re-creation of the fall of the Mughal Empire, and their atmosphere of loss and longing, such as Sohrab Modi's *Mirza Ghalib* (1954), while recent years have seen a small revival in the genre in five films written by Khalid Mohamed. Three of these were directed by Shyam Benegal, a trilogy said to be based on Mohamed's own family (*Mammo* 1994, *Sardari Begum* 1996, and *Zubeidaa* 2001) and two films directed by Mohamed himself (*Fiza* 2000 and *Tehzeeb* 2003). *Fiza* is one of the few mainstream Hindi films that engages with the 1992/3 riots in Bombay (see also *Bombay*, dir. Mani Ratnam, 1995) through the eyes of a Muslim family, while Benegal's films are closer to the middle cinema.

Middle cinema has produced its own type of Muslim socials, such as Saeed Akhtar Mirza's *Salim Langade pe mat ro* ('Don't weep for Salim the Lame', 1989), which showed the lives of working-class Muslims in Bombay's Do Tanki area, or Vishal Bharadwaj's *Maqbool* (2004), which blends the Muslim social and the gangster film into a reworking of Shakespeare's *Macbeth*. From this cinema, one of the best films is *Garam hawa* (1973, dir. M.S. Sathyu), which is somewhat historical but also deals with the theme of Partition (see below) but this time only in the context of a Muslim family.

Many films have been made about Partition but they have mostly shown the unimaginable violence of the terrible time. *Garam hawa* is set in the aftermath of Partition, when the border between India and Pakistan was still open and Muslim families who had not thought of leaving their homes before began to wonder if they had made the right decision as the social and political climate had changed in ways they had not expected. This film shows families in Agra, the heartland of India, who were suddenly made to feel like strangers in their own homes. The suffering of these people, not through brutality but through the loss of their values and their human ties as their worlds moved under their feet, and yet the hope of some final possible future, makes this one of the most powerful films made about the impact of Partition. This can be typified in just one shot, the image of Salim (Balraj Sahni), walking in front of the Taj Mahal, the symbol of love and of India but also a Muslim shrine and a part of

Figure 3.4 Garam hawa (1973, dir. M.S. Sathyu). Salim (Balraj Sahni) walks by the Taj Mahal, an image that emphasises the film's theme that the Muslim community is part of Indian society rather than that of the new state of Pakistan.

everyday life to a person born and brought up in Agra, which shows so simply how the Partition changed the sub-continent forever. The film has few songs but there is a memorable *qawwali* to Salim Chisti, when a young couple, Shamshad and Amina, visit Fatehpur Sikri, not as tourists but as pilgrims to the tomb of Salim Chisti, showing their religious attachment to their home city. The lyrics of the *qawwali*, as so often with Muslim devotional songs, outline not only the devotion of the pilgrims in the spiritual sense but also of earthly love and hopes.

Representations of Muslims in non-Islamicate genres

The Hindi film, outside the Islamicate genres, regards Muslims as the Other. Caution must be exercised in taking this to be the same as a wider political and social positioning of Muslims in India because in the film the Muslim often seems to be just one of a series of Others. These include those from different regions and other religions, a situation in which religion is just one of the many markers of identity rather than a serious engagement with Islamic culture or belief. However, the importance of the cinematic representation should not be underestimated as it has some grounding in wider views of Muslims in Indian society, both as others see them and as they see themselves, and because the filmic views become seen as representative.

While earlier films including Muslims had to do with national integration (*Padosi*, 1941, dir. V. Shantaram), or showed them as kindly, though often eccentric, friends (*Kabuliwala*, 1961, dir. Hemen Gupta; *Yaadon ki baraat*, 1973, dir. Nasir Husain) or onlookers, typified by the 'Abdul Chacha' stereotype, many films preferred not to show any Muslim characters, even though their absence made for a striking silence. Such films would include *Jab jab phool khile* (1965, dir. Suraj Prakash), in which the boatman is presented as a Hindu called Raja, although all the boatmen are Muslims, and even though he yells the Muslim cry, '*Afoo Khuda!*'

Even if Muslims and Islam were referred to only in passing in *Nastik* (1954, dir. I.S. Johar), the few Partition films that appeared in the 1950s and 1960s showed Muslims marked by language, culture and clothing as well as faith, such as in *Dharamputra* (1961, dir. Yash Chopra) and *Chhalia* (1960, dir. Manmohan Desai).

It was really in the 1970s that films began to show lower-class Muslims rather than aristocrats associated with a glorious past. This significant change seems to have been largely associated with India's greatest superstar, Amitabh Bachchan, who played mostly 'secular' Hindus, in that he was often shown to be a non-believer who nevertheless had a deep respect for Islam. However, while he rebelled against his mother's Hinduism, he also went to the temple to die (e.g. in *Deewaar*, 1975, dir. Yash Chopra).

He played a Hindu whose great friend was a Pathan in *Zanjeer* (1973, dir. Prakash Mehra), he played a Hindu adopted by a Muslim in *Muqaddar ka Sikandar* (1978, dir. Prakash Mehra) and a Christian (*Amar, Akbar, Anthony*, 1977, dir. Manmohan Desai), who regarded all religions with respect. Iqbal Masud (n.d.) writes:

> Kader Khan [the script writer] in *Muqaddar ka Sikandar* and later on in *Coolie* introduced a note of religious mysticism. In *Muqaddar* Amitabh Bachchan does not play a 'Muslim' role but he evokes the nuances to build up the portrait of a Dervish fulfilling an exalted mission. In *Coolie* he portrays a Muslim coolie who becomes a revolutionary. The old Mehboob syndrome of Muslim radicalism is reproduced in *Coolie*. Amitabh carries a hawk named Allah Rakha on his wrist. This is a direct reference to the poet Iqbal's hawk (Shaheen) – a central symbol in his poetry. Shaheen for Iqbal represented the aspiring, soaring spirit of man as in the line *Tu Shaheen hai parwaz hai kaam tera* (you are a hawk, your destiny is flight).
>
> Amitabh similarly soared in that film despite its formula trappings. The emotionally charged scene of departing Hajis, the pilgrims sailing to Mecca for the major Muslim festival of Id-ul-Baqr, at Bombay docks is played with a genuine empathy which enfolds the viewer. *Coolie* represents the rise and integration of the Common Muslim in the working masses of the country rebelling for change.

Figure 3.5 Coolie (1983, dir. Manmohan Desai). Iqbal (Amitabh Bachchan) is saved from death by his *chador*, the cloth covering Haji Ali's tomb.

(See Chapter 4 for further discussion of *Coolie*, 1983, dir. Manmohan Desai.)

There have been relatively few films that mention the Partition of India, the time of the worst communal conflicts in Indian history, and the largest migration in human history when 10 million people migrated as the Islamic Republic of Pakistan was created alongside the secular republic of India. Some try to show that Hindus and Muslims are 'really the same', so a Hindu extremist has to come to terms with the fact that he was born a Muslim (*Dharamputra*, 1961, dir. Yash Chopra), or how other bonds are broken in the upsurge of violence of this time (*Tamas*, 1986, dir. Govind Nihalani;[32] *Pinjar* 2003, dir. Chandra Prakash Dwivedi). (The impact of the Partition on a Muslim family in *Garam hawa* is discussed above.)

Hey! Ram (2000, dir. Kamal Haasan), which begins around the time of Partition, while ultimately carrying a Gandhian message and showing scenes of Hindu barbarity, albeit often retaliatory, gives more emphasis to graphically violent scenes which depict Muslim atrocities, inspired by Jinnah; meanwhile it portrays the Rashtriya Swayamsevak Sangh (National Voluntary Service) as largely sympathetic even though Gandhi's assassins came from its ranks. *Gadar* (2001, dir. Anil Sharma) is careful not to be anti-Muslim, and the Sikh hero marries a Muslim and does not ask her to change her religion, although the film is anti-Pakistan. It is Pakistan which underlines the problematic representation of the Muslim in Hindi film, and this is typified in films that deal with the issue of Kashmir (notably *Roja*, 1992, dir. Mani Ratnam and *Mission Kashmir*, 2000, dir. Vidhu Vinod Chopra). In other films terrorists usually have some Pakistan connection, as in *Sarfarosh* (1998, dir. John Matthews Matthan).

Films about the Bombay riots of 1992/3 in which over 1,000 Muslims were killed include: *Bombay* (1995, dir. Mani Ratnam), in which a Hindu man and a Muslim woman have just moved to Bombay and *Fiza* (2000, dir. Khalid Mohamed), in which the son/brother becomes a terrorist.

Muslims are often shown alongside Hindus in gangster films; this is a form of realism as the Bombay underworld is indeed a mixture of Hindus and Muslims as shown in *Satya* (1998, dir. Ram Gopal Varma). In *Sarfarosh* (1998, dir. John Matthews Matthan), a Muslim police officer is taken off the case involving a Pakistani criminal network as it is felt that he cannot be trusted not to feel loyal to Muslims, even if Pakistani. One of the chief Pakistani villains is able to move around India as he is a *ghazal* singer, which brings the question of Islamicate culture under suspicion. This film was banned in Malaysia and West Asia (Kaul 2001). An interesting film is *Ghulam-e Mustafa* (1997, dir. Parto Ghosh), in which Nana Patekar, who is said to have his right-wing Hindu sympathies, plays a Muslim hit man who has to protect a Hindu Brahmin family and overcome the open hostility and prejudice that the mother initially feels towards him. Although her views seem shocking, similar sentiments are voiced quite openly – at least out of the hearing of Muslims. She is finally won over by Mustafa's qualities of devotion and loyalty and he becomes one of the family, once again the idea being that the differences between communities are easily negotiable.

In recent years, two films may mark a new way of depicting Muslims. The first is *Dhoom* (2004, dir. Sanjay Gadhvi), in which a motorbike mechanic is marked as a Muslim only by his name, Ali, while the film makes no other reference to his Muslim-ness. A more complicated negotiation takes place in *Veer-Zaara* (2004, dir. Yash Chopra), where the difference in religion is seen as one of many differences between people that has to be acknowledged rather than be seen as a point of conflict. The film stresses other similarities between people, in this case Punjabi-ness, as the Pakistani Punjabi Muslim and the Indian Punjabi Hindu find. In this film, Sikhs, who are also Punjabis, act as mediators between Hindus and Muslims. Although their community was devastated by the Partition, with many of their sacred places being difficult for them to access in Pakistan, the Sikhs are shown as having no bitterness or anger. The Sikh nanny regards Zaara's Muslim family as her own; while the Sikh priest tells Veer that Zaara's devotion is such that anyone would be moved by it. Veer may well be a Sikh, as he wears a necklace that shows him as such, but his uncle and aunt who brought him up seem to be Punjabi Hindu and south Indian Hindu. The problems between the two lovers are attributed in part to a villain but also to the states that have divided them, and eventually the lovers are able to overcome these barriers with the help of a Pakistani Muslim lawyer. Perhaps only India's top producer, Yash Chopra (see Dwyer 2002a), could have taken such a risky topic. Despite not achieving the blockbuster success of his usual films, *Veer-Zaara* swept all the awards for the year and Yash Chopra was invited to a lunch with the visiting President of Pakistan, General Musharraf, where the band played music from the film.

These recent films show a move away from depictions of noble UP aristocrats to working-class, 'secular' Muslims and (for the first time, I believe) Punjabi Muslims, even if most of them are still enormously wealthy. However, it is too soon to know if these mark a trend in Hindi film's depiction of Muslims.

Concluding remarks

As mentioned above, these films are about Islam as the basis of culture (language, literature, music, clothing and so on) and they do not usually include any mention of religion as belief beyond devotion and as practice. The Islamicate genres rarely show non-Muslims and when they do, Muslims are always shown as respectful to Hindus and they never disrespect the religion in any way. Most Muslims are depicted as religious figures, in a broader culture which places a high value on religiosity. The representation of Muslims in non-Islamicate genres is often problematic, as is Hindi cinema's representation of all communities other than north Indian Hindus (see Chapter 4).

The real significance of these representations is in the importance of the cinema itself. Hindi cinema dominates public culture's images and representations, being to a great extent a source of fantasy for the whole country and for Indian cinema's vast overseas audiences. It is no exaggeration to say that wider views of Muslims may be derived from images and representations in the films for both Muslims and non-Muslims who form the audiences.

There are disputes within the Muslim communities themselves, who are aware of the power of these images, about their representation in film. Some Muslims condemn the film industry altogether, arguing that it and its personnel do not speak for Indian Muslims.[33] There are also protests by the community about the way it is represented in the films, whether on matters of divorce or simply of accurately historical representations that contradict current sensibilities.[34]

Yet other representations are celebrated by some sections of the Muslim community in India and in the international audience for the Hindi film, who are said to have particularly appreciated *Veer-Zaara*. Many people from different communities enjoy what Iqbal Masud called the 'cultural elegance' of the Uttar Pradesh Muslim, and certainly many people who are new to Hindi cinema find these films more appealing than visions of modern India.

Islam is not seen as a problem in Indian cinema providing it is within the Islamicate context rather than the world of politicised or globalised Islam. All the Muslims in Hindi films seem to be very rooted in South Asia, and connections to other Islamic countries are nearly always linked with terrorism, particularly with Pakistan and the Gulf. The other major source of tension is romance between Hindus and Muslims, which occurs only when these tensions play a major role in the narrative (as in Mani Ratnam's *Bombay*, 1995, and *Veer-Zaara*). In other words, Islam as culture and belief is 'acceptable' but the issues of the international community and of inter-communal relations are still highly sensitive.

Although this chapter is not about 'Filming the gods' as mentioned above, it raises the problem that all viewers have to face, namely how the Hindi film's images shape and form the public image of the Muslim in other communities and impact on the community's own self-image. It seems that the Islamicate images may represent Muslims' own image of themselves – at least an image to the section of the community that views films. (The Muslim audience is always regarded by the film producers as a major part of their audience, hence there are no major films released during Ramadan, although there are no figures to prove this. The overseas

Muslim audience, notably in the Gulf States and in the UK is considerable.) This is in part specific to the image of a minority community which is often marked and caricatured. Cinema is currently engaging with problems of representing difference and how difference be incorporated into the idea of the nation and indeed the wider audience. As Faisal Devji (1992: 1) points out, 'The Muslim ... represents a fundamental anxiety of nationalism itself: of the nation as something unachieved.'

Chapter 4

The religious and the secular in the Hindi film

Religious and secular

This chapter examines how religion, religions, religious communities, religious beliefs and religious practices are depicted in the 'non-religious' genres, focusing on the dominant genre of the Hindi film, the social. The discussion includes collective practices and beliefs, which may or may not be explicitly labelled as religious. The chapter also raises questions of secularism and the way that these films show the presence and absence of religious elements to draw conclusions about religion as part of a wider range of cultural practices.

Secularism has several meanings even within western societies, for as Asad (2003: 193) argues, religion produces the secular by defining what belongs to which domain. It would be an enormous project to present a comparative study of what secularism might mean in the west and in India and then to examine the relationship between secularism and film. In India there are several widely held interpretations of secularism, where the term's references range from a political exclusion of religion to one of atheism, then relate these to the Hindi film.

Secularism has long been regarded as one of the defining features of modernity (Giddens 1990) and as absent from the public sphere as defined by Habermas. In recent years, it has been argued that while secularism may be a feature of modernity in the formerly Christian west, even there it is uneven and incomplete. Recent research now shows that there are other modernities where secularism may not have a place, notably modernities produced by religion such as an Islamic modernity (Roy 2004, Devji 2005). Although Ashis Nandy has long argued for other modernities in India, little has been written about a possible Hindu modernity.

Two major types of secularism that are often confused should be distinguished: one as a political practice or doctrine and one as an epistemic category or ontology (Asad 2003). It is largely accurate to say that in the west the state is mostly separate from religion, while religion has been pushed more into the private sphere with private faith, whether in traditional religions or new religions and new spiritualities or New Age beliefs. Yet even within the west, secularism varies across cultures and societies, for example it seems more entrenched in Europe than the US. However, even within Europe the varieties of secularism differ, notably between the UK, where there is an established church, and France, where secularism means the prohibition of the display of religious symbols in schools and other institutions of the state (see Asad 2003: 5).

In India there has been much discussion of secularism as a political practice or doctrine but it is not the subject of this chapter beyond mentioning that the term is much contested and has spawned an enduring debate.[1] Although India is constitutionally a secular state, it cannot be so in the same sense as western-style secularism because the very categories of religion differ and there is no church to separate from the state. The present (2005) government, the Congress Party, claims to espouse secularist values in that it does not speak for any one religious group (and is proud of having a Muslim President, albeit appointed by its predecessors, and a Sikh Prime Minister and Roman Catholic leader) and is actively supported by minorities, notably Muslims. Congress argues that all religions have equal status and that religion is not part of the state. However, Congress is accused by the BJP, the supporters of a policy of Hindutva (Hindu nationalism), of being 'pseudo-secularist' because they support different laws for minorities, thus producing religious communities, whereas they themselves are actually the true secularists. Others argue that India is not secular but has high-caste Hinduism masquerading as secularism. So while India is constitutionally politically secular, its constitution has produced religious and caste communities and has not prevented communalism.

In everyday speech, it is clear that secularism has another range of meanings in India.[2] It rarely means the separation of the religious and the non-religious or 'equal disregard' for all religions, which can come close to meaning atheism, but it usually means 'equal regard for all religions'.[3] This in turn usually means 'high regard' as religiosity is generally highly valued in India. It is the former pluralistic meaning that is used in the film industry where the word 'secular' is often employed to describe the industry itself or the films that it makes.

This contestation of the term 'secular' is not surprising, given that new forms of secularism have to be produced in order to respond to the specific religion itself, as there are no universal distinctions of what belongs to the religious and what to the secular. This view is supported by Talal Asad's argument that religion produces secularism by its own ideas of what is sacred and what is religious (2003: 193). In other words, religion and secularism have to be examined together as the sacred and the secular are dependent on each other and this very relationship in turn produces new ideas of religion, ethics and politics.

Religion, secularism and the film industry

The Hindi film industry prides itself on being secular, and it is secular in the sense of 'equal respect' being given to each religion. The diversity of the industry goes back to its earliest days, at least in Bombay, where Bengali Hindus worked alongside Germans (New Theatre), while in other companies many Muslim stars worked alongside Hindus, Jews and Parsis. After independence, when many Punjabi Hindus who had fled the partition came to Bombay, they worked alongside Muslims. A notable example is B.R. Chopra, who left Lahore in August 1947, and, for his 1950s films such as *Ek hi raasta* (1956) and *Naya daur* (1957), had a story-writing team that was mostly Muslim (including Akhtar ul-Imam and Akhtar Mirza); his lyricist was Muslim (Sahir Ludhianvi), his music directors Hindu (O.P. Nayyar, Hemant Kumar), his singers Muslim (Mohammad Rafi) and Hindu (Lata Mangeshkar) while his stars were Muslims (Dilip Kumar, Meena Kumari) and Hindus (Vyjayanthimala, Ashok Kumar).

Manto (1998) also shows how mixed the world of the film people was in terms of religious backgrounds, and there were many deep friendships, affairs and marriages across communities (Raj Kapoor and Nargis; Kishore Kumar and Madhubala) in the 1940s, just as there are today (Shahrukh Khan, Aamir Khan both married Hindus while Hrithik Roshan married a Muslim). This is all well known by the fans, who often regard the stars themselves as gods, even having temples dedicated to them.[4] However, their behaviour, while often accepted, is not seen as something to emulate for the 'ordinary people' (see Dwyer 2000a: 115–42).

The film industry does not, on the whole, try to elide the differences between the different religions – nor indeed, between different regional backgrounds – but festivals, life rituals, etc. are celebrated together, whatever the community. However, one notable feature of the industry is the absence, at least at the higher levels, of anyone lower caste or Dalit. There are certainly some castes that are numerically significant in the industry (notably the Punjabi Khatris) but there does not seem to be any other association around caste.

The Hindi film industry's treatment of religion is probably not that dissimilar from Hollywood where everyone knew who was Jewish, Roman Catholic and so on. Although many of the Hollywood moguls were Jewish, it seems their studios celebrated 'national' (often Christian) festivals such as Christmas and Thanksgiving. No eyebrows were raised at the involvement of Jewish people in creating the American dream of the Christian festival through film, notably with songs like the 'secular' 'White Christmas' written by Irving Berlin (Israel Baline).

One much over-hyped feature of the industry is that actors had to 'conceal' their religious identities by changing their names, so Yusuf Khan became Dilip Kumar, Begum Mumtaz Jehan became Madhubala and Mahajabeen became Meena Kumari. However, concealment was not the aim as everyone in the industry and beyond knew these were stage names and no attempt was made to hide people's religious backgrounds. While no one ever changed his or her name to a Muslim name, many Hindus also changed their names (Ashok Kumar Ganguly to Ashok Kumar, Kulbhushan Nath Pandit to Raaj Kumar, Hari Krishna Goswami to Manoj Kumar and so on) in order to have modern, neutral names, as many Hollywood and other movie stars took stage names that sounded more fashionable or less 'ethnic' (Frederick Austerlitz to Fred Astaire, Lucille Le Sueur to Joan Crawford, Camille Javal to Brigitte Bardot and so on). Similarly in the west, there was no attempt to conceal religious origin, as Woody Allen, who changed his name from Allen Stewart Konigsberg, has always played up his Jewish ethnicity.

The industry has many practices which are directly religious. The films themselves often open with religious images, whether RK Film's sequence of Prithviraj Kapoor worshipping Shiva, or Mukta Arts' use of *Om* and the recitation of the *Gayatri mantra*, or Mehboob Khan's communist hammer and sickle with the popular Urdu verse: 'No matter what evils your enemies wish for you, it is of no consequence. Only that can happen which is God's will.' (The poem is anonymous though variously attributed to Irshad Lucknowi and Agha Hashr Kashmiri.)

The industry itself uses religious practices such as having an auspicious moment (*muhurat*) for the first shot, which usually incorporates Hindu rituals such as the breaking of a coconut. Many offices have images of Hindu deities in them, which are worshipped. Astrology, which is not exclusive to any religious tradition and whose popular usage in India tends to blend western and Indian forms, is important for working out dates for releases and other significant events, while numerology and other practices lead to the changing of spellings of names of films (such as Rakesh Roshan's 2006 film *Kkrish*) and of the actors (Kareena Kapoor has changed the spelling of her name to Karrena and Kariena).[5]

In recent years, certain cults have become important in the film industry, notably that of the Venkateswara temple in Tirupati (Andhra Pradesh) and that of Sai Baba of Shirdi (Maharashtra). While the former is more closely associated with the Telugu and Tamil industries, several members of the Bombay film industry are known to be devotees, and Amitabh Bachchan visited for a special ceremony for his sixtieth birthday in 2002. It is the richest shrine in India, with an annual income said to be of around Rs 800 crore (approx. £100 million).

The first major devotee of Sai Baba in the film industry was Raj Kapoor, who made regular visits to the shrine. (See Chapter 2 on the devotional film.) Sai Baba, who is claimed as a Hindu and a Muslim, is regarded as 'secular' in the definition given above, in that he is held in equally high regard by Hindus and Muslims. It is not surprising that given this 'secular' religiosity, the proximity of his shrine to Bombay, the simplicity of the rituals involved and his granting of miracles, that he has become such a focus of devotion to many in the industry.

Religion, secularism and the social genre

While other genres of Hindi cinema have cyclically emerged and disappeared, the dominant genre of the Hindi film since the 1940s has been the omnibus 'social' genre. Its generic boundaries are even fuzzier than those of other notoriously loosely defined Hindi films, as all films have romance, action, songs and dance, etc. However, since the producers, consumers and critics recognise generic categories, such as the gangster film, the action film, the war film and so on, the social tends to be the category to which any film whose genre is not clear is assigned. It means a melodrama set in the contemporary period, where the hero (more rarely the heroine) seeks to reconcile romantic love to the demands of the family and the community/nation.

The social genre is not directly about religion but often shows direct and indirect signs of religion and religiosity, as practice and belief as well as in its depiction of myth and the sacred. However, the genre is never called 'The Hindu social' (cf. The Muslim social in Chapter 3), because Hindu beliefs and practices are dominant in the social, as is true of Indian culture in general where Hindu religious references may pass almost unnoticed, and so it does not need marking as Hindu and this may even lead to the genre being regarded as 'secular' as many of the signs of religion are also those of culture and society. In other words, Hinduism is the invisible norm, the standard default position.

This chapter examines the social and some other films that are not part of the three 'religious' genres examined in the preceding chapters, to see the extent to which they manifest a Hindu imagination (to draw from Andrew Greeley 2000, in which he examines 'the Catholic imagination') or a secular imagination that Hinduism would produce. The somewhat amorphous category of the social film is so vast, and the presence of religion is so diverse, that I do not attempt to historicise the social in its political and social context. Such potted histories often flatten the complexities of these connections, oversimplifying them to read that Nehruvian dominance of the 1950s meant all films were secular in a Nehruvian way or that the dominance of Hindutva in the 1990s meant that all films were tinged with saffron. Instead, the chapter is focused on manifestations of the religious in the films in diverse areas such as narrative, language and so on. I do place them in their context, but like generic categories, themselves showing changes in mentality, these manifestations too have cyclical and exceptional occurrences.

While it is almost impossible to have no mention of religion in film (given that even the characters' names refer to their religion), there is usually no depiction of religious practice or belief in genres that are explicitly concerned with modernity and being modern. Some of the early genres of Indian cinema, such as the stunt film, which present striking images of modernity, have no space for religion, which is seen as being outside the domain of the modern. Wadia Movietone's films of 'Fearless' Nadia (Mary Evans) from the 1930s and 1940s (such as *Diamond queen*, 1940, dir. Homi Wadia) are good examples of this as they are not in any way anti-religious but the stunts, chases and fights do not leave any room for religion. Nadia is clearly a foreigner, with her blond hair and light eyes, but she is often referred to as the *Bambaiwali* ('woman from Bombay') and there are no suggestions of her religious origins, although her characters usually have Hindu (i.e. unmarked) names.

The film noir, such as *CID* (1956, dir. Raj Khosla), which again focuses on the modern, is usually silent about religion. In *CID*, the depiction of the icons of modernity, such as telephones, guns, cars, newspapers, verges on the obsessive, in particular the relay of phone calls at the beginning of the film. Some social films are also unmarked by religion, with class difference, rather than caste difference, being the usual impediment to marriage. Striking exceptions are *Acchut kanya* (1936, dir. Franz Osten) and *Sujata* (1959, dir. Bimal Roy).

However, these films were probably unusual in that even the social reform film such as *Duniya na mane* (1937, dir. V. Shantaram) showed several religious practices (worship of deceased parents, celebration of

Figure 4.1 Devika Rani as Kasturi, the 'untouchable girl' in *Achut kanya* (1936, dir. Franz Osten). Ashok Kumar plays the Brahmin boy.

festivals, wearing of *kumkum* – the vermilion mark on the forehead of married women – the Marathi version of the film was called *Kunku*), which give the heroine a more sympathetic or virtuous position, given the radical viewpoint she expresses on forced marriages. However, this film is a good counterpoint to the modernist film to show that a realist modern view can incorporate religion as cultural practice.

In the 1940s, there was a generic shift away from mythologicals, devotionals and stunts towards the omnibus genre of the social, which came to be the dominant genre. Given that this was the time of one of the major social upheavals in India (the world war, followed by independence, Partition and mass migration) and major communal tensions, the cinema was surprisingly quiet on all these issues.

Perhaps it was in the spirit of Nehruvian secularism that films often focused on human values rather than religious values, with the reformist films of Bimal Roy (*Sujata*, 1959, about 'untouchability' and *Do bigha zamin*, 1953, about urban migrants), and of B.R. Chopra (*Naya daur*, 1957, about industrialisation; *Ek hi raasta*, 1956, about widow remarriage). B.R. Chopra's production of Yash Chopra's *Dhool ka phool*, 1959, had an abandoned child brought up by an elderly Muslim, Abdul Chacha (Uncle Abdul), who believes the child is *Khudah ki amanat* ('entrusted by God'). Both Muslims and Hindus reject the child because they do not know his origins. This leads Abdul Chacha to sing a famous song which verges on humanism/atheism in its criticism of religious prejudice:

> *Tu Hindu banega na Musalman na banega.*
> *Insaan ki aulad hai, insaan banega.*
> You won't become a Hindu or a Muslim.
> You are the son of a human and you'll become a human.

It may also be that the films of this period were so preoccupied with creating a new mythology for a new nation, to bind it together into a community, that nationalism becomes almost a religion at this point. Films like Mehboob Khan's *Mother India* (1957), despite the abundance of Muslims working on the film, has many elements of Hindu mythology (see below for more on this film), yet has a partly 'secular' approach, albeit more complicated than that in his *Andaaz* (1949), where foreign ways and behaviour are seen to lead to criminality and imprisonment.

Even in the 1960s, when many films showed the rise of a new youth culture, and the beginnings of consumerism that were creating a new subjectivity, overt religious practices and belief are rarely absent, even if religion seems to be more associated with elders. This includes the Nasir Husain youth films, especially those with Shammi Kapoor which focus on romance, comedies and dancing. The 1970s see a rise in depictions of religious community if not in religious belief and practice, while the use of mythological references in the socials increases before the 1990s bring in more celebratory depictions of religious ceremonies and practices, often thought to be aimed at the overseas market.

Hindi films are never, to the best of my knowledge, anti-religious, and there is nothing similar to the Tamil DMK films such as *Parasakthi* (1952, dir. Krishnan-Panju), in which the deities themselves are called pieces of stone (although cut by the censors this can be lip-read) and the priest tries to rape the heroine (see Pandian 1991). Hindi socials may criticise priests and people who act in the name of religion (and many of the devotionals in Chapter 2 criticised Brahmins), and a striking example of this is *Nastik* (1954, dir. I.S. Johar). *Nastik* means 'One who says there is not (any authority in the Vedas)' but is used to mean 'atheist'.

Nastik is the story of Anil (Ajit), a refugee travelling with others on a train, with his sister and little brother, after their parents have been killed in the Partition riots. Kavi Pradeep's famous song '*Kitna badal gaya insaan!*' is picturised against a backdrop of actual footage of refugees and also stylised shots of *mullahs* and priests arguing. His little brother dies while the *mahant* ('priest') refuses to visit poor people. Anil is sent to gaol on false witness for attempting to kill the priest, and he becomes an atheist. His sister becomes a prostitute and kills herself. The priest realises Anil wants to kill him so he goes on a pilgrimage with his daughter to Dwarka, Rameshwaram, Benaras, Hardwar and Puri, where Anil is shown looking at the deities but not worshipping, except that this constitutes a form of *darshan*. Anil decides to take revenge by making the priest's daughter (Nalini Jaywant) fall in love by flirting with her, luring her out in a boat in a storm, when the spirit of the river, who appears as a figure with a halo, saves her. They marry in secret, escape in a boat on the Ganges pursued by her father but they fall in the water. Anil thinks she is dead but her father saves her and she gives birth to a son. When the child becomes sick, she goes to a popular Baba ('preacher') for healing who turns out to be Anil, who is just a fake. However, the child's illness makes him re-find God.

Although the film was banned (*Filmfare* 3(9), 30 April 1954), it went on to have a golden jubilee (run of fifty weeks), probably because of its success in dealing with the issue of the Partition, and the subsequent loss of faith and search for meaning in the world. Although Anil becomes an atheist, his re-finding of faith through love, repentance and through his interaction with the deities, even though he had no belief in them, fits into the wider worldview of the Hindi film.

Films that do not mention religion are few and far between, and the remarkable persistence of religion in the cinema is notable both in direct references to or depictions of religion (communities, practices, beliefs, divine intervention) and in indirect expressions (religious beliefs and moral systems of films) that are seen in many films.

A striking feature of modern India is the presence of the religious, whether in images, gesture, language, festivals, rituals and so on. A removal of these elements would make the Hindi film seem not only unrealistic but would also take away from its emotions, its spectacle and so on, and these features need to be examined.

The facile expression that 'Hinduism is not a religion but a way of life' is based on a misunderstanding of 'religion' as only 'belief' rather than also 'culture' and 'practice'. Hinduism, a term which is many centuries younger than the religion it describes, refers to diverse, if not always contradictory, religious beliefs and practices. Some forms of Hinduism are centred on culture and on practice, where the world is sacred, while others are based on belief and devotion to a god or a higher principle, though still drawing on culture and practice. All these forms are found in the social film and my aim here is to describe and analyse some of these occurrences. I also look at what they tell us about Hinduism, about film's view of Hinduism and other religions and how they interact. I conclude with some remarks about religion and secularism in modern India.

Representation of communities

Although the Hindi film features the upper-caste, north Indian Hindu male as the norm, other religious and regional communities appear, distinguished by their names (which show region, religion and caste among other markers), dress, language, festivals, ceremonies, music and so on.

It is almost impossible to give a name without showing the character's religion. A few films do this, such as *Rangeela* (1995, dir. Ram Gopal Varma), in which the hero, Munna (meaning approximately 'Kid'), could be either Hindu or Muslim. Another strange example, already mentioned in the previous chapter, is *Jab jab phool khile* (1965, dir. Suraj Prakash), in which the exotic Kashmiri *shikari* ('boatman') is called Raja (a Hindu name) although all the *shikaris* are Muslim, and Raja yells, '*Afoo Khuda*!', a Muslim expression for 'O God!'

Very few films show lower castes or Dalits,[6] unless the film is specifically about caste issues (*Acchut kanya*, *Sujata* mentioned above; also devotional films such as *Dharmatma*, 1935, dir. V. Shantaram) or wants to make a point about Dalit uplift (*Lagaan*, 2001, dir. Ashutosh Gowariker). Even with the rise of lower castes as a political group in north India, they have not featured in films unless these are directly concerned with the topic as in *Bandit Queen* (1994, dir. Shekhar Kapur). Although in recent years the reference of Hindi films has broadened to take in other regional groups and some genres, such as the gangster film, include mostly lower-class characters of various regions and religions, cinema remains one of the main ways, along with practices and rituals of the state, that upper-caste Hinduism penetrates India.

Hindus from other regions of India are usually shown as figures of fun, especially south Indians, whose Hindi accents are much mocked, for example the music teacher in *Padosan* (1968, dir. Jyoti Swaroop) or the Gujaratis in *Kal ho na ho* (2003, dir. Nikhil Advani). (The diasporic Indians, however westernised, retain the same characteristics as their Indian equivalents, so the Punjabis in *Kal ho na ho* mock the Gujarati attempts at a wedding song.) At other times, region can be an obstacle to a couple's union as in *Ek duuje ke liye* (1981, dir. K. Balachander), in which the boy is Tamil and the girl is Punjabi. The same repetition of comedy and hostility is found in the depiction of people who belong to other religions.

The major 'other' religion in India is Islam. It is the largest of the minority religions and the one that is taken the most seriously, and, along with Hinduism, is referred to as 'the two communities'. Its complex depictions (and also inter-communal marriages and Partition films) have been discussed in Chapter 3. It was seen there that these depictions changed over time and genre with no single depiction of the Muslim emerging. Muslims are often exoticised, sometimes alien, sometimes the loyal friend, the politicised figure, sometimes a terrorist. This is the only community that is taken seriously but relations between the two groups are nearly always problematic and intermarriage is almost impossible, *Veer-Zaara* (2004, dir. Yash Chopra) being a notable exception (see Chapter 3).

Sikhs and Jains are often regarded as quasi-sects of Hinduism, the latter barely featuring at all. The only striking example of a Jain is that of Adinath, the reformist gaoler, in *Do aankhen barah haath* (1957, dir. V. Shantaram), who leads a 'human experiment' into criminal reform. His religious beliefs and practices are never shown, but his name is that of a Jain. Sikhs feature usually as warriors in war films, where their brave nature is always emphasised. They are often seen as the butt of jokes for being a bit simple as in *Kuch kuch hota hai* (1998, dir. Karan Johar). Curiously, there are no Sikhs in *Dilwale dulhaniya le jayenge* (1995, dir. Aditya Chopra), the overseas Punjabi's return to the homeland, whereas in *Veer-Zaara*, the Sikhs negotiate between Hindus and Muslims and the Pakistani girl, Zaara, first goes to India to take her Sikh nanny's ashes back to her homeland.

Other religions are scarcely acknowledged, especially those that have few followers in India or are confined to certain areas and hence not recognised in the popular imagination nationally. For example, there are few references to Jewish people apart from the old staples of the Parsi theatre set during the Roman Empire – *Yahudi*, 1958, dir. Bimal Roy and *Yahudi ki ladki*, 1933, dir. Premankur Atorthy, and *Yahudi ki ladki*, 1957, dir. S.D. Narang), although there have been several prominent Jewish actors in Indian cinema (including Sulochana and Nadira). Parsis, who form a prominent community in Bombay, do not appear too often in films, probably because they are not a well-known community beyond

मेंहदी लगाके रखना... डोली सजाके रखना
लेने तुझे ओ गोरी... आएँगे तेरे सजना

YASH CHOPRA'S
Dilwale Dulhania Le Jayenge

DIRECTED BY ADITYA CHOPRA
MUSIC JATIN-LALIT LYRICS ANAND BAKSHI CINEMATOGRAPHY MANMOHAN SINGH

Figure 4.2 Dilwale dulhaniya le jayenge (1995, dir. Aditya Chopra). Raj (Shahrukh Khan) and Simran (Kajol) as British Asians who teach their parents about Indian traditions. The couple are dressed for the engagement ceremony in the film, which has been much copied in real life.

Maharashtra and Gujarat. Their representation is usually as in *Qurbani* (1981, dir. Feroz Khan), where middle-class Parsis are shown as comical figures, much amusement being provided by the fact that their language is a mixture of Gujarati and accented Hindi, they have lots of children and drive a vintage car.

Christians, although found across India, are often associated with Goa in particular, and their representation is not complex, although it has changed over time. Christian men are usually comics and drunks (Jack Braganza in *Bobby*, 1973, dir. Raj Kapoor, and Anthony in *Amar, Akbar, Anthony*, 1977, dir. Manmohan Desai) or criminals called Robert and Peter. Women are professionals (nurses and teachers) or are mostly shown as women of dubious virtue, often gangsters' molls immortalised in Ajit's much-quoted dialogues as Mona Darling and Lily – 'Don't be silly' – or dancing girls such as Miss Edna (Madhubala) in *Howrah Bridge* (1958, dir. Shakti Samanta).[7]

Although Christians protested about the way the heroine's sexuality was shown in *Julie* (1975, dir. K.S. Sethumadhavan), in *Bobby*, the Christian girl, Bobby, was shown as a standard heroine, even if her clothes were a little more skimpy than usual. There were no objections to the youngsters' relationship from either family on the grounds of religion (he is Hindu, she Christian), only of class.

In recent years, Sanjay Leela Bhansali has made two films about Christians, one about Goans, *Khamoshi – the musical* (1998), and one about Anglo-Indians in Simla, *Black* (2005). There seem to be only aesthetic reasons – locations, churches, candles, clothes and music – for their being Christians as there is no reference to their being minorities or having different beliefs and practices. (*Kal ho na ho* has an interesting twist on the depiction of Indian Christians but is discussed below as the religious aspects of the film are more complicated than the straightforward depiction of community.) *Black* had no reference to the Irish Catholic origins of the family that their name (McNally) suggests, and graduation ceremonies by candlelight in a building that could be a church or a convocation hall and the wearing of black to an engagement party seemed strange.

One of the striking features in the showing of Christianity is not of the community itself, but of the respect that Hindus always show to Christian places of worship, and they are often shown actually praying in a church. The most likely reason for this could be that many people in the industry went to convent schools and other educational institutions run by the Church.

Manmohan Desai made several films about families separated and reunited (almost constituting a separate genre called 'lost and found'), and one of his earliest films was about a Partition separation. His films often showed characters from different religions, his most famous being *Amar,*

Akbar, Anthony, which is now a byword in religious plurality. Three boys are separated from their parents on Independence Day, when their father leaves them at the foot of a statue of Mahatma Gandhi. Each is brought up by different parents, one a Hindu (Amar), one a Muslim (Akbar) and one a Christian (Anthony). The mother gets to know Akbar and Anthony but as she was blinded in an accident she does not realise they are her sons. The religious situation is kept more simple as the boys all fall for girls from their own communities. The Hindu's romance is sincere and reforming, whereas the Muslim man is an exhibitionist, though his beloved is a doctor, whom he woos by singing (camp) *qawwalis* ('*Purdah re purdah*') at an event where she wears a *burqa*, and brings eunuchs to shame her father into permitting the romance. The Christian is a drunk and a small-time crook but his girlfriend is virtuous, although her father is a gangster.

The fact that the boys' real parents are Hindus and the Hindu son is a policeman reinforces the underlying Hindu-ness of all Indians. However, there is much lip-service paid to the religiosity of the Catholic priest and the sincere prayers of Akbar to Shirdi Sai Baba, whose devotees are shown clearly as both Hindus and Muslims. The prayers result in his blind mother's miraculous cure as two rays of light emanate from the eyes of the image of Sai Baba.

Gods in the world

While representation of communities shows us religious beliefs and practices, the social films also show direct representations of the gods who intervene in the world. This is through the divine word in the case of Islam or through the efficacy of their images, usually in what would be described as a miracle. While the miracle does not seem surprising in the 'religious' genres, its appearance in the social film is as a plot device to give sanction to the story or to a character's actions and can seem disjunctive with the relationship between characters and narratives elsewhere in the film. However, as the discussion below will show, this is not actually out of step with other elements of the film that may be less overtly 'religious'.

The intervention may be associated with 'Islamic' sources. For example, in *Coolie* (1983, dir. Manmohan Desai), Iqbal (whose girlfriend, Julie, is a Christian, and whose friend, Sunny, is a Hindu) is a Muslim who is proud of his coolie's badge number 786 (the numerological value of '*Bismillah al-Rahman al-Rahim*'/'In the name of God, the gracious and the merciful'). There are several 'miracles' during the film, for example, someone's memory is restored when a print showing calligraphy from the Quran falls or, during a song to God in which she prays for her life, lightning surrounds Iqbal's mother to protect her. However, the most dramatic miracle is at the climax as Iqbal climbs the minaret at the tomb of Haji Ali. He survives the bullets shot at him by his enemy, Zafar (a Muslim) because he recites the *kalma* (the affirmation 'there is no God but God and Mohammed is His Prophet') and is draped in the *chador* (cover) of Haji Ali's tomb, which has verses from the Quran embroidered on it, and because he writes '786' in his blood on the paint. The three bullets that are lodged in Iqbal's body are removed during surgery while prayers are said for him outside the operating theatre by his Muslim parents. However, this is given a 'secular' angle as each bullet is removed in between cuts to the coolies' prayers said in a temple, a church and a *gurdwara*. (Amitabh Bachchan suffered a near-fatal injury on the sets of *Coolie* and it was felt that it was divine intervention from the prayers of all faiths that brought him back to life.)

It may be said that in Hindu thought, the gods are often in this world, and regularly manifest themselves on earth, often as *avatars* or incarnations or as themselves. Their images, usually in two or three dimensions, are regarded as efficacious (Pinney 2004). It is not surprising then that in films divine intervention happens through the image itself rather than a manifestation of the deity in human or part-human form. In *Dil to pagal hai* (1997, dir. Yash Chopra), small crystal images of Ganesh inspire the protagonists to keep their faith. The social film is unlike the religious films in that we rarely see an actual manifestation of the divine and often the miracle is not clearly an act of direct intervention but is suggested by montage and editing. This is the case in *Hum aapke hain kaun . . .!* (1994, dir. Sooraj Barjatya), in which Rama intervenes indirectly to bring the older brother and sister together (referred to in the song '*Wah wah Ramji*'/'Well done, Rama!'), whereas an interchange of looks between an image of Krishna and Tuffy the dog lead the dog to carrying a letter which reveals the true situation and will ultimately bring together the younger brother and sister.

As the Hindi film narrative is often disrupted, notably by the songs, these instances of the miraculous do not disturb the audience because they are presented as 'real' and as part of the realistic, melodramatic worldview that permeates the rest of the film. A belief in miracles is common to most cultures and their presence in the Hindi film is not noted as disruptive by the audience members themselves, who might well be disappointed if the images and gods did not respond to their devotees.

Mythology

The use of mythology in the social film is clearly very different from that outlined in the mythological genre discussed in Chapter 1. In the social, mythological stories are brought into the everyday world, where they are retold as part of daily life until the division between religious and the

Produced by
Kamal Kumar Barjatya
Rajkumar Barjatya
Ajit Kumar Barjatya

Screenplay & Direction
Sooraj R. Barjatya

Rajshri Productions (P) Ltd. Present

Yours Forever..!
English　　　　　Eastmancolor

Music
Raamlaxman

Lyrics
Hema Sardesai

English Version by
Opender Chanana

Figure 4.3 Hum aapke hain koun . . . ! (1994, dir. Sooraj Barjatya). Publicity still from the song '*Didi tera dewaar deewana*', sung to mark a pregnancy ritual.

mundane is blurred. In these retellings, belief is not necessarily implied any more than by the use of Greek and Roman mythology in Europe, which has been foundational to European culture. While no one today may believe in the fates that created Oedipus' destiny or that Narcissus truly underwent a metamorphosis, these stories have been told and retold over the centuries and now are most famous in the modern narratives of Freudian psychoanalysis. The social film often provides an arena in which familiar stories are retold or referred to as the everyday is framed by myth, which can be used to narrate the way the world is and the way it should be.

The major way in which mythology appears in the social film is the referencing of the mythological stories, usually those of the two great epics, the *Mahabharata* and the *Ramayana*. These can be an episode within a film so in *Awaara*, when the judge refuses to take his pregnant wife back after she has been held captive by another man, the story of Sita is immediately invoked and is referred to directly within the film. The mythological reference can be unstated but run through the entire film, so Mani

Ratnam, giving his own interpretation of his much-discussed film, *Roja* (see Chapter 3), says that this story of a woman seeking to claim her husband's life from the threat of death is Savitri, who pleaded with Yama, the god of death, for Satyavan's life. The most frequently used motifs are in the case of brothers where a family quarrel with a child who has a different mother evokes the *Ramayana* (*Kabhi khushi kabhie gham*, 2001, dir. Karan Johar); while, much more frequently, the story of a wronged brother and a fortunate brother is that of Karan and Arjun from the *Mahabharata*.

The melodrama of a film may be made more tragic by the evocation of a mythological story. For example, *Main tulsi tere aangan ki* (1978, dir. Vijay Anand) could just be a 'weepie' in which a dancing girl commits suicide when the father of her child has to make a new life with a respectable woman. However, it draws on the mythological associations as the dancing girl is called Tulsi, the name of the sacred basil who is wedded to Vishnu, but it also refers to the story of Vrinda, a prostitute who fell in love with Krishna (an incarnation of Vishnu), who could not marry him so remained, like the *tulsi*, outside in his *aangan* (courtyard), the public area of the house.

Sometimes in a film, the characters are named after gods or mythological figures, which resonates in the film, even if the story is dissimilar. While Subhash Ghai's film *Kisna* (2005) was felt to do this in a heavy-handed way, his *Khalnayak* (1993) successfully evoked the purity of the heroine, named Ganga (the holy river) and Ram (the righteous), and in case the audience had missed it, there was a small lecture on this, connecting the deities to the characters in the film's narratives.[8]

Figure 4.4 Kabhi khushi kabhie gham (2001, dir. Karan Johar). A domestic ritual, an *aarti*, becomes an occasion for the display of a family's wealth and devotion.

Films may draw on several mythological themes and referents, notably in *Mother India* (1957, dir. Mehboob Khan), where even though the director was a practising Muslim, he understood the way in which mythology added to the depth of the film, helping to turn it into a national epic. The film uses the mythology of various goddesses in the main heroine, Mother India, such as Bhu Devi (the earth), Lakshmi (the goddess of wealth), Radha (the lover of Krishna, who is not, according to some, a goddess), and the new goddess of the nation, Mother India (sometimes called Bharat Mata, but this title was not used for the film itself, to emphasise her 'secular' nature); meanwhile her husband was called Shyam (a name of Krishna), her 'good' son Ram, and her rebellious son, Birju (another name of Krishna).[9] The analyses of the mythological references in the film have largely been framed by Freudian readings, notably the Oedipal myth, which maps suspiciously smoothly onto the film and its off-screen romance between the heroine, Nargis, and Sunil Dutt (who plays Birju).

The films have created their own myths, within the texts themselves as well as in the stories of the stars themselves, in the sense that Wendy Doniger (2004) describes:

> in the broadest sense: stories that are not necessarily connected with a particular religion but that have the force of religious beliefs, that endure in the cultural imagination as religious texts do, and that deal with deeply held beliefs that religions, too, often traffic in. Such myths are often invoked by people in real-life situations that duplicate the situations they have heard about in myths.

Mother India would be a good example of this, as the story of the peasant woman struggling against all odds, protecting her honour and that of the village, and making personal sacrifices for the good of the village has become a myth in itself. Nargis famously referred to dams (which Nehru is said to have called 'the temples of modern India', which featured prominently in the film) to attack the cinema of Satyajit Ray, which she accused of portraying negative images of India to the west. In the 1990s, when Sanjay Dutt, the son of Nargis and Sunil Dutt, was arrested under TADA (an anti-terrorist law), part of the shock was that he was the son of 'Mother India'. Another good example is *Devdas*, the several versions of which I shall examine below in this chapter to discuss the way they use a language of love that draws on religion while also evoking mythology.

Though several of the major figures involved in the making of *Mother India* were Muslims, the religious references were all Hindu or Hindu-based. However, as mentioned above, Mehboob Productions used a popular, anonymous verse at the beginning of the film, which can be said to be at least Islamicate if not Islamic, while showing the communist symbol of the hammer and sickle.

Religion, language and love

Hindi cinema draws on various lyric traditions for its language of love and romance, which are found throughout the films but particularly in the film songs, and which form one of the major attractions of the films. Several of these traditions are connected with religious devotion and the figures of speech established in the lyrics are found regularly throughout the songs. This does not mean that the songs themselves are religious, but their sensibility and their ways of thinking are associated with these traditions. These songs are then used beyond the films themselves as a public language of love which sets a way of expressing emotions and feelings where the religious may be central or may only be a faint echo of its original meaning.

Mysticism and other religious experiences are associated with erotic love as this is the only way in which these experiences have a physiological foundation. This is done not only through words, but also through the image or the person, and in cinema the process of scopophilia, the pleasure of looking, is another powerful source of desire, which we saw in Chapters 1 and 2 was associated with the practice of *darshan* in much of Indian experience.

The Indian lyric tradition creates analogies of earthly love with spiritual or divine love throughout its history, through classical Sanskrit and Tamil lyrics, the medieval traditions of *bhakti* and into the lyrics of Urdu and the modern Indian languages (Dwyer 2000a, Ch. 2). Even the emergence of modern/postmodern ideals of love (see Dwyer 2000a) has not made this language any less religious (indeed one of my arguments in this book is that modern in India does not mean non-religious). Some of these traditions are more closely associated with the Hindi film song lyric and I now discuss these at more length. Several types of lyric tradition and indeed religious tradition are found in one film and these are not aimed at being exclusive. Two famous examples are *Pyaasa* (1957, dir. Guru Dutt) and *Awaara* (1951, dir. Raj Kapoor), which draw on a eclectic range of religious references.

Most of the lyrics in *Pyaasa* are in the tradition of the Urdu lyric which is associated with Islamicate culture (see Chapter 3), yet the examples here do not have many religious overtones but are associated with the socialist and often atheistic spirit of the Progressive Writers' Movement. The film also includes a song in the style of a *Mirabhajan* (a devotional song, supposedly composed by the *bhakta* Mira), 'Aaj sanam more ang laga lo', which evokes the Hindu *bhakti* tradition. However, the visual imagery of the film more frequently draws on Christian imagery as Vijay is shown reading a magazine with a picture of Christ on it, then he appears at his own 'memorial' where he adopts the posture of the crucified Christ in the backlit doorway.

Awaara, which takes the 'modern' view that it is nurture not nature that makes a criminal, refers to the story of Sita (as mentioned above) but in one of its most famous sequences, the dream scene, has very mixed religious references in the desire of Raju for redemption through Rita's love for him, where she is presented in a sort of heaven, while he is in a hell, tormented by devils, and the various sets show statues of the deities the Trimurti (the composite image of Shiva, Vishnu and Brahma), of the Devi (the Goddess) and of Nataraj (Dancing Shiva).

These references are very different from the evocation of Hindu *bhakti* in *Mughal-e Azam* (1961, Dir. K. Asif), where the *bhajan* '*Mohe panghat pe*', about Krishna the lover, is sung at the Janmashtami festival (the birth of Krishna) to show the religious tolerance of the Mughal court, where the Empress is a Hindu and the Emperor joins in her celebrations. Of course, the song also refers to the earthly love of the Prince for the dancing girl who is singing the song.

Although the relationships portrayed in *bhakti* literature are often transgressive, they are also some kind of model of human relationships. Yet it can be dangerous to draw too many parallels with real life. For example, in *Bandini* (1963, dir. Bimal Roy), the father is blamed for reading Bengali Vaishnava lyrics in front of his daughter and her lover and hence exciting their passions.

However, religion is also used in films to 'justify' transgressive – or overtly sexual – relationships. *Satyam shivam sundaram* (1978, dir. Raj Kapoor) shows the heroine, Zeenat Aman, wearing less and less clothing, the more devotional the songs are and the more they invoke Radha and Krishna.[10] In this film, her worshipping of the *lingam* (phallus) was certainly depicted in an erotic manner and even though Raj Kapoor was an establishment figure there was trouble with the censors for these scenes in which 'ejaculatory symbols are inflated to gigantic dimensions' (Rajadhyaksha and Willemen 1999: 439). Although the film was meant to be about spiritual or inner beauty rather than external beauty as the heroine, Roopa ('beauty'), is scarred, Kapoor himself said in an interview, 'Let people come to see Zeenat Aman's tits, they'll go out remembering the film' (George 1994: 134). Kapoor went even further with his 1985 *Ram teri Ganga maili hai* ('Ram, your Ganges is polluted'), in which the heroine, named after the sacred river itself, Ganga (Mandakini), was supposed to represent the corruption of woman by unscrupulous men and of India by politicians. However, it was Mandakini's completely transparent wet saris, used on publicity stills, in which she appeared nude with a clear display of her nipples, that caused outrage. These films showed a pornographic rather than an erotic display of the female body. Both films are great favourites with adolescent boys even until today.

The language of *bhakti* is also used elsewhere in songs to create an atmosphere of purity and devoted love, especially where some transgression has occurred. For example, in *Daag* (1973, dir. Yash Chopra), when Sonia (Sharmila) finds her husband Sunil (Rajesh Khanna), living with another woman, he sings her a love song, '*Mere dil mein aaj kya hai?*' ('What is happening in my heart today?'), where he sings of his devotion to her:

> *Mujhe devta banaakar*
> *Teri chaahaton ne puja*
> *Mera pyaar kah raha hai*
> *Main tujhe khuda bana doon*
> Your love made me a god
> And worshipped me
> My love says
> I should make you a god.

The lyrics happily move between 'Hindu' vocabulary such as *devta* 'deity', *puja* 'worship' and *pyaar* 'love' to the Persian word *khuda* 'God' and this is not seen as in any way remarkable.

In Chapter 3, the religious associations of Islamicate lyrics in the *ghazal* and also of the *qawwali* were mentioned, where the lyrics are ambiguous as to whether they are referring to divine or earthly love. The words of doomed passion and unrequited love are not necessarily religious in the film song, even though they use words associated with Islamicate cultures. Sometimes these traditions are referred to, when Hindu characters suddenly sing 'Allah' in their songs, not out of any Islamic devotion but because of the song traditions, so in *Teesri manzil* (1966, dir. Vijay Anand), a modern dance song '*Aaja aaja, main hoon pyaar tera*' ('Come here, I am your love'), suddenly says '*Allah Allah inkaar tera*' ('My God, don't deny me').

In *Dil se* (1998, dir. Mani Ratnam), Gulzar reworked the lyrics of the famous Sufi poet Bulleh Shah for the song 'Chaiya chaiya'. The song contains traditional images of Urdu poetry, for example '*Jinke sar ho ishq ki chhanh, paon ke neeche jannat hogi*' ('the one on whose head the shadow of love falls, has paradise beneath his feet') or

> *Taaweez banake pahanoon usse*
> *aayat ki tarah mil jaaye kahin.*
> *Mera nagma vahin mera kalama vahin.*
> I'll make a charm and wear it,
> I'll get her as if by a miracle.
> She is my song, she is my declaration of faith.

However, times had changed so that many protests were made against the song by Islamic groups, although this follows an old tradition of declaring love as religion or even replacing religion; to quote Ghalib:

Jaan tum par nisaar karta hun
Main nahin jaanta dua kya hai
I sacrifice my life for you
I don't know what prayers are.

Friendship is also a form of devotion equal to faith as Sher Khan (Pran) sings in *Zanjeer* (1973, dir. Prakash Mehra), '*Yaari hai imaan mera*' (Friendship is my religion).

As well as their traditional ambiguity between religious devotion and human love, *qawwalis* are often used in purely secular meanings, for example '*Kajra re*' in *Bunty aur Babli* (2005, dir. Shaad Ali Sahgal), which is more of a dance or 'item number'. Some *qawwalis* aim at a religious feeling across all faiths, such as the celebrated '*Na to karavan ki talash hai*' ('I'm not looking for a travelling caravan'), where God is said to be found equally in all religions.

While it might seem that some of this language would appear to be somewhat archaic in today's modern Hindi film, this is not the case. In fact, this language often survives as it shows the seriousness and devotion of love and its power being greater than and outlasting humans. I bring together these various observations on mythology, on language and on other forms of religious practice by looking at the story of Devdas, who has become a new mythological figure as the doomed lover beyond cinema to the extent that one can say, 'He's a real Devdas', and whose story has been told with different religious elements over the many versions that have been made throughout the history of Indian cinema (see Dwyer 2004c).

The character of Devdas was created in the eponymous novel of Saratchandra Chatterjee (1876–1938), which was much loved by the Bengali middle classes and which became popular across India through translation, before being filmed several times in various Indian languages.

Devdas Mukherjee, the son of a rich landowner, is a difficult child but a close friend of Parvati (Paro) Chakrabarty until he goes to Calcutta for his education. Paro's parents hope that Devdas and Paro will marry but the Mukherjees will not consider her as a daughter-in-law as the family is socially inferior and from the same village. The rebuffed Chakrabartys decide to marry Paro to a wealthy widower. Paro goes to Devdas' room at night but he says he cannot fight his family, he heads back to Calcutta, then returns again to the village. Paro refuses to forgive him, saying that he just wants to hurt her and she is marrying a better man; Devdas scars her face by hitting her. Paro becomes an ideal wife in an unconsummated marriage to an older man and a stepmother to children her own age, while Devdas, having fallen into the company of Chunni Babu, takes to drink and dancing girls. The courtesan, Chandramukhi, falls in love with him but he abuses her and rejects the possibility of love with her, while

also expressing his need and his sympathy. Devdas returns home to collect
his large inheritance after his father's death. Paro comes to meet him and
begs him to stop drinking but he returns to Calcutta. Chandramukhi aban-
dons her profession and goes to a village to follow a simple life, until she
returns to Calcutta in search of Devdas who has gone missing. She has
to take up her old profession to make money for his care, but he sets off
for a journey around India. He goes to Paro's village to keep his promise
of returning to her before he dies but her family refuse to let her meet
him. Devdas dies in front of her house without meeting her. She falls into
a swoon and never recovers from her grief.

Although the novel, the 1935 and the 1955 films are different given
their form and the times in which they were made, they keep a similar
narrative and are in the spirit of a certain type of realism. The latest film
stands apart so I discuss it only briefly after the other versions.

The 1935 Bengali version of the film (*Devdas*, 1935, dir. P.C. Barua),
about which Ashis Nandy writes (2000), is said to exist only in archives
in Dhaka and I have not had an opportunity to see it, but the simultaneously made Hindi version is very close to the original story. Made by
New Theatres, which was committed to middle-class literary values, the
film incorporates songs in a realistic manner. In the 1955 version, Bimal
Roy, the cameraman on the Saigal films, shows his trademark realist
cinema. Only the beauty of the three major stars brings more glamour to
the film, especially Vyjayanthimala's dancing as Chandramukhi.

This film is centrally concerned with the absence of the marriage of
Devdas and Paro. Yet, even though they die without ever having had a
sexual relationship with each other (or even anyone else), Paro and Devdas
appear to be a married couple from their childhood to his death. The
transformation of their childhood love into romantic love is presented as
a smooth transition, and this love is the unchanging centre at the heart
of this film about decay and disappointment. Paro's devotion to Devdas
has overtly religious elements, whether in the editing of the film that shows
him as her deity when she is lighting the lamp or the way they can
communicate telepathically (in the films not the book). Paro is saintly,
innocent and her (enforced) chastity makes her the ideal of childhood love
for Devdas – ever pure rather than the adulterous (if only mentally so)
love of a married woman for another man. She is even ready to risk
bringing disgrace on her family when she wants to bring a sick Devdas
home or when she tries to run out onto the road to him before he
dies. Their connection is emphasised in the film versions in a way it is
not in the novel, in that Paro feels Devdas' pain through her scar and at
the end they can communicate telepathically. The pure quality of their
love is emphasised in the music and lyrics of the films, with reference to
imagery of Krishna's pastoral loves, and in the 1955 film the lyrics are
by Sahir Ludhianvi, the great romantic lyricist of Hindi cinema, who wrote

the lyrics for *Pyaasa* (see above) as well as all Yash Chopra's films up to Sahir's death in 1981.

Devdas himself sings in the earlier version with K.L. Saigal, which is as expected, given that Saigal was a famous singing star. In the 1955 film, the children Paro and Devdas sing a song 'O *albele panchhi*' about a bird that has come from far that they want to keep, but otherwise they do not sing any more songs. Two songs are picturised on Paro, both sung by travelling Vaishnavas. The first, '*Aan milo Shyam saawre*', is a devotional song to Krishna about Radha pining for him when he leaves their childhood home, which makes Paro cry as she misses Devdas, drawing parallels to the sanctity of their childhood spent in a rural idyll. The second song is '*Saajan ki ho gayi*', about a young girl falling in love and forgetting all her childhood friends and family, which again makes Paro cry as she realises she will never forget Devdas and will never fall in love with her husband. Chandramukhi has two big dances but does not have songs that express her quasi-maternal devotion to Devdas and which might otherwise sanctify it.

The 2002 version of the film (dir. Sanjay Leela Bhansali) moves away from realism into a fully *filmi* or Bollywood style. Every scene shows a sumptuous extravagance which descends into a relentless kitsch. The childhood elements of Paro and Devdas' relationship are played down and the film instead shows their close physicality, again in a rather camp and asexual manner. However, the song lyrics and the music still carry these elements of religious devotion.

When Paro is getting married, the following song lyrics are sung, clearly not about her husband but about Devdas who is shown with her throughout the song:

> *hamesha tumko chaaha aur chaaha aur chaaha.*
> *hamesha tumko chaaha aur chaaha kuchh bhi nahin*
> *tumhen dil ne hai puja puja puja aur puja kuch bhi nahin*
> *na na nahin . . . kuchh bhi nahin . . .*
> I always loved you, loved you and loved you.
> I always loved you, and loved nothing else
> My heart worshipped you, worshipped you, and worshipped nothing
>   else.
> No, nothing . . . nothing at all . . .

Another song, '*More piya*', is of Krishna and Radha, which again draws parallels with the devotion of Devdas and Paro as a childhood bond that has the aura of the holy about it. This song is sung by Paro's mother, while Paro and Devdas are by the river, a visual image resonant with that of Krishna and Radha meeting on the banks of the Yamuna River.

In the 2002 version of the film, Chandramukhi has a song '*Kahe ched mohe*', which refers to the Krishna and Radha myth again, and brings her love for Devdas into the same sphere as that of Paro and Devdas, although she is a courtesan rather than a childhood friend. Paro and Chandramukhi dance together for the *Durga Puja* ('festival of the goddess'), where they both sing a song, '*Dola re dola*', about dancing and love. Another of Chandramukhi's songs, '*Maar daala*', uses words associated with Islamic prayers, as she begs God to give her her lover:

> *haan magar du'aa men jab yeh haath uthaaya*
> *khuda se du'aa men tumhen maang daala*
> *maang daala, Allah.*
> *ham par yeh kisne hara rang daala?*
> *khushi ne hamaari hamen maar daala*
> *hamen maar daala*
> *Allah maar daala ...*
> Yes, but when I raised my hands in prayer,
> I asked God for you!
> God, I asked for you!
> Who spread this green colour over me?
> My happiness killed me!
> It killed me,
> God, it killed me.

The use of 'Muslim' words here (*du'aa*, *Khuda* and *Allah*), and the reference to raising hands to pray in the style of Muslims, draws on the traditional association of courtesans with the Islamicate word, described in Chapter 3 above. Yet for all the religious vocabulary used in the Hindi film lyric for the language of love, the association of the language of love and that of religion remains an area for further investigation.

Hindu family values

In the 1990s, journalists and critics began to talk about Hindi films having 'Hindu Family Values', a new phenomenon in cinema though not new in religion, in which alongside strong traditions of renouncers, the house-holder also figures as the sustainer of religion and caste through his worship and other practices and through his pilgrimages (Madan 1987). These values, as the name suggests, include giving importance to religion and the family, with new visions of domesticity and of morality. They keep the religious as part of the everyday and have had a great appeal to India's new middle classes as they also allow them to enjoy the new consumerism that grew in this decade with the economic liberalisation of India.

The films are set in a world of plenitude, in particular those of the Yash Raj Films and Dharma Productions, which depict religion as consumerist practice and repackage traditions to suit this new modern

world. These films reinforce the presence of religiosity, fate, divine intervention and ever-more extravagant celebration of festivals much as scenes
of worship that had always been popular in Hindi films. The appeal was
a new form of modernity which incorporated religious values. The films
were in part a return to tradition but they were also an invention of a
new tradition. These films have also created certain styles of religious
practice which are now emulated in real life such as the 'Yash Chopra
wedding', and songs from the festivals and ceremonies shown in the films
are sung at weddings and the clothing is copied directly.

The values offered by these films also appealed to the diaspora as transnational communities, because the family has become more important
than the state itself, so 'Indian-ness' no longer means living within India.
These films also created a more 'positive' image of a rich consumerist
India, able to stand on at least equal terms with others in the world.

These values have often been hard to distinguish from the political rise
of Hindutva in the 1990s but they focus on the family rather than on
the political.[11] Dwyer (2006a) argues that factors such as censorship,
economics, diasporic audience and the nature of the industry have kept
Hindutva away from the film. Although the media themselves mediate
politics and reshape and reform it the complexities of the relationships
between Hindi film and politics are unclear (Prasad 1998 is one of the
few serious engagements with this topic).

From the 1990s onwards, film began to show more engagement with
the representation of Muslims (see Chapter 3), although the communities
often protested about their depictions. Although the films do not show
marital or romantic relationships across the communities, friendships and
other relationships began to become more frequent and less remarkable.
As mentioned in Chapter 3, in *Veer-Zaara* (2004, dir. Yash Chopra), religion and even political borders are shown to be less divisive than
previously, where the emphasis is on a sense of Punjabi-ness overriding
such divisions.

Melodrama and fate

Although much of the above is concerned with direct representation of
religion, the rest of the chapter looks at elements which perhaps one might
not initially consider under the category of religious, such as the role of
fate in melodrama, and argues that this shows widely held beliefs which
may well constitute the religious.

Melodrama, a mode dominated by excess, with its world of coincidence,
happenings, timings and chance meetings, was long regarded as a pejora-
tive term, but has largely been rehabilitated, at least in the world of film
studies. Much of this study has used Brooks (1976) as a foundational text,
although this book examines the roots of the melodrama in the novel and

the stage in Europe before the beginnings of cinema. Melodrama's emergence in the west was tied to the rise of modernity and the middle classes. Brooks (1976: 42) argues that it creates a new ethical and moral world with the breakdown of divine order or desacralisation and the rise of secular ethics – ways of giving new meaning as the moral world moves from the social to the personal or the familial (1976: 15–16). In other words, melodrama is related to the rise of the modern in the west.

Melodrama from the west entered Indian cultural forms via the urban theatre and literature and has now permeated the Hindi film. However, its transformation in Indian culture, not just formally but also in the realm of meaning, raises questions of the role of religion in the Hindi melodrama. Despite the pioneering work of Rosie Thomas and Ravi Vasudevan on melodrama in India cinema, the melodramatic mode which creates an ethical, moral world has not been examined in terms of the religious.

Ashis Nandy has long argued that just as there is no one premodernity, so there is no single modernity. His suggestions of other modernities in India need to be considered here as it seems that as there are Islamic modernities so there may well be Hindu modernities or secular (in the Indian sense noted above) modernities where religion plays a part. It seems that the melodrama in Hindi cinema includes religion, even though all its trappings are modern, and this merits some discussion.

Melodrama in Indian cinema is creating a new world order that is neither religious nor secular in the western sense of being without religion, but secular in the Indian sense discussed above, that is it is a general – even popular – faith. In Hindi cinema, the world never becomes random, and never becomes a world without God like the world of western secularism. This can be best examined by looking at fate, a concept in India that is neither Hindu nor Muslim, but part of shared common beliefs.

Melodrama in the west is associated with the desacralisation of the world, but there is a strong belief in fate (Brooks 1976: 15). Fate is not strictly part of Christian belief (although predestination has long been debated) but it seems to be a popular belief which is traceable in Europe to pre-Christian origins as fate is well known in Classical (Greek and Roman) and Germanic mythology. It is not fate as the term is used today, as meaning some impersonal force over which one has no control and against which it is pointless to struggle. In Greek mythology, it was the fates who spun their web which decided people's fate. They were not dispensing justice: it can be seen that Oedipus is a sinner but his sin is not his fault and so he does not deserve the fate he gets. Fate in India seems different from both these concepts of fate in the west but little has been written about it and melodrama provides a point at which colonial and postcolonial ideas meet premodern and modern ideas.

A common link to Hinduism, Jainism and Buddhism is a belief in *karma*, or the idea that one's actions bear fruit. However, the term does not have the same meaning even within these groupings, as it varies over time and different varieties of belief. Roughly, it may be said that *karma* is an impersonal force which lies beyond the will of the gods, so that human actions are regulated by superhuman laws.[12] Although *karma* is complex, it is generally held to exist across births, so what may look unjust in one's present life is actually a result of *karma*. It is not referred to as often in films as more popular words for fate and destiny, but one clear example is *Karz* (1980, dir. Subhash Ghai), whose many religious themes (O'Flaherty 1981) include rebirth. It is not surprising that it has several direct references to *karma*, including in its trailer: 'The karma of past lives comes back to you.' (There have been several films called *Karma*, including Ghai's 1986 film, which is more about action and revenge than religion.) However, *Karz* is largely a remake of a Hollywood film, *The reincarnation of Peter Proud* (1975, dir. J. Lee Thompson) and, although about reincarnation, it is more about justice and revenge for a previous life than about *karma* itself.

Hindi films pay more attention to fate and destiny, whose actions can be seen across one lifetime, than to *karma*. The popular belief in India, both Hindu and Muslim, is that one's fate is written on one's forehead at birth (Gujarati: *nasib lamna par lakhyu che* – 'one's fate is written on one's forehead'; Urdu *sar-navisht*, lit. 'head writing' or 'fate'). While in Hinduism, this destiny can be connected with *karma* in that what is written depends on one's *karma* from a previous birth, fate seems to be a popular survival in Islamic thought, as it has been in Christianity, where it is a mixture of natural justice and God's will. Most of the words used for fate in the film are derived from Arabic – *muqaddar*, *kismet*, *takdeer* and *naseeb* – and thus are associated with the Islamic world, while few equivalent words of Sanskrit ('Hindu') origin, such as *niyati* and *daiva*, are used for reasons that remain unclear.

Fate in India is not random as in western belief but one gets what one deserves. Even if one does not seem to be getting what one deserves, this is often due to the slower action of *karma* but justice will be restored. One cannot question what fate has in store. In *Waqt* (1965, dir. Yash Chopra), the merchant laughs at the possibility that fate may have its own plans for the family at the beginning of the film, but at the end, when they are restored after numerous traumas, he acknowledges that one never knows what is in store.

However, fate can be overwritten by divine and by human action. The gods can give *anugraha* or 'grace, favour' in saving those they want to. This action is seen in the instances of direct intervention, referred to above. Human action, while it may well be in line with fate or *karma*, may also depend on other human qualities. One is morality and virtue.

Certain characters in films are traditionally embodiments of all kinds of virtue – moral, intellectual and aesthetic – notably the hero, whose action in the film springs from a search for love not only for pleasure but also for what is right. This type of hero is seen in most films but he may be replaced by a figure, typified by Amitabh Bachchan's 'Angry Young Man', who was wronged by society and struggles to establish his own morality. However, this inevitably leads him into conflict with wider society, usually embodied by the police or a 'good brother', and he has to die in punishment for his transgression. Examples of this would include *Deewaar* (1975, dir. Yash Chopra) and *Muqaddar ka Sikander* (1978, dir. Prakash Mehra).

While the heroine may also have these characteristics, the major female figure of virtue is usually the mother, often a widowed mother, who will not abandon her principles however easy the alternatives. One of the clearest examples of this would be Radha in *Mother India* (1957, dir. Mehboob Khan), although the reason for so much suffering lying in her fate is not clear. Other women suffer for their transgressions but their virtue may be rewarded. So Tulsi in *Main tulsi tere aangan ki* (1978, dir. Vijay Anand) dies but is honoured after her death and her son is restored to his rightful place, and Vandana in *Aradhana* (1969, dir. Shakti Samanta), is reunited with her son and honoured for her suffering, while Sahibjaan (in *Pakeezah*, 1971, dir. Kamal Amrohi) not only marries her lover but also is admitted into the high society from which her mother was rejected.

Apart from this popular belief in fate which is shared by people from several religious communities, there are other beliefs, such as astrology, gemology and numerology as well as numerous 'superstitions', which may not be religious per se but which also show that the world is not just random but is controlled by something or someone superhuman or divine. These beliefs vary greatly as to the scope they give in negotiating with the predetermined in order to gain some control over one's own destiny through rituals, fasts and so on.

These beliefs and practices raise questions about the boundaries of religion and about whether the world created within the Hindi social films is just a 'moral universe' as seen in the melodramatic mode in cinema (Brooks 1972) or whether it is part of the general experience of cinema approaching that of a religion in itself (Lyden 2003). Leaving the second issue for the next chapter, the rest of this chapter examines the religious world of the Hindi film.

Concluding remarks

Cinema is the place where Ashis Nandy's ideas of other modernities needs to be explored, not least as it is the place that brings together the modern and the religious, in a way that is often viewed as secular. It may be that this secular form is also a manifestation of a Hindu imagination that shapes the worldview of the Hindi film. This chapter shows that the religion very much present in this cinema, as Hinduism – or at least in the forms found here – is a religion of the here and now not of another world. The Hindi film presents an enchanted world where gods are still present, and miracles are almost part of the everyday and their miraculous nature is barely noticed, a world not so far away from the real world where on some days the images of the gods drink the milk they are offered.

The Hindu imagination as manifest in film is a way of understanding the world that is not an essentialising feature of India but a feature of Hinduism itself. These are only tentative suggestions but its presence in other cultural forms such as literature, art and music also seems likely and may merit further investigation.

Hinduism is a problematic label that is used to describe a broad set of practices and beliefs or an imagination. The imagination here is not about doctrine but is a mixture of popular beliefs and generally held views that are part of everyday life. It does not exclude members of other communities, so Muslims are separate from this world in terms of religion and much cultural practice but this is the world that is presented as the norm in India. Muslims in the industry have taken a major role in the creation of this imagination and it is secular in the Indian sense of equal respect for all religions. (It was mentioned above that Jewish people in Hollywood helped create the American dream, which is founded in Christianity, or American secularism.)

As mentioned above, the cinema shows the upper-caste Hindu as the norm, as have state practices. Cinema's influence on religion can be seen simply in the ways that rituals are picked up from films. Notable examples include the regional practice of stealing shoes at weddings, which has spread all over the country after the popularity of the song and the ritual in *Hum aapke hain kaun ...!* (1994, dir. Sooraj Barjatya). *Veer-Zaara* (2004, dir. Yash Chopra) had a popular song for the winter festival of Lori that invented a tradition of breaking sugar canes which was re-enacted at Lori parties two months after the film's release.

It seems that the nature of the religious in the Hindi film is often open to question and its interpretation is complex. *Kal ho na ho* (2003, dir. Nikhil Advani) is a love story which raises issues about communities as the girl is partly Christian and the boys are both Hindu, but it can be read in part as a fairytale.

Naina Catherine Kapur (Preity Zinta) lives in New York with her two siblings and her grandmother and mother, who fight constantly. The quarrels are in part because the Punjabi grandmother never accepted her son's love marriage to a Christian but more because she blames her daughter-in-law for his suicide.

One night, as the Kapurs pray for an angel to come into their life, the film cuts to swelling music and swooping shots of Shahrukh Khan against the skyline of Manhattan, an Indian angel coming to NYC to answer these prayers. This is reinforced as the Kapurs ask for light in their lives and he is presented in the snow as a source of light to the world. His theme music is the resonant title song, whose words are about living one's life to the full, whether or not there is a tomorrow. Aman Mathur (Shahrukh) has come from India for medical treatment for his heart, which is failing him physically, even though he is the only person in the beginning of the film whose emotional heart is properly functional. As an angel he teaches everyone about love, and all wounds are healed, all bonds reinstated, apart from his own as he has to leave this world and let those who are left behind get on with their newly enriched lives.

This story does not belong to one religious tradition or another but shows simply a popularly held belief in divine intervention. It was interesting to notice that the miracle of the angel was barely noted but the film was seen as a classic 'love triangle' where the hero sacrifices his immediate happiness in the knowledge that he is about to die.

Chapter 5

Concluding remarks

In the last fifteen years Indian society has undergone some of the greatest changes it has seen since Independence in 1947. Several key events at the beginning of the 1990s inaugurated the processes that occurred during the decade. These years saw the rise and fall of the political parties who support Hindutva or policies of Hindu nationalism, while economic reforms brought in a new age of consumerism and liberalism that has taken root across the Indian metropolises.

While other major social transformations also took place during this decade, such as the rise of lower castes (Jaffrelot 2003), this period can be said to be one in which a new social group, 'the new middle classes', dominated India economically, politically, socially and culturally (Dwyer 2000a). The impact of these new groups was felt outside of India as they were part of transnational family networks and the diaspora that became increasingly important as a market for Hindi films, alongside other global audiences.

This decade also saw a media revolution (satellite and cable television since 1991), a communications revolution (the mobile phone and the Internet) and new technologies (the audio cassette, the CD, the VCD and the DVD). The dynamics of the interaction of these new media with the film industry have been fast and there has barely been time to analyse them.

Religious genres, which had been phenomenally popular as religious soaps on terrestrial television (notably Ramanand Sagar's *Ramayana* and B.R. Chopra's *Mahabharata*), soon spread throughout the cable and satellite channels along with other religious programming (lectures, music programmes), and now religious channels such as Astha and Sanskar are growing in popularity. Audio cassettes and CDs of religious music have continued to sell well, while VCDs and DVDs have allowed religious films to recirculate. Religious content has also flourished in other media, so the Internet now offers online *pujas* ('worship') as well as access to texts, religious history and so on, while even mobile phones offer SMS blessings and religious ringtones.

Much of this material in the new media is recycled from the religious films. It is impossible to predict where this is all going, and even the present situation remains unclear. One emerging trend is that the consumption of these new media is very different from that of cinema. Although cinema attendance in India has grown with new viewing trends such as the multiplex, the trend for mediated religion is away from an audience in a theatre hall towards a consumer in a domestic space. This must be viewed with caution as the work of Mankekar (1999) on viewing the television *Mahabharata* suggests Indian viewing practices may be different and these new media may allow the creation of new audiences. This is true of other media as audio cassettes and CDs are played in taxis, autorickshaws and other public places, while VCDs are shown on television screens during festivals.

These new technologies allow more rapid dissemination of religious content to the diaspora, and increasingly these groups are active as consumers and producers. Just as Islam has been affected by globalisation, especially among the Muslim diaspora (Devji 2005, Roy 2004), one may expect to see the emergence of a new form of globalised Hinduism as the religioscape spreads through the world, linked by these new media. It remains to be seen what form this globalised Hinduism will take.

Although these new media may have initially been viewed as a threat to film (and the DVD seems to be a particular problem for piracy), they actually reinforce film, which remains more spectacular, has better technology and brings audiences together in pleasant surroundings, notably the new multiplexes in shopping malls. The changes in film technology, especially those of digitally produced special effects, have led to talk of a new film of the *Mahabharata* with superstars Aamir Khan and Shahrukh Khan playing Karan and Arjun (although it remains to be seen if the audience will accept Muslims, albeit superstars, in these roles).

Cinema is part of the wider project of modernisation. It deals with material progress, sometimes with moral progress but it has deep ambiguities which are its strengths and which make its study so rewarding. Lyden (2003) suggests that the very nature of film evokes the religious. I read this with the caution exercised by Asad (2003:181–201) in his analysis of the proposition that nationalism is a form of religion, where he shows that this widely held view does not stand up to close scrutiny. While there is much that is religious in the nature of film itself, it does not necessarily constitute a religion. The differences between American cinema and religion and Indian cinema and religion are such that great care should be taken in drawing parallels between the two. More research needs to be done into the pleasures of the religious aesthetic, of faith and of belief in a moral universe in India and in Indian cinema (see Burch Brown 2000).

It may be that Indian cinema has specific traits that incline it more towards the religious than other cinemas. One must consider the aesthetics of Hindi cinema, such as its deployment of the miraculous, stars, *darshan*, tableaux, sets, song and dance, and the aesthetic of astonishment and its evocation of wonder and reverence. Of course it is not just the text itself, but the way the audience perceives it. One only has to think of how Gandhi came to be seen as a divine figure (Amin 1984, Pinney 2004). While all film stars are different from mere mortals through the mechanisms of stardom (Dwyer 1998), Hindi film stars are often perceived as gods by their fans, who may dedicate temples to them. Research has already shown the close associations in India of religion and performance, though this is yet to be analysed in cinema (Bharucha 1998 and Kapur 1993a, 1993b, 1990). Bharucha (1998: 40) notes: 'There is, I believe, an intensely private space in the believer's consciousness that is activated during prayer, worship, meditation or ecstasy.'

Cinema creates a group identity for people who believe in the congregation (*satsang*) and its miraculous effects, and its 'aesthetic of astonishment' (Gunning 1997) for an audience that believes in miracles and in stars as gods. Most people react to cinema as something ineffable: we know cinema, we feel cinema but we find it hard to analyse.

It is promising that the scholarly discipline of film studies is slowly beginning to engage seriously with religion. For some years the dominant paradigms were Freud and feminism, which undoubtedly were productive for engaging with melodrama with its study of the unconscious, dreams, desire, and fantasy. We still do not have a better language than this, and so we persist with it, despite our awareness of its limitations. Of course, for religious films, one has to be aware that psychoanalysis sets itself up as a new religion (Phillips 1993, Ch. 11). The theories of postmodernism and the breakdown of grand narratives are not accepted by the majority, neither in the west nor in India.

In *Filming the Gods*, most of the readings can be said to be meanings that are known to the audience and also based on the views of the film makers, critics and audiences, though for the first time they are historicised and contextualised rather than interpreted individually, and as a mistaken teleology.

These films, however cynical critics may be, do create religious sentiment in viewers and audiences and may contribute towards a hybrid Hinduism, whether they are taking it from the world around them or whether they are creating it themselves. The films' focus on the family, on the group, on the nation, on the transnational Indian community is all part of a search for a new morality and a new happiness. This raises the question of a Hindu imagination, for these films suggest that religion is more important than nationalism. As British Muslims now often prefer to define themselves as Muslims rather than as Pakistani or Indian, so perhaps a new Hindu imagination may be emerging where the British or North American person of Indian origin is no less Hindu than an Indian.

This does not imply any necessary association with Hindutva or Hindu nationalism but with a form of popular belief that has not been redefined in these Semitic terms, nor in any form of systematic belief. If this is indeed a Hindu imagination, it needs to be defined, analysed and historicised.

Asad (1993: 39–45) points out that in the west, religion has been diminished and denied a public space. It is no longer regarded as a powerful, knowledge-producing worldview but is a passive belief, its universal categories relegated to the beliefs of the individual. While Asad discusses religion and secularism in the context of Islam and Christianity, and Gauchet (1994) and Taylor (2002) in that of Christianity, no one has yet examined the relationship of modernity to secularism and Hinduism in this manner.

Secularist nationalism in India placed the religious in the private not in the public sphere (cf. Chatterjee 1986 and 1993). Yet it is not clear how this division can be made in India where the secular is so different from its western (Christian) form. Secularism is produced by religion and most of our understandings of it are based on European society (Asad 2003 and Madan 1997). In Hinduism, there does not seem to be a possibility of separate domains for the sacred and profane. The division would be between pure and impure *pavitra* and *apavitra* – which are by no means equivalent. The gods of Hinduism are here in the everyday world, which is sacred itself, a goddess, known as Bhu, Vasundhara and many other names. It remains to be seen how Hinduism would produce a secular imagination, and what it would be.

The media have created ways of representing religious groups and identities. Some of these draw from precolonial divisions but they also show how profoundly the colonial representation of caste and community has been fixed in the Indian imagination. The cinema, although it rarely mentions caste, has also constructed new religious identities, and I have noted several for women including the worship of Santoshi Maa and the spread in popularity of rituals such as that of Karva chauth (a fast for a husband's welfare).

The discussion in Chapter 3 shows that there is clearly an Islamicate imagination, a depiction of a culture where the Muslim figure is in the centre of the world while God is also present, not just in Sufi shrines and sacred objects, but also has agency and can cause miracles to occur. Even when Muslims appear in 'non-religious' films, they are shown as religious and often devout figures, who belong to this world. The complex relationships between the communities are often alluded to in the films. Hindus are shown to be respectful to Islamicate culture and even to worship at Muslim shrines. Muslims can pay their respects to Hinduism, and some Muslim rulers were known for giving grants to Hindu temples, but they cannot worship the images.

The media have played a major part in forming this Islamicate imagination, of image, text and music, drawing from sources as diverse as Mughal art to Parsi theatre and chromolithographs to popular stories. The Islamicate films have built on these images and created their own representations of beauty, architecture, religiosity and music. The figure of the courtesan has been central to this and now every courtesan's song and dance will have to reflect this world, where even a Hindu, such as Chandramukhi in *Devdas* (2002, dir. Sanjay Leela Bhansali), has to present herself as part of this culture. The beauty and elegance of the 'lost world' of Lucknow is contrasted with a supposed Hindu – and colonial – lack of refinement.

The Hindu imagination seems more elusive, although Greeley's argument for the existence of a Catholic imagination has some clear parallels (Greeley 2000). One shared feature is that Greeley is looking at the Catholic imagination in a society where Catholics are aware of, and in part defined by, their relations to other religious groups. The films examined in this book also suggest that communities are defined and self-aware in India in part, at least, through their definition against others. In India, while there is some syncretism, the religious communities are also separate but they interact and shape themselves in relation to others (notably Hindu reform movements of the nineteenth century as figures such as Swami Dayanand tried to make Hinduism, at least in the form of the Arya Samaj, follow the religions of the book).

Although it seems too early to posit a well-defined Hindu imagination, cinema is the best place to look for the presence or absence of the Hindu and of the secular imagination anywhere in India. It needs to be examined in conjunction with ideas of other modernities, where one may begin with the fact that although cinema is *the* art form of modernity, it is never free from religion.

This Hindu imagination must not be confused with Hindu-ness as Hindutva. For many people this eruption of the religious in the most modern forms of media may be frightening and associated with extremism and fanaticism. There is no reason that religion should be a force for evil but it may be a giver of strength, joy and pleasure. The Hindu gods must be worshipped and celebrated and the films go some way to keeping them in the world. Many images of Ram today, in particular those promoted by Hindutva, may be of the warrior king, ready to fight, but for many he remains an object of devotion and love. The history of the images of the gods in the media show the audience is making an active appropriation of meanings for new situations in life.

Pauline Kael at the Arts Club of Chicago in 1975 pointed out the importance of Catholic directors in Hollywood (Altman, Coppola and Scorsese), in that their sensuous style was not about religion; rather their work was connected with religious themes and moral conduct. Cinema is an important forum to examine these key issues in western society, which now values emotions and feelings above all else and where sexual identities have become more important than other ways of thinking about oneself (see Anderson and Mullen 1998). Many of the arts in the west no longer pay attention to minds and souls, virtues, love, duty, self-sacrifice and character, but instead concentrate on bodies, from surfaces to orifices. Hindi films still ask important questions about bodies, souls, morals and selves, and it is these themes which make it so much more interesting than much of Hollywood. Indian cinema's serious consideration of religion is part of understanding Indian history and society, if one is prepared to engage seriously with it.

Notes

Introduction

1   D.G. Phalke, quoted in Rajadhyaksha 1999: 49.
2   Unidentified, though most probably *The life and passion of Christ* (1903), a British film of the Horitz Passion Play. Another possible contender is *La vie et la passion du Jésus Christ* (1905, dir. Lucien Nonguet and Ferdinand Zecce).
3   These issues are discussed in papers in edited volumes such as Babb and Wadley 1995, Brosius and Butcher 1999, and de Vries and Weber 2001.
4   Birgit Meyer has pointed out that the religious is already a form of mediation between its practitioners and the spiritual realm. See the 'Introduction' to Meyer and Moors 2006.
5   This is not to downplay the importance of religion in these spheres. See Roy 2005 for a short overview of religion in India in historical and political history.
6   See, for example, Asad 1993, Durkheim 2001, Eliade 1959, Smith 1998.
7   See, for example, Dwyer 2006d, Flood 1996 and Fuller 1992. Although often defined as Hindus, many groups such as Sikhs and Dalits reject this label. See Ilaiah 1996.
8   Asad 1993, Devji 2005 and Roy 2004.
9   Exceptions are Kapur's essay on *Tukaram* (Kapur 2000) and several essays on the 1975 film *Jai Santoshi Maa*, see Chapter 1 below.
10 Most published research concerns Christianity and Hollywood cinema. These are reviewed in bibliographic essays by Nolan 2003 and Mitchell 2005. Key texts are Baugh 1997, Kracauer 1997, Lyden 2003, Marsh and Oritz 1997, May and Bird 1982, Martin and Ostwalt 1995, Miles 1996, Schrader 1972. There are several studies of these representations beyond Europe and America such as in Brent Plate 2003.
11 Compare with Christian art in Burch Brown 2000.
12 Pinney 1997 and 2004 in particular. See also Jain 1998.
13 For a more detailed discussion of the historical film and Indian history see Mukhopadhyay 2004.
14 Prasad 1998 is a sophisticated analysis of Indian cinema in relation to politics.

1 The mythological film

1   The best account of the history of Indian cinema remains Barnouw and Krishnaswamy 1980.
2   See Dharap 1985, Phalke 1987, Pinney 1997: 91–3, Rajadhyaksha 1993, Rangoonwalla 1975, and Shoesmith 1987.

3 Wadia 1977. I am grateful to the late Riyad Vinci Wadia for allowing me access to the Wadia Movietone Archive.

4 The major purpose of this Committee was an enquiry into the state of censorship of cinema in British India. It had three British and three Indian members, its Chair was Diwan Bahadur T. Rangachariar, a lawyer from Madras. They travelled the whole country, interviewed almost a thousand witnesses, male and female, from all communities both in and outside the industry.

5 See Asad 2003: 181–201 on why nationalism is not a religion.

6 The film which may have inspired Phalke, mentioned in Introduction, n.2, was a film of a Passion Play.

7 DeMille's films were much appreciated in India; one of India's Movie Moghuls, Mehboob Khan (see Chapter 3 below), met him on a visit to Hollywood and was delighted to be called 'India's DeMille' (see Reuben 1994).

8 He later became an exhibitor, ending up as the wealthy manager of the Gaiety Cinema in Bombay. See http://www.victorian-cinema.net/bhatvadekar. htm, viewed 14 March 2005.

9 Though see Chapter 2 below on the competing claims of a devotional, *Pundalik*.

10 The historical was also hugely popular during this time, whether Indian or imported from Hollywood (Mukhopadhyay 2004: 51–2) and can be compared to the mythological films as different ways of reconsidering the past. These would be similar to the Shivaji Utsav which Bal Gangadhar Tilak began in 1896 and the Ganapati Utsav he began in 1894. Both festivals were intended to promote traditionalism of indigenous, national culture.

Most of the western Indian historicals were made outside Bombay, in the cities where the Maratha elite lived – Poona, Nasik and Kolhapur. The Maharashtra Film Company, which made many Shivaji films, was based in Kolhapur and received support from its ruler, who was a direct descendant of Shivaji (Mukhopadhyay 2004: 56) and a supporter of anti-Brahminical causes and caste reforms.

11 See bibliography for a list of abbreviations.

12 Dharamsey 1994 lists the films of the silent period.

13 I have no idea what categories such as 'semi-Oriental' are as I have not seen examples of these films.

14 I am using the term here in the restricted sense of semi- or quasi-divine figures of mythology rather than the protagonist of a narrative.

15 Wendy Doniger, aka Wendy Doniger O'Flaherty, has made many excellent studies of early Indian mythology (see bibliography). She gives an early 'positioning' on her understanding of myth in O'Flaherty 1973.

16 There are Christian mythological traditions in Kerala but they lie beyond the scope of this chapter.

17 These are also the frameworks of various 'secular' narratives. See Chapter 4 below.

18 The core parts of the *Mahabharata* were composed around the second century BC, although there are older portions. Other texts, such as the *Bhagavad Gita*, were interpolated until it reached its present form of over 100,000 stanzas (*shlokas*), well into the first millennium.

19 See Lutgendorf 1991a on the performance traditions of this version.

20 The collected papers in Babb and Wadley 1995 form a key study of these mediated religious forms. (Chromolithographs is the preferred term for popular prints also known as oleographs and 'calendar art'. See Pinney 2004.)

21 Kathryn Hansen 2000, 2004 and Anuradha Kapur 1993a, 1993b are the leading scholars of Parsi Theatre.
22 See Kapur 1993a on the mythological in Parsi Theatre.
23 See Hansen 2000 and 2004. See Chapter 3 below for a discussion of Urdu.
24 Kapur 2000 emphasises the frontality of the image throughout but this remains open to debate.
25 This term is used most often in the context of religious worship, where it is a two-way look between the devotee and the deity that establishes religious authority. However, it is also used to establish social and political authority. It is a look that establishes an authoritative figure or icon and the space around him or her, assigning positions in a hierarchy but these are open to negotiation and change. Prasad 1998: 76–7, which draws on Babb 1981 and Eck 1985, also Vasudevan 2000: 139–47.
26 Rajadhyaksha 1994 describes many of these in some detail.
27 In the National Film Archive (NFAI), Pune. P.K. Nair 1980: 107.
28 In the NFAI, Pune. P.K. Nair 1980: 107.
29 See P.K. Nair 1980 and Rajadhyaksha 1994 for other silent films in the NFAI.
30 English translations printed in Rangoonwalla 1970.
31 See n.2 above.
32 Barnouw and Krishnaswamy 1980, Dharap 1985 and Rajadhyaksha 1987 are the major sources for Phalke's life.
33 See Introduction, n.2.
34 See Bordwell and Thompson 1994: 16–7 on Méliès and Cubbit 2004.
35 In the NFAI, Pune. Rajadhyaksha and Willemen 1999: 243.
36 Obituary 'Kamalabai Gokhale – an acting legend', *The Afternoon Despatch & Courier*, Friday 23 May 1997: 15.
37 In the NFAI, Pune. Rajadhyaksha and Willemen 1999: 243.
38 Pinney 2004:73 suggests a print showing Hanuman flying above the burning Lanka may have been made by Phalke himself.
39 In the NFAI, Pune. Rajadhyaksha and Willemen 1999: 243.
40 In the NFAI, Pune. Rajadhyaksha and Willemen 1999: 243.
41 Dharap 1985: 40 notes Phalke's commitment to *swadeshi*.
42 Cf. Larkin 2002 on the public space of cinema halls in colonial Nigeria.
43 Reproduced in Barnouw and Krishnaswamy 1980: 21.
44 With the possible exception of Kashmir as a paradise on earth for Punjabis, as noted by Meenu Gaur in her forthcoming research on Kashmir in South Asian cinema.
45 Gujarati: '*bhasha marathi '-ardhi samjaay-ardhi na samjaay chataa pan Balgaandharva Maa Modaknu sangit hindu paarsi, musalmaan sarvane ghelaa banavi de che.' Mauj Majah* 28 August 1932: 22.
46 In *Filmland* 4 March 1933: 16–7.
47 *Mauj Majah* 26 March 1933: 26.
48 I am grateful to Ramdas Bhatkal for drawing my attention to this novelist, whose several works were made into films including *Kunku/Duniya na mane*, 1937, dir. V. Shantaram. He has often been confused with the first Marathi novelist, Hari Narayan Apte (1864–1919).
49 The version I saw in the NFAI and the VCD I have of the film do not have subtitles and I may have missed some fine dialogue.
50 *Bombay Chronicle* Sat. 8 Dec. 1934: 3.
51 *Bombay Chronicle* Sat. 19 Jan. 1935: 4.
52 *Bombay Chronicle* Sat. 26 Jan. 1935: 4.

53 *Bombay Chronicle* Sat. 16 March 1935: 8.
54 *Bombay Chronicle* Sat. 20 Apr. 1935: 4:
55 *Bombay Chronicle* Sat. 1 March 1941: 10.
56 See http://www.vijaybhatt.net, viewed 9 December 2004.
57 Babubhai Mistry, India's master of trick photography and special effects, worked on Prakash's *Khwaab ki duniya*, the story of an invisible man, for which he earned the title 'Kaala Dhaaga' for his use of black thread in scenes. (See more below on Mistry.)
58 *Bombay Chronicle* Sat. 14 Feb. 1942: 10.
59 *Bombay Chronicle* Sat. 28 Mar. 1942: 8.
60 *Picturpost* 15 May 1954: 58.
61 Statement of Mr M.K. Gandhi, Sabarmati, dated 12 November 1927. ICC III: 56.
62 ('Matters that matter') *Picturpost* 15 March 1944: 13–5.
63 *Picturpost* 15 March 1944: 13.
64 *Filmfare* 8 June 1956: 43.
65 E.g. http://store.nehaflix.com/religious.html. Thanks to Kush Varia for referring this site.
66 *Filmfare* 16 April 1954.
67 *Filmfare* 16 Feb. 1957: 7.
68 *Filmfare* 15 Oct. 1954: 4.
69 *Filmfare* 5 Aug. 1955: 21.
70 The low status of these films can be seen from reviews in upmarket journals such as *Filmindia*, which reviews one of these films: ' "Tulsi Vrunda" another mythological hocus! The entire picture is a crude affair. It seems to be planned for old-fashioned idiots who like to see their folklore on the screen. Ishwarlal hardly looks a good Jalandhar who was a great warrior. Ishwarlal, with a paunch that walks before him, lends doubtful effeminity to the role . . . "TV" is essentially a picture for *ghati* women from the villages. It is not at all a picture for the cities', *Filmindia* July 1947: 72. (*Ghati* is an abusive term for non-westernised Indians.) This film is not listed in Rajadhyaksha and Willemen 1999, unless it is connected with the Tamil film *Tulasi Jalandhar*, dir. Kadaru Nagabhushanam, 1947.
71 *Bombay Chronicle* Sat. 10 June 1950: 8.
72 *Bombay Chronicle* Sat. 1 July 1950: 8.
73 *Bombay Chronicle* Sat. 8 July 1950: 8.
74 *Bombay Chronicle* Sat. 22 July 1950: 8.
75 *Bombay Chronicle* Sat. 26 Aug 1950: 8.
76 *Bombay Chronicle* Sat. 21 July 1951: 3.
77 For a rich description of the film by Philip Lutgendorf, see http://www.uiowa.edu/~incinema/Mahabharat.html, viewed 5 January 2005.
78 Chandrakant made action and mythological films, in Hindi, Punjabi and Gujarati. Many of his films were with Dara Singh.
79 http://www.oddfilms.com/bizarro.htm, viewed 5 January 2005.
80 See Lutgendorf 2003 for a rich description of the film.
81 See Lutgendorf 2003: 23 for a summary of the *vratkatha*. A Hindi version in Roman script is available online, see http://www.dalsabzi.com/Mantras/santoshi_mata_ki_katha.htm, viewed 12 March 2005.
82 Abu-Lughod 2002 notices a similar phenomenon among Egyptian women's choice of new religious practices.
83 *Sati* films, about long-suffering women, had been popular from the beginning of Indian films, notably the story of Sati Anasuya.

84 http://bhajans.bhanot.net/bhaj29.html, viewed 20 March 2005.

85 http://www.thehotspotonline.com/moviespot/bolly/BollyHorror/bollyhorror.
    htm, viewed 10 March 2005.

86 http://www.illuminatedlantern.com/cinema/features/snakes.html, viewed 16
    March 2005; also http://www.thehotspotonline.com/moviespot/bolly/reviews/
    d/DoodhKarz.htm, viewed 16 March 2005. Thanks to Kush Varia for these
    references.

87 Waheeda Rehman dances a more 'classical' or 'religious' snake dance in
    Guide (1965, dir. Vijay Anand), while another features as a comic item in
    Bride and prejudice (2004, dir. Gurinder Chadha).

88 Sathe 1984: 107 has a subheading, '1913–1942: le Gujarat choisit la langue
    hindie (Gujarat chooses the Hindi language)'.

89 Notable exceptions being films of the 'middle' cinema type that are made in
    the Gujarati language such as *Bhavni Bhavai* (1980, dir. Ketan Mehta), based
    on the Gujarati folk theatre form, Bhavai, but having its cinematic roots in
    the 'middle' cinema.

90 Thanks to Kush Varia for his advice on these films.

91 This was true for the Vaishnava *acharyas* mentioned in Chapter 2 below.

92 'Mythological pictures have drawn money by shovels from this presidency'
    4 Feb. 1931–31 Dec. reported in '1934: What happened – and what will
    happen', *Moving Picture Monthly 1935* Annual: 26.

93 'In the Studios – On the Screen: The East India Film Company: For the last
    six months the East India Film Company have been making strenuous efforts
    to place their affairs on a better footing … During the latter half of 1934,
    the company released four super pictures, Sultana, Mumtaz Begum, Sita
    Vanwas and Lava-Kush … Sita Vanwas is a Tamil talkie, while Lava Kush
    is a Telugu talkie. Ramayan in Tamil and Savitry in Telugu produced by
    this company broke all records for continuous run in South India', *Bombay
    Chronicle* Sat. 26 Jan. 1935: 4.

94 On the Tamil film industry see Baskaran 1981 and 1996.

95 See Pandian 1991 for a study of this film and Pandian 1992 on MGR (M.G.
    Ramachandran, Tamil film superstar and later Chief Minister of Tamil Nadu),
    the DMK and the Tamil film industry.

96 Cf. a short essay by his biographer, S. Venkat Narayan 1985.

97 Tirupati is the richest shrine in India and has recently become the focus of
    worship for many north Indian film stars who often visit the temple before
    beginning a film.

98 Mankekar 2002 notes that Sikhs and Muslims also watched the *Mahabharata*.

99 I have made an argument for this case in the contemporary Hindi film. See
    Dwyer 2005.

100 See Rajagopal 2001 for a detailed study of the interaction of Hindutva poli-
    tics and this television serial.

101 Mankekar 1999 has a detailed ethnography of viewing this series.

102 *Bombay Chronicle* Sat. 20 Nov. 1948: 4. Note the *Encyclopaedia*'s view of
    Kanu Desai's work in their review of Vijay Bhatt's *Ram Rajya* (see above),
    'The big-budget art direction was a classic contribution by neo-classical kitsch
    artist Kanu Desai', Rajadhyaksha and Willemen 1999: 299.

103 *Bombay Chronicle* Sat. 27 Nov. 1948: 4.

104 *Bombay Chronicle* Sat. 4 Dec. 1948: 4.

105 *Bombay Chronicle* Sat. 12 Apr. 1947: 8.

106 *The Motion Picture Magazine* May 1947: 177–8.

107 *Bombay Chronicle* Sat. 11 Nov. 1944: 6.

108 B.D. Dogra, quoted Gokarn n.d.: 69.
109 For an exhaustive catalogue of Indian nationalism and cinema see Kaul 1998.
110 *Bombay Chronicle* Sat. 1 June 1946: 8.
111 *Bombay Chronicle* Sat. 26 July 1947:8.
112 *The Motion Picture Magazine* February 1947:12.
113 *Bombay Chronicle* Sat. 11 March 1950: 8.
114 V.G. Damle 'Cultural aspect of mythological films', *The Mirror* 4 Feb. 1940.

2 The devotional film

1 Advertisement reproduced in Kaul 1998: 17.
2 Reviewed *Bombay Chronicle*, Sat. 25 Oct. 1947: 8.
3 A fragment of this film survives in the NFAI, where Tukaram has a vision of the lord.
4 *The Mirror* 26 Dec. 1942.
5 I have seen the silent film *The Catechist of Kil-arni*, dir. R.S. Prakash, 1923, a Roman Catholic missionary propaganda film about 'Untouchables' set in south India, which does not seem to belong to this genre.
   I do not discuss saints from Christian traditions although I found a reference to a film about St Philomena in the *Bombay Chronicle* Sat. 15 April 1950: 8:

> Triple version Life of St Philomena: The life of that great saint, Philomena, contains elements of childlike simplicity and moments of truly heroic intensity. It is shortly to be filmed by Religious Pictures Corporations and will be in Tamil, Hindi and English. Preliminary work on this film is in progress and efforts are being made to fully live-up to the greatness of the subject. Outdoor shots are to be filmed in Mysore and Goa and the production is under the personal supervision of WP Fernandes. The dialogues and the direction of the Tamil version is being handled by Mr SS Vasan.

6 See Ramanujan 1999: 279–94 on the *sants* and other *bhaktas*.
7 On this poem and the genealogy of classical Tamil poetry and Tamil *bhakti* literature, see Ramanujan 1999.
8 Other forms of nationalism were also prevalent at this time. *The Mirror* 13 Aug.: 1939 notes that *Sant Ramdas* was banned in Kolhapur as it gives the *sant* more prominence than Shivaji and social unrest was feared.
9 File P/T 28881, OIOL, Proceedings of the first session of the Indian Motion Picture Congress held on 7/8 May 1939. Thanks to Urvi Mukhopadhyay for this reference.
10 For a concise, clear view of Gandhi's philosophy and religion see Parekh 1997; see also Hardiman 2003 for a more historical view.
11 He took his principle of *nishkam karma* ('action without regard for its results') from here but ignored the fact that its teachings are in opposition to his principle of *ahimsa* ('non-violence').
12 Many Hindu reformers, such as Brahmo Samaj, had drawn on Christian traditions, and the Christian hymn 'Lead kindly light' became something of a favourite in India.
13 See Pinney 2004, Chapter 6 on political chromolithographs 1890–1950. Among the several films on Bhagat Singh, the most recent shows him to be an atheist, *The legend of Bhagat Singh* (2002, dir. Rajkumar Santoshi). As with other recent films about freedom fighters, its major policy seems to be

the attack on Gandhi and the Congress. See also *Veer Savarkar* (2001, dir. Ved Rahi, Marathi).

14 See quote from IIC III: 56.

15 M. Shivram 'Mahatma Gandhi ane sinema', *Mauj Majah* 7 May 1933: no page.

16 *The Mirror*, Bombay, 14 May 1939: 5.

17 'K Ahmed Abbas writes a letter to Mahatma Gandhi', *Filmindia* October 1939: 4 and 5. Reprinted in Bandyopadhyay 1993: 141–5.

18 *Bombay Chronicle* Sat. 28 Feb. 1948: 8.

19 *Bombay Chronicle* Sat. 10 Apr. 1948: 8.

20 www.historytoday.com/dm_getArticle.asp?gid=12554. Viewed 13 March 2005.

21 Key films being *Bhakta Cheta* (1940), *Avvayiyyar* (1953) in Tamil, and Chittor V. Nagaiah's films in Telugu, which include *Bhakta Potana* 1942), *Thyagayya* (1946) and *Yogi Vemana* (1947). See Rajadhyaksha and Willemen 1999: 204.

22 The most famous was Fida Husain for his role as Narsi Bhagat. Kathryn Hansen, personal communication.

23 Pagnis' association with Tukaram was such that his photographs were put up in houses and even in temples. Watve 1985: 19.

24 *Filmland* 4 March 1933: 17–8.

25 *Filmland* 4 March 1933: 17–8.

26 On the end of Prabhat Films see Bhole 1980.

27 Karve 1988:158, cited in Fuller 1992: 211. See also Mokashi 1987.

28 V. Shantaram 'The eternal conflict', *Filmfare* 6 Jan. 1956: 32–3.

29 *Bombay Chronicle* Sat. 7 Dec. 1935: 9.

30 *Bombay Chronicle* Sat. 7 Dec. 1935: 15.

31 *Bombay Chronicle* Sat. 21 Dec. 1935: 15.

32 A very good website for information about Tukaram is http://www.tukaram. com. It makes no mention of the film.

33 Directorate of Film Festivals (1981) 'Sant Tukaram': 102–3. (Anonymous.)

34 V. Shantaram 'The eternal conflict', *Filmfare* 6 Jan. 1956: 32–3.

35 Vishnupant Pagnis 'My two "saint roles"', *The Mirror*, 11 Nov. 1939.

36 Kapur 2000: 239. I do not really understand the meaning of 'secular' that Kapur suggests here.

37 Directorate of Film Festivals (1981) 'Sant Tukaram': 102–3. (Anonymous.)

38 *The Mirror* 18 Aug. 1940.

39 K.A. Abbas, *Bombay Chronicle* 25 May 1940, quoted in Watve 1985: 35.

40 *Bombay Chronicle* 1 June 1940, quoted in Watve 1985: 37.

41 *Bombay Chronicle* 8 June 1940, quoted in Watve 1985: 37–40.

42 *The Mirror* 16 June 1940: 7.

43 Thanks to Shreeyash Palshikar for this information.

44 See below for comments on the effect of the removal of miracles from the life of Meera in Gulzar's 1979 film.

45 He was the son of Rev. Modak, a member of the Bombay Legislative Council. *The Mirror* 11 Feb. 1940.

46 *The Mirror* 17 Mar. 1940.

47 All from a feature in *The Mirror* 17 April 1943 (no page).

48 *The Mirror* 20 Sept. 41: 38.

49 *Bombay Chronicle* Sat. 27 Sept. 1941: 10.

50 *Bombay Chronicle* Sat. 11 Oct. 1941:10.

51 Janabai is found by Namdev's father during a pilgrimage to Pandharpur. He takes her home, where Namdev and Janabai both become devotees of Vithoba.

They are like siblings. Janabai gets money so that Namdev can start a business, but he loses money, at which point his wife Rajai goes back to her mother. When Namdev goes on pilgrimage with Dnyaneshwar, Janabai tries to pay the loan off but Vitthal himself appears to pay it. He helps her with the housework but he falls asleep grinding rice. She puts a blanket on him, which he takes to the temple, leaving her his necklace. The villagers say she stole it, and sentence her to death, but Vitthal rescues her.

52 'Sant Namdev Opens: Suramya Pictures devotional hit Sant Namdev is being released. The stars are Lalita Pawar, Jayaram Shiledar, Sumati Gupte and Shahu Modak. All these artists are familiar with the mythological field, and Sant Namdev is expected to prove very successful with Marathi audience who are familiar with the story' *Bombay Chronicle* Sat. 24 June 1950: 8.

53 *Filmfare* 26 Nov. 1954: 19.

54 Vijay Bhatt made *Chaitanya Mahaprabhu* in 1954, with Bharat Bhushan and Durga Khote, top stars of mythologicals/devotionals, with R.C. Boral, who had scored several of New Theatres' devotionals, as music director to give it a Bengali feel. It was critically acclaimed (e.g. *Filmfare* 22 Jan. 1954) but did not make a great impact at the box office.

55 *Bombay Chronicle* Sat. 26 Dec. 1942: 7.

56 *Bombay Chronicle* Sat. 30 Jan. 1943: 8.

57 *Bombay Chronicle* Sat. 6 Mar. 1948: 8. Vijay Bhatt's website lists *Bhakta Surdas* 1947 and *Bilwamangal* 1948 as both in Hindi.

58 Baburao Patel's *Filmindia* was known for its eccentricity but the review of this film, 'Muslim "Meerabai" grossly slanders Hinduism!' attacks the film on the basis of its misrepresentation of Hindu marriage but largely because its director was a Muslim who migrated to Pakistan. *Filmindia* Sept. 1947: 53–7. (The star of the 1932 film was Zubeidaa, a Muslim, and this seems to have attracted little comment.)

59 http://www.hindu.com/thehindu/mp/2002/01/21/stories/2002012100030300. htm, viewed 5 Feb. 2005.

60 *Bombay Chronicle* Sat. 29 Nov. 1947: 8.

61 Kabir's dates are uncertain and disputed by various groups of his followers. These are the dates given by Vaudeville 1974: 55.

62 See Chapter 3 for a discussion of Islamicate films.

63 *Bombay Chronicle* Sat. 14 Nov. 1942: 8.

64 *Bombay Chronicle* Sat. 5 Dec. 1942: 8.

65 Advertisement for screening at Minerva in *The Mirror*, 19 December 1942: no page.

66 See Shackle 1986 and 1988, McLeod 1989.

67 *Bombay Chronicle* Sat. 6 Dec. 1947: 8.

68 *The Mirror* 28 May 1939.

69 For more details see http://www.sangeetham.com/musiri2.htm. Viewed 13 March 2005.

70 This was already discussed in a satirical article, 'Sensation in heaven! Saints to protest to God against their screen-biographies', in *The Mirror* 20 July 1941: 17–19.

71 *Bombay Chronicle* 1 June 1940, 8 June 1940.

72 See Rajni Bakshi, 'Quest for Universal Religion', http://indiatogether.org/opinions/rbakshi/vanand/vanand-p1.htm, viewed 30 January 2005.

73 The synthesis of two traditions has been discussed in other cults, for example, in Stewart 2002.

74 Interview, April 2003.

3 The Islamicate film

1   Kesavan has taken this term from Marshall Hodgson's *Venture of Islam*. See Kesavan 1994.

2   Irani worked with several important Muslims such as Abdulally Esoofally with whom he co-owned the Alexandra Theatre and later co-founded Imperial, and he was also in partnership with Gujarati Hindus such as Bhogilal K.M. Dave, the co-founder of Star, who later set up the Sharda Film Company.

3   For more on Gujaratis and cinema see Mehta 1993.

4   As they were not political, they were not discussed in Pinney 2004.

5   These images and calligraphy are seen to be highly efficacious in films such as *Coolie* (1983, dir. Manmohan Desai).

6   For a lively, chatty biography of Mehboob see Reuben 1994.

7   As the Ottoman Empire was founded only in the fifteenth century, I am not sure in what historical period the film is set.

8   Including King 1994, Lelyveld 1994, Rai 2001, 2005, Shackle and Snell 1990.

9   *Junglee*, dir. S. Mukherjee, 1961, is in Urdu, according to its censor certificate.

10 This is not to say there has not been a significant Hindi component in Hindi cinema. Writers such as Radheshyam Kathavachak (b. 1890) have actively promoted Hindi, and Trivedi (forthcoming) counterbalances Kesavan 1994 which argues for the Urdu roots of the cinema.

11 The late Iqbal Masud and I had long conversations about Islamicate films, which helped shape many of my ideas on the topic.

12 Thanks to Faisal Devji for this reference.

13 There have been a few collaborations or exchanges between Indian and Pakistani artists and writers in recent years but these are still exceptional. For example, *Khamosh pani* (2003, dir. Sabiha Sumar).

14 Muhammad Sadiq, in his widely read history of Urdu literature, is deeply ambivalent about the form (Sadiq 1995), which Pritchett 1994 attributes to the influence of the new poetics created by Azad and Hali in the nineteenth century.

15 Mirza Asadullah Beg Khan (1797–1869); Ghalib 'Victorious' is a pen name.

16 This recent history of the *ghazal* as a song lyric has been traced by Peter Manuel, 1991.

17 Jatindra Nath Mitra 'A review of Indian Pictures', *Filmland*, Puja issue, 1934.

18 Director, producer, actor, Fatima Begum (1905–83), was also the wife of a Nawab and mother of several female stars of the early cinema http://www.hindustantimes.com/news/specials/slideshows/20s/20–6.htm. Viewed 1 March 2003.

19 I am indebted throughout this section to Urvi Mukhopadhyay for various discussions and for her Ph.D. thesis, Mukhopadhyay 2004.

20 The Orientalist features are not necessarily to be associated with the film's German director, who made many hit films in India outside this genre, including the realist social *Acchut Kanya* in 1936.

21 Advertisement, *Times of India* 20 March 1929, quoted in Mukhopadhyay 2004: 69.

22 Urvi Mukhopadhyay drew my attention to the written statement of Mr Mukandi Lala, Bar-at-Law, Dpty President, United Province's Legislative Council, to the Indian Cinematograph Enquiry Committee, 1927–8, 362 in File no. V/26/970/3, OIOL.

23 Mukhopadhyay 2004: 96 from papers in the National Archives New Delhi.

24 Such as *Devdas*, Bimal Roy, 1955, and *Sahib, bibi aur ghulam/King, queen and knave*, Abrar Alvi, 1961. See Chakravarty 1993: 261–305 for a longer account of the history of the courtesan film.

25 Muslims formed the majority population of most north Indian cities before independence, which is one of the reasons why many of the courtesans were Muslims.

26 See Kasbekar 2000 on viewing dances.

27 See also Uberoi 1997 on podoerotics.

28 See Dwyer 2000a on the importance of the star in Hindi films.

29 The novel is usually *Umrao Jan Ada* while the film is *Umrao Jaan*.

30 Ghalib wrote an account of this time in his *Dastanbu* and in his extensive correspondence. See Russell and Islam 1994.

31 Interview with Nasreen Kabir, *Movie Mahel*, Hyphen Films.

32 This was made as a television series in India but shown as a film in the UK.

33 There was a famous television interview when Shabana Azmi, actor and social activist, also a Muslim, asked Imam Bukhari of the Jama Masjid why he did not join the jihad which he had been urging Indian Muslims to join. He replied, 'Main naachne-gaane wali tawaif ko jawaab nahin deta.' ('I don't answer to a singing and dancing prostitute.') Shabana Azmi told journalists that this showed Bukhari is no real Muslim as he disrespects women, artistes and liberals. (For the full version of this story see Dasverma 2001.)

34 RICC 41 mentions objections being made to famous Muslim women, usually historical figures, being shown out of *purdah* as they object to showing anyone venerated as holy. A.R. Kardar (see above), a Muslim writes an article 'Why I don't direct "Muslim subjects"', explaining it is simply too much trouble. *The Mirror* 29 Sept. 1940.

4 The religious and the secular in the Hindi film

1 On the considerable corpus of academic writing on the rise of communalism and secularism see Roy 2005: 5–7.

2 The metalanguages of the Hindi film are English and Hindi (journalism as well as within the industry), where the 'social' is called by its English name in both languages or less frequently in Hindi as *samaajik* ('social'). I have not heard 'secular' used to describe films or the industry in any language other than English. The Hindi equivalent, *dharmanirpekshata* (lit. 'disregarding religion') is not used when talking about films or the industry where the English word is preferred, whatever the language of the discussion.

3 See Dwyer 2006a, Madan 1997 and Nandy 1985.

4 A temple to Amitabh Bachchan was recently opened in Calcutta: http://movies.indiainfo.com/features/amit-temple.html. Viewed 15 September 2005.

5 Niraj Mancchanda is well-known in Bombay for his advice to the stars on these matters. See http://astrology.indiainfo.com/astrologers/nirajmancchanda/index.shtml. Viewed 15 September 2005.

6 Many Dalits regard themselves as non-Hindus, cf. Illaiah 1996.

7 See Jerry Pinto 2006 on Helen for discussions of a Christian actress in Indian cinema and on the general portrayal of Christians in Hindi cinema.

8 One of the Shiv Sena's many objections to the lesbian relationship in *Fire*, 1996, dir. Deepa Mehta, was that the characters were called Radha and Seeta.

9 See Chatterjee 2002, Dwyer 2000a: 129–37, Thomas 1989.

10 A former censor notes, 'all sorts of sexual cavorting was justified if it was cloaked in a "mythological" garb', Sarkar 1982: 50.

11 A group of Hindutva supporters came to an earlier version of Dwyer 2006a, which I presented at Queen Mary College, University of London. One of their objections to the Hindi cinema was that it put more emphasis on family than on religion. My response was that the emphasis on the family is very much part of Hindu traditions.

12 Fuller 1992: 245–52, Gombrich 2005, O'Flaherty 1980.

Bibliography

Official sources and abbreviations

RICC   *Report of the Indian Cinematograph Committee, 1927–8.* (aka The Rangachariar Committee.) Calcutta: Government of India Central Publication Branch, 1928.

ICC, I   *Indian Cinematograph Committee 1927–8, Evidence Vol I. Bombay.* Calcutta: Government of India Central Publication Branch.

ICC, II   *Indian Cinematograph Committee 1927–8, Evidence Vol II. Witnesses examined at Lahore, Peshawar, Lucknow and Calcutta with their statements.* Calcutta: Government of India Central Publication Branch.

ICC, III   *Indian Cinematograph Committee 1927–8, Vol III. Oral evidence of witnesses examined at Madras, Rangoon, Mandalay, Calcutta (one witness), Jamshedpur, Nagpur and Delhi, with their written statements.* Calcutta: Government of India Central Publication Branch.

ICC, IV   *Indian Cinematograph Committee 1927–8, Vol IV. Written statements of witnesses not orally examined, memoranda from provincial governments & miscellaneous papers.* Calcutta: Government of India Central Publication Branch.

ICC, V   *Indian Cinematograph Committee 1927–8, Vol V. Oral evidence of witnesses examined in camera with the written statement of Mr Tipnis: the memorandum of the government of Burma; the chairman's inspection notes on cinemas & studios visited.* Calcutta: Government of India Central Publication Branch.

NFAI   National Film Archive of India.

RFEC   *Report of the Film Enquiry Committee 1951.* (aka The Patil Committee.) New Delhi: Government of India Press: New Delhi.

RECFC   *Report of the Enquiry Committee on Film Censorship.* (aka The Khosla Committee.) New Delhi: Ministry of Information and Broadcasting, Government of India, 1968.

RWGNFP   *Report of the Working Group on National Film Policy.* New Delhi: Ministry of Information and Broadcasting, Government of India, May 1980.

Periodicals and newspapers

Bombay Chronicle
Filmfare
Filmindia
Journal of Religion and Film
Mirror
Mauj Majah (*Gujarati*)
Motion Picture Magazine
Picturpost
Rajatpat (*Hindi*)
Times of India
Manushi, Special Issue: 'Women Bhakta poets.' Jan.–June 1989, Nos. 50–52.

Books, articles, theses

Abu-Lughod, Lila (2002) 'Egyptian melodrama – technology of the modern subject?' In Faye D. Ginsburg, Lila Abu-Lughod and Brian Larkin (eds) *Media worlds: anthropology on new terrain*. Berkeley: University of California Press: 115–33.

Ahmad, Aijaz (ed.) (1971) *Ghazals of Ghalib*. New York: Columbia University Press.

Alam, Muzaffar (2004) *The languages of political Islam*: *India 1200–1800*. London: C. Hurst & Co.

Altman, Rick (1999) *Film/genre*. London: British Film Institute.

Amin, Shahid (1984) 'Gandhi as Mahatma: Gorakhpur District, Easten UP, 1921–2.' In *Subaltern Studies III*. Delhi: Oxford University Press: 1–61.

Amin, Shahid (2004) 'On representing the Musalman.' In *Sarai reader 2004*: *crisis/media*. Delhi: Sarai: 92–7. Also at www.sarai.net/journal/04_pdf/001intro. pdf. Viewed 2 February 2005.

Anderson, B. (1991, 2nd ed.) *Imagined communities*: *reflections on the origin and spread of nationalism*. London: Verso.

Anderson, Digby and Peter Mullen (eds) (1998) *Faking it*: *the sentimentalisation of modern society*. London: Penguin.

Appadurai, Arjun (1997) *Modernity at large*: *cultural dimensions of globalization*. Delhi: Oxford University Press.

Arora, Poonam (1997) 'Devdas: India's emasculated Hero, sado-masochism and colonialism.' http://social.chass.ncsu.edu/jouvert/v1i1/devdas.htm. Viewed 28 May 2004.

Arudra (1984) 'Le cinema telugu.' In Aruna Vasudeva and Philippe Lenglet (eds) *Les cinémas indiens*. CinémAction 30. Paris: Editions du Cerf: 114–19.

Asad, Talal (1993) *Genealogies of religion*: *discipline and reasons of power in Christianity and Islam*. Baltimore: Johns Hopkins University Press.

Asad, Talal (2003) *Formations of the secular*: *Christianity, Islam, modernity*. Stanford: Stanford University Press.

Babb, Lawrence A. (1981) 'Glancing: visual interaction in Hinduism.' *Journal of Anthropological Research*, 37(4): 387–401.

Babb, Lawrence, A. (1987) *Redemptive encounters*: *three modern styles in the Hindu tradition*. Berkeley: University of California Press.

Babb, Lawrence and Susan Wadley (eds) (1995) *Media and the transformation of religion in South Asia*. Philadelphia: University of Pennsylvania Press.

Bahadur, Satish (1976) 'The context of Indian film culture.' In *Film Miscellany*, December. Pune: Jagat Murari, director of the Film and Television Institute of India: 90–107.

Bandyopadhyay, Samik (ed.) (1993) *Indian cinema: contemporary perspectives from the thirties*. Selected by Dhruba Gupta and Biren Das Sharma. Jamshedpur: Celluloid Chapter.

Barnouw, Erik and S. Krishnaswamy (1980, 2nd ed.) *Indian film*. New York: Oxford University Press.

Barthes, Roland (1973) *Mythologies*. Ed. and trans. by Annette Lavers. London: Paladin Books.

Barthes, Roland (1977) 'Change the object itself: mythology today.' In *Image, music, text*. London: Fontana: 165–9.

Baskaran, S. Theodore (1981) *The message-bearers: the nationalist politics and the entertainment media in South India 1880–1945*. Madras: Cre-A.

Baskaran, S. Theodore (1996) *The eye of the serpent: an introduction to Tamil cinema*. Madras: East–West Books.

Baugh, Lloyd (1997) *Imaging the divine: Jesus and Christ-figures in films*. Kansas City: Sheed & Ward.

Bazin, André (2002) 'Cinema and theology: the case of Heaven over the marshes.' Ed. and trans. by Bert Cardullo. *Journal of Religion and Film*, 6(2) http://www.unomaha.edu/~wwwjrf/heaven.htm. Viewed 30 December 2003 [1951].

Bergesen, Albert J. and Andrew M. Greeley (2000) *God in the movies*. New Brunswick: Transaction Publishers.

Bharucha, Rustom (1994) 'On the border of fascism: manufacture of consent in Roja.' *Economic and Political Weekly*, 29(23), 4 June: 1390–5.

Bharucha, Rustom (1998) *In the name of the secular: cultural practice and activism in India today*. Delhi: Oxford University Press.

Bhaumik, Kaushik (2001) 'The emergence of the Bombay film industry, 1913–1936'. Unpublished D.Phil., University of Oxford.

Bhole, Keshavrao (1980) 'When the sun set on Prabhat.' Trans. Gauri Deshpande. *Cinema Vision* 1(2): 56–62.

Bordwell, David and Kristin Thompson (1994) *Film history: an introduction*. London: McGraw-Hill.

Bourdieu, Pierre (1984) *Distinction: a social critique of the judgement of taste*. Trans. Richard Nice. Cambridge, Mass.: Harvard University Press.

Brooks, Peter (1976) *The melodramatic imagination: Balzac, Henry James, melodrama and the mode of excess*. New Haven: Yale.

Brosius, Christiane and Melissa Butcher (eds) (1999) *Image journeys: audio-visual media and cultural change in India*. New Delhi: Sage Publications.

Bruzzi, Stella (1997) *Undressing cinema: clothing and identity in the movies*. London: Routledge.

Burch Brown, Frank (2000) *Good taste, bad taste, and Christian taste: aesthetics in religious life*. New York: Oxford University Press.

Butalia, Urvashi (2000) *The other side of silence: voices from the Partition of India*. London: Hurst & Co.

Byatt, A.S. (2004) 'Soul searching.' Review, *The Guardian*, 14 February 2004: 4–6.

Cavell, Stanley (1981) *Pursuits of happiness: the Hollywood comedy of remarriage*. Harvard Film Studies. Cambridge, Mass.: Harvard University Press.

Cavell, Stanley (1984) *Themes out of school: effects and causes*. Chicago: University of Chicago Press.

Chabria, Suresh and Paolo Cherchi Usai (eds) (1994) *Light of Asia: Indian silent cinema, 1912–1935*. New Delhi: Wiley Eastern.

Chakravarty, Sumita S. (1993) *National identity in Indian popular cinema, 1947–1987*. Austin: University of Texas Press.

Chatterjee, Gayatri (1992) *Awāra*. New Delhi: Wiley Eastern.

Chatterjee, Gayatri (2002) *Mother India*. London: British Film Institute.

Chatterjee, Partha (1986) *Nationalist thought and the colonial world: a derivative discourse?* London: Zed Books for the United Nations University.

Chatterjee, Partha (1993) *The nation and its fragments: colonial and postcolonial histories*. Delhi: Oxford University Press.

Chatterjee, Saratchandra (1996) *Devdas and other stories*. Ed. and trans. by V.S. Naravane. New Delhi: Roli Books.

Cubitt, Sean (2004) *The cinema effect*. Cambridge, Mass.: MIT Press.

D'Emilio, John and Estelle B. Freedman (1997) *Intimate matters: a history of sexuality in America*. Chicago: University of Chicago Press. [1988].

Dabholkar, Govind R. (Hemadpant) (1999) *Shri Sai satcharita: the life and teachings of Shirdi Sai Baba*. Trans. by Indira Kher. New Delhi: Sterling Publishers Private Limited.

Dalmia, Vasudha (1997) *The nationalization of Hindu traditions: Bharatendu Harischandra and nineteenth-century Banaras*. Delhi: Oxford University Press.

Das, Veena (1981) 'The mythological film and its framework of meaning: an analysis of Jai Santoshi Ma.' *Indian International Quarterly*, 8(1), Special Issue ed. Pradip Krishen: 43–56.

Dasverma@aol.com (2001) 'An interesting article, an interview with Shabana Azmi (an MP, actress, activist).' http://lists.cs.columbia.edu/pipermail/ornet/2001-October/002380.html. Viewed 29 November 2004.

Davis, Richard H. (1997) *Lives of Indian images*. Princeton: Princeton University Press.

Derné, Steve (2000) *Movies, masculinity, modernity: an ethnography of men's filmgoing in India*. Westport, Conn.: Greenwood Press.

Devji, Faisal (1992) 'Hindu/Muslim/Indian.' *Public Culture* (5)1, Fall: 1–18.

Devji, Faisal (1999) 'A nation in suspense: Muslim sentiment in colonial India.' Unpublished MS.

Devji, Faisal (2005) *Landscapes of the jihad: militancy, morality, modernity*. London: C. Hurst & Co.

Dharamsey, Virchand (1994) 'Indian silent cinema, 1912–1934: a filmography.' In Suresh Chabria and Paolo Cherchi Usai (eds) *Light of Asia: Indian silent cinema, 1912–1935*. New Delhi: Wiley Eastern: 73–212.

Dharap, B.V. (1983) 'The mythological or taking fatalism for granted.' In Aruna Vasudev and Philippe Lenglet (eds) *Indian cinema superbazaar*. New Delhi: Vikas Publishing House: 79–83.

Dharap, B.V. (1985) 'Dadasaheb Phalke: father of Indian cinema.' In T.M. Ramachandran (ed.) *70 years of Indian cinema (1913–1983)*. Bombay: Cinema India International: 33–48.

Dickey, Sara (1993) *Cinema and the urban poor in south India*. Cambridge: Cambridge University Press.

Directorate of Film Festivals, New Delhi (1981) *Filmindia: Looking back 1896–1960*. New Delhi.

Dirks, Nicholas B. (2000) 'The home and the nation: consuming culture and politics in Roja.' In Rachel Dwyer and Christopher Pinney (eds) *Pleasure and the nation: the history, consumption and politics of public culture in India*. Delhi: Oxford University Press: 161–85.

Dogra, Bharat B. (1977) 'Mythological films: seduction of the faithful.' *Filmfare*, January 7–20: 50–1.

Doniger, Wendy (2000) *The bedtrick: tales of sex & masquerade*. Chicago: University of Chicago Press.

Doniger, Wendy (2004) 'The mythology of self-imitation in passing: race, gender and politics.' The Henry Myers Annual Lecture, delivered at SOAS, 20 September.

Doniger, Wendy (2005) *The woman who pretended to be who she was: myths of self-imitation*. New York: Oxford University Press.

Dumont, Louis (1998, complete rev. ed.) *Homo hierarchicus: the caste system and its implications*.Trans. Mark Sainsbury, Louis Dumont and Basia Gulati. Delhi: Oxford University Press.

Durkheim, Emile (2001) *The elementary forms of religious life*. Trans. Carol Cosman. Oxford: Oxford University Press.

Dwyer, Rachel (2000a) *All you want is money, all you need is love: sex and romance in modern India*. London: Cassell.

Dwyer, Rachel (2000b) '"Indian values" and the diaspora: Yash Chopra's films of the 1990s.' *West Coast Line*, 32–34/2, Autumn 2000: 6–27; also in Parthiv Shah (ed.) *Figures, facts, feelings: a direct diasporic dialogue*. New Delhi: Centre for Media and Alternative Communication: 74–82.

Dwyer, Rachel (2000c) 'The erotics of the wet sari in Hindi films.' *South Asia*, 23 (2), June: 143–59. Translated into Flemish: 'De natte sari-sutra: vestimentaire erotiek in de moderne Hindi-film.' *AS: mediatijdschrift*, 170: 26–43.)

Dwyer, Rachel (2001) *The poetics of devotion: the Gujarati lyrics of Dayārām, 1777–1852*. London: Curzon.

Dwyer, Rachel (2002a) *Yash Chopra*. In World Directors series. London: British Film Institute/Berkeley: University of California Press/New Delhi: Roli Books.

Dwyer, Rachel (2002b) 'Real and imagined audiences: Lagaan and the Hindi film after the 1990s.' *Etnofoor*, 15(1/2) December, Special volume: 'Screens': 177–93.

Dwyer, Rachel (2004a) 'Representing the Muslim: the "courtesan film" in Indian popular cinema.' In Tudor Parfitt and Yulia Egorova (eds) *Mediating the other: representations of Jews, Muslims and Christians in the media*. Jewish Studies series. London: Routledge/Curzon: 78–92.

Dwyer, Rachel (2004b) 'International Hinduism: the Swaminarayan sect.' In K.A. Jacobsen and P. Kumar (eds) *South Asians in the diaspora: histories and religious traditions*. Leiden and Boston: Brill: 180–99.

Dwyer, Rachel (2004c) '*Yeh shaadi nahin ho sakti!* (This wedding cannot happen!).' In G.W. Jones and Kamalini Ramdas (eds) (*Un*)*tying the knot: ideal and reality in Asian marriage*. Asian Trends, 2. Singapore: Asia Research Institute, National University of Singapore: 59–90.

Dwyer, Rachel (2005) *100 Bollywood films*. London: British Film Institute. Roli Books: New Delhi.

Dwyer, Rachel (2006a) 'The saffron screen?: Hindi movies and Hindu nationalism.' In Birgit Meyer and Annalies Moors (eds) *Religion, media and the public sphere*. Bloomington: Indiana University Press: 422–60.

Dwyer, Rachel (2006b) 'Kiss and tell: expressing love in Hindi movies.' In Francesca Orsini (ed.) *Love in South Asian traditions*. Cambridge: Cambridge University Press: 289–302.

Dwyer, Rachel (2006c) 'Planet Bollywood: Hindi film in the UK.' In Nasreen Ali, Virinder Kalra and S. Sayyid (eds) *Postcolonial people: South Asians in Britain*. London: C. Hurst & Co.: 366–75.

Dwyer, Rachel (2006d) *What do Hindus believe?* London: Granta.

Dwyer, Rachel and Christopher Pinney (eds) (2000) *Pleasure and the nation: the history, consumption and politics of public culture in India*. Delhi: Oxford University Press.

Dwyer, Rachel and Divia Patel (2002) *Cinema India: the visual culture of the Hindi film*. London: Reaktion/New Brunswick: Rutgers University Press/Delhi: Oxford University Press.

Dyer, Richard (1977) 'Entertainment and utopia.' *Movie* (24), Spring: 2–13.

Dyer, Richard (1998) *Stars*. Supplementary chapter by Paul McDonald. London: British Film Institute.

Eck, Diana L. (1985, 2nd ed.) *Darsan: seeing the divine image in India*. Chambersburg: Anima.

Eickelman, Dale F. and Jon W. Anderson (1999) *New media in the Muslim world*. Bloomington: Indiana University Press.

Eliade, Mircea (1959) *The sacred and the profane: the nature of religion*. Trans. by W.R. Trask. New York, London: Harcourt Brace Jovanovich.

Elsaesser, Thomas (1985) 'Tales of sound and fury: observations on the family melodrama.' Reprinted in Bill Nichols *Movies and methods, Vol II*. Berkeley: University of California Press:165–89. [1972]

Flood, Gavin (1996) *An introduction to Hinduism*. Cambridge: Cambridge University Press.

Freud, Sigmund (1953) 'Three essays on the theory of sexuality.' In *The standard edition of the complete psychological works of Sigmund Freud, Vol VII*. London: Hogarth Press and the Institute of Psycho-analysis. [1905]

Frow, John (2006) *Genre*. New Critical Idiom. London: Routledge.

Fuller, C.J. (1992) The camphor flame: popular Hinduism and society in India. Princeton: Princeton University Press.

Gandhy, Behroze and Rosie Thomas (1991) 'Three Indian film stars.' In C. Gledhill (ed.) *Stardom: industry of desire*. Routledge: London: 107–31.

Gauchet, Marcel (1997) *The disenchantment of the world: a political history of religion*. Trans. Oscar Burge. Foreword by Charles Taylor. 'New French Thought'. Princeton: Princeton University Press.

Gay, Peter (1986) *The bourgeois experience, Victoria to Freud. Vol II: the tender passion*. Oxford: Oxford University Press.

George. T.J.S. (1994) *The life and times of Nargis*. New Delhi: Indus.

Geertz, Clifford (1973) *The interpretation of cultures: selected essays*. New York: Basic Books.

Giddens, Anthony (1990) *The consequences of modernity*. Cambridge: Polity.

Giddens, Anthony (1992) *The transformation of intimacy: sexuality, love and eroticism in modern societies*. Cambridge: Polity.

Gillespie, Marie (1995) *Television, ethnicity and cultural change*. London: Routledge.

Gledhill, Christine (ed.) (1987) *Home is where the heart is: studies in melodrama and the woman's film*. London: British Film Institute.

Gledhill, Christine (1991) 'Signs of melodrama.' In C. Gledhill (ed.) *Stardom: industry of desire*. Routledge: London: 207–32.

Gledhill, C. (2000) 'Rethinking genre.' In C. Gledhill and L. Williams (eds) *Reinventing film studies*. London: Arnold: 221–43.

Gokarn, Kusum (n.d) 'Popularity of devotional films (Hindi).' Unpublished NFAI Research Project.

Gold, Daniel (1987) *The lord as guru: Hindi sants in the northern tradition*. Delhi: Oxford University Press.

Gombrich, Richard (2005) 'Karma.' In Rachel Dwyer and Subir Sinha (eds) *Keywords*. http://www.soas.ac.uk/centres/centreinfo.cfm?navid=912. Viewed 15 December 2005.

Gopalan, Lalitha (2002) *Cinema of interruptions: action genres in contemporary Indian cinema*. London: British Film Institute.

Gopalan, Lalitha (2005) *Bombay*. London: British Film Institute.

Greeley, Andrew (2000) *The Catholic imagination*. Berkeley: University of California Press.

Guha-Thakurta, Tapti (1992a) 'The ideology of the "aesthetic": the purging of visual tastes and the campaign for a new Indian art in late nineteenth/early twentieth century Bengal.' *Studies in history*, 8(2) n.s.: 237–81.

Guha-Thakurta, Tapti (1992b) *The making of a new 'Indian' art: artists, aesthetics and nationalism in Bengal, c.1850–1920*. Cambridge: Cambridge University Press.

Gunaki, Basavaraj (2003) *Shirdi Saibaba: an epic*. Shirdi: Shri Saibaba Sansthan.

Gunning, Tom (1986) 'The cinema of attraction: early film, its spectator and the avant-garde.' *Wide Angle*, 8:3–4.

Gunning, Tom (1997) 'An aesthetic of astonishment: early film and the (in)credulous spectator.' In Linda Williams (ed.) *Viewing positions: ways of seeing film*. New Brunswick: Rutgers University Press: 114–33.

Gutman, Judith M. (1982) *Through Indian eyes*. New York: Oxford University Press.

Haggard, Stephen (1988) 'Mass media and the visual arts in twentieth-century South Asia: Indian film posters, 1947–present.' *South Asia Research*, 8(2), May: 78–88.

Hansen, Kathryn (1992) *Grounds for play: the nautanki theatre of north India*. Berkeley: University of California Press.

Hansen, Kathryn (2000) 'The *Inder Sabha* phenomenon: public theatre and consumption in greater India (1853–1956).' In Rachel Dwyer and Christopher Pinney (eds) *Pleasure and the nation: the history, politics and consumption of public culture in India*. Delhi: Oxford University Press: 76–114.

Hansen, Kathryn (2004) 'Language, community and the theatrical public: linguistic pluralism and change in the nineteenth-century Parsi theatre.' In Stuart Blackburn and Vasudha Dalmia (eds) *India's literary history: essays on the nineteenth century*. New Delhi: Permanent Black: 60–86.

Hansen, Miriam (1991) *Babel & Babylon: spectatorship in American silent film.* Cambridge, Mass.: Harvard University Press.

Hansen, Thomas Blom (1999) *The saffron wave: democracy and Hindu nationalism in modern India.* Princeton: Princeton University Press.

Hansen, Thomas Blom (2001) *Wages of violence: naming and identity in postcolonial Bombay.* Princeton: Princeton University Press.

Hardiman, David (2003) *Gandhi in his time and ours: the global legacy of his ideas.* London: C. Hurst & Co.

Hasan, Mushirul and Asim Roy (eds) (2005) *Living together separately: cultural India in history and politics.* New Delhi: Oxford University Press.

Hawley, John S. and Mark Juergensmayer (eds and trans.) (1988) *Songs of the saints of India.* New York: Oxford University Press.

Heath, Stephen (1981) *Questions of cinema.* Bloomington: Indiana University Press.

Horsfield, Peter, Mary E. Hess and Adan M. Medrano (eds) (2004) *Belief in media: cultural perspectives on media and Christianity.* Aldershot: Ashgate.

Hughes, Stephen Putnam (1996) 'Is there anyone out there? Exhibition and formation of silent film audiences in South Asia.' Unpublished Ph.D. University of Chicago.

Hughes, Stephen P. (2000) 'Policing silent film exhibition in colonial South India.' In Ravi Vasudevan (ed.) *Making meaning in Indian cinema.* Delhi: Oxford University Press: 39–64.

Ilaiah, Kancha (1996) *Why I am not a Hindu: a Sudra critique of Hindutva, philosophy, culture, and political economy.* Calcutta: Samya.

Illouz, Eva (1997) *Consuming the romantic utopia: love and the cultural contradictions of capitalism.* Berkeley: University of California Press.

Inden, Ron (1999) 'Transnational class, erotic arcadia and commercial utopia in Hindi films.' In Christiane Brosius and Melissa Butcher (eds) *Image journeys: audio-visual media and cultural change in India.* New Delhi: Sage Publications: 41–66.

Jaffrelot, Christophe (1996) *The Hindu nationalist movement and Indian politics, 1925 to the 1990s.* London: C. Hurst & Co.

Jaffrelot, Christophe (2003) *India's silent revolution: the rise of the lower castes.* London: C. Hurst & Co.

Jain, Kajri (1998) 'Gods in the Bazaar.' *South Asia*, XXI (no. 1): 91–108.

Johnston, Robert K. (2000) *Reel spirituality: theology and film in dialogue.* Grand Rapids, Mich: Baker Academic.

Joshi, Manohar Shyam (2002) *Patkatha lekhan: ek parichay.* New Delhi: Rajkamal Prakashan.

Kabir, Nasreen Munni (1999) *Talking films: conversations on Hindi cinema with Javed Akhtar.* Delhi: Oxford University Press.

Kabir, Nasreen Munni (2005) *Talking songs: Javed Akhtar in conversation with Nasreen Munni Kabir and sixty selected songs.* Delhi: Oxford University Press.

Kakar, Sudhir (1981, 2nd edn.) *The inner world: a psycho-analytic study of childhood and society in India.* Delhi: Oxford University Press.

Kakar, Sudhir and John M. Ross (1986) *Tales of love, sex and danger.* Delhi: Oxford University Press.

Kamath, M.V. and V.B. Kher (1991) *Sai Baba of Shirdi: a unique saint.* Mumbai: Jaico Publishing House.

Kapur, Anuradha (1990) *Actors, pilgrims, kings and gods: the Ramlila at Ramnagar*. Calcutta: Seagull Books.

Kapur, Anuradha (1993a) 'The representation of gods and heroes: Parsi mythological drama of the early twentieth century.' *Journal of Arts and Ideas*, 23–4:85–107.

Kapur, Anuradha (1993b) 'Deity to crusader: the changing iconography of Ram.' In Gyanendra Pandey (ed.) *Hindus and others: the question of identity in India today*. New Delhi: Penguin: 74–109.

Kapur, Geeta (1987) 'Mythic material in Indian cinema.' *Journal of Arts and Ideas*, 14–15: 79–108.

Kapur, Geeta (2000) *When was modernism: essays on contemporary cultural practice in India*. New Delhi: Tulika.

Karve, Irawati (1988) 'On the road: a Maharashtrian pilgrimage.' In Eleanor Zelliot and Maxine Berntsen (eds) *The experience of Hinduism: essays on religion in Maharashtra*. Albany: State University of New York Press: 147–73. [Orig. essay in Marathi, 1951]

Kasbekar, Asha (2000) 'Hidden pleasures: negotiating the myth of the female ideal in popular Hindi cinema.' In Rachel Dwyer and Christopher Pinney (eds) *Pleasure and the nation: the history, politics and consumption of public culture in India*. Delhi: Oxford University Press: 286–308.

Kaul, Gautam (1998) *Cinema and the Indian freedom struggle*. New Delhi: Sterling Publishers Pvt Ltd.

Kaul, Gautam (2001) 'The *Gadar* between real & reel history.' http://www.tribune india.com/2001/20010707/windows/main1.htm. Viewed 29 November 2004.

Kaviraj, Sudipta (1995) *Unhappy consciousness: Bankimchandra Chattopadhyay and the formation of nationalist discourse in India*. Delhi: Oxford University Press.

Kesavan, Mukul (1994) 'Urdu, Awadh and the tawaif: the Islamicate roots of Hindi cinema.' In Zoya Hasan (ed.) *Forging identities: gender, communities and the state*. New Delhi: Kali for Women: 244–57.

King, Christopher (1994) *One language, two scripts: the Hindi movement in nineteenth century North India*. Delhi: Oxford University Press.

Kolatkar, A. (1978) *Jejuri*. London: Peppercorn.

Kracauer, Siegfried (1997) *Theory of film: the redemption of physical reality*. With introduction by Miriam Bratu Hansen. Princeton: Princeton University Press.

Landy, Marcia (1996) *Cinematic uses of the past*. Minneapolis: University of Minnesota Press.

Larkin, Brian (1997) 'Indian films and Nigerian lovers: media and the creation of parallel modernities.' *Africa*, 67(3): 406–40.

Larkin, Brian (2002) 'The materiality of cinema theaters in northern Nigeria.' In Faye D. Ginsburg, Lila Abu-Lughod and Brian Larkin (eds) *Media worlds: anthropology on new terrain*. Berkeley: University of California Press: 319–36.

Lelyveld, David (1994) '*Zuban-e Urdu-e Mu'alla* and the idol of linguistic origins.' *Annual of Urdu Studies*, 9: http://www.urdustudies.com/Issue09/index.html. Viewed 10 March 2003.

Lincoln, Bruce (1999) *Theorizing myth: narrative, ideology and scholarship*. Chicago: University of Chicago Press.

Lutgendorf, Philip (1991a) *The life of a text: performing the Ramcaritmanas of Tulsidas*. Berkeley: University of California Press.

Lutgendorf, Philip (1991b) 'The secret life of Ramcandra of Ayodhya.' In Paula Richman (ed.) *Many Ramayanas*: *the diversity of a narrative tradition in South Asia*. Berkeley: University of California Press: 217–34.

Lutgendorf, Philip (1995) 'All in the (Raghu) family: a video epic in cultural context.' In Lawrence Babb and Susan Wadley (eds) *Media and the transformation of religion in South Asia*. Philadelphia: University of Pennsylvania Press: 217–53.

Lutgendorf, Philip (2003) 'Jai Santoshi Maa revisited.' In S. Brent Plate (ed.) *Representing religion in world cinema*: *filmmaking, mythmaking, culture making*. New York: Palgrave Macmillan: 19–42.

Lyden, John (1997a) 'Continuing the conversation: a response to Clive Marsh.' *Journal of Religion and Film*. Reader discussion. http://avalon.unomaha.edu/jrf/disctopc3.htm#John%20Lyden. Viewed 2 February 2005.

Lyden, John (1997b) 'To commend or to critique? The question of religion and film studies.' *Journal of Religion and Film*, 1(2). http://avalon.unomaha.edu/jrf/tocommend.htm. Viewed 2 February 2005.

Lyden, John C. (2003) *Film as religion*: *myths, morals and rituals*. New York: New York University Press.

Madan, T.N. (1987) *Non-renunciation*: *themes and interpretations of Hindu culture*. Delhi: Oxford University Press.

Madan, T.N. (1997) *Modern myths, locked minds*: *secularism and fundamentalism in India*. Delhi: Oxford University Press.

Mankekar, Purnima (1999) *Screening culture, viewing politics*: *an ethnography of television, womanhood, and nation in postcolonial India*. Durham: Duke University Press.

Mankekar, Purnima (2002) 'Epic contests: television and religious identity in India.' In Faye D. Ginsburg, Lila Abu-Lughod and Brian Larkin (eds) *Media worlds*: *anthropology on new terrain*. Berkeley: University of California Press: 134–51.

Manto, Sadat (1998) *Stars from another sky*: *the Bombay film world of the 1940s*. Trans. Khalid Hasan. New Delhi: Penguin.

Manuel, Peter (1991) 'The popularization and transformation of the light-classical Urdu Ghazal-song.' In Arjun Appadurai, Frank J. Korom and Margaret A. Mills (eds) *Gender, genre and power in South Asian expressive traditions*. Philadelphia: University of Pennsylvania Press: 347–61.

Manuel, Peter (1993) *Cassette culture*: *popular music and technology in north India*. Chicago: University of Chicago Press.

Marsh, Clive and Gaye Ortiz (eds) (1997) *Explorations in theology and film*: *movies and meaning*. Oxford: Blackwell.

Marsh, Clive (1998) 'Religion, theology and film in a postmodern age: a response to John Lyden'. *Journal of Religion and Film*, 2(1). http://avalon.unomaha.edu/jrf/marshrel.htm. Viewed 2 February 2005.

Martin, Joel W. and Conrad E. Ostwalt Jr (eds) (1995) *Screening the sacred*: *religion, myth, and ideology in popular American film*. Boulder, Colo: Westview Press.

Masselos, J. (1991, 2nd ed.) *Indian nationalism*: *an history*. New Delhi: Sterling.

Masud, Iqbal (n.d.) 'Muslim ethos in Indian cinema.' http://www.india-emb.org.eg/section%203/sec%203%20eng/MUSLIM%20ETHOS%20IN%20INDIAN%20CINEMA.html. Viewed 29 November 2004.

Matthews, David (1997) *An anthology of Urdu verse in English*. (Original poems in Devanagari script.) Delhi: Oxford University Press.

Matthews, David J., Christopher Shackle and Shahrukh Husain (1985) *Urdu literature*. London: Third World Foundation for Social and Economic Studies.

May, John R. (ed.) (1997) *New image of religious film*. Kansas City: Sheed & Ward.

May, John R. and Michael Bird (eds) (1982) *Religion in film*. Knoxville: University of Tennessee Press.

McLeod, W.H. (1989) *The Sikhs: history, religion and society*. New York: Columbia University Press.

Mehta, Suketu (2005) *Maximum city: Bombay lost and found*. London: Headline Review.

Mehta, Ushakant (1993) *Gujarat chalchitra parampara*. Trans. by Bamsidhar Sharma from Gujarati into Hindi. Delhi: Rajesh Prakashan.

Meyer, Birgit (2003) 'Pentecostalism, prosperity and popular cinema in Ghana.' In S. Brent Plate (ed.) *Representing religion in world cinema: filmmaking, myth-making, culture making*. New York: Palgrave Macmillan: 121–43.

Meyer, Birgit and Annalies Moors (eds) (2006) *Religion, media and the public sphere*. Bloomington: Indiana University Press.

Miles, Margaret (1996) *Seeing and believing: religion and values in the movies*. Boston: Beacon Press.

Mishra, Vijay (2002) *Bollywood cinema: temples of desires*. London: Routledge.

Mitchell, Jolyon (2005, 3rd ed.) 'Theology and film.' In David F. Ford with Rachel Muers (eds) *The modern theologians: an introduction to Christian theology since 1918*. Oxford: Blackwell Publishing: 736–59.

Mitchell, Jolyon and Sophia Marriage (eds) (2003) *Mediating religion: conversations in media, religion and culture*. London: T & T Clark.

Mitra, Ananda (1993) *Television and popular culture in India: a study of the Mahabharat*. New Delhi: Sage.

Mokashi, D.B. (1987) *Palkhi: an Indian pilgrimage*. Albany: State University of New York Press.

Morgan, David (2005) *The sacred gaze: religious visual culture in theory and practice*. Berkeley: University of California Press.

Mukhopadhyay, Urvi (2004) 'The perception of the "medieval" in Indian popular films: 1920s–1960s.' Unpublished Ph.D., SOAS, University of London.

Nair, P.K. (1980) 'Silent films in the archive.' *Cinema Vision*, 1(1): 104–13.

Nandy, Ashis (1985) 'An anti-secularist manifesto.' In *The romance of the state and the fate of dissent in the tropics*. Delhi: Oxford University Press: 34–60.

Nandy, A. (1988) *The intimate enemy: loss and recovery of self under colonialism*. Delhi: Oxford University Press. [1983]

Nandy, Ashis (1995a) 'An intelligent critic's guide to the Indian cinema.' In *The savage Freud and other essays on possible and retrievable selves*. Delhi: Oxford University Press: 196–236.

Nandy, Ashis (2000) 'Invitation to an antique death: the journey of Pramathesh Barua as the origin of the terribly effeminate, maudlin, self-destructive heroes of Indian cinema.' In Rachel Dwyer and Christopher Pinney (eds) *Pleasure and the nation: the history, politics and consumption of public culture in India*. Delhi: Oxford University Press:139–60.

Nandy, Ashis (2002) *Time warps: silent and evasive pasts in Indian politics and religion.* London: C. Hurst & Co.

Narayan, S. Venkat (1985) 'The phenomenon called NTR – actor turned politician.' In T.M. Ramachandran (ed.) *70 years of Indian cinema (1913–1983).* Bombay: Cinema India International: 203–14.

National Film Development Corporation (1998) *Indian cinema, a visual voyage.* New Delhi: Publications Division, Ministry of Information and Broadcasting, Government of India.

Neale, Steve (1980) *Genre.* London: British Film Institute.

Neale, Steve (1986) 'Melodrama and tears.' *Screen,* 27(6): 6–22.

Neale, Steve (1990) 'Questions of genre.' *Screen,* 31(1): 45–66.

Neale, Steve (2000) *Genre and Hollywood.* London: Routledge.

Niebuhr, H. Richard (1951) *Christ and culture.* New York: Harper and Row.

Niranjana, Tejaswini (1994) 'Integrating whose nation?: tourists and terrorists in "Roja".' *Economic and Political Weekly,* 29(3), 15 January: 79–82.

Nolan, Steve (2003) 'Film and religion.' In Jolyon Mitchell and Sophia Marriage (eds) (2003) *Mediating religion: conversations in media, religion and culture.* London: T & T Clark: 369–83.

O'Flaherty, Wendy Doniger (1973) *Asceticism and eroticism in the mythology of Shiva.* London: Oxford University Press.

O'Flaherty, Wendy Doniger (1980) *Women, androgynes, and other mythical beasts.* Chicago: University of Chicago Press.

O'Flaherty, Wendy Doniger (1981) 'The mythological in disguise: an analysis of *Karz.*' In 'Indian popular cinema: myth, meaning and metaphor.' *India International Centre Quarterly,* 8(1), Special Issue, ed. Mira Sinha: 23–30.

Oldenburg, Veena Talwar (1989) *The making of colonial Lucknow 1856–1877.* Delhi: Oxford University Press.

Orsini, Francesca (2006) *The Hindi public sphere, 1920–1940: language and literature in the age of nationalism.* Delhi: Oxford University Press.

Orsini, Francesca (ed.) (2005) *Love in South Asian traditions.* Cambridge: Cambridge University Press.

Pandian, M.S.S. (1991) 'Parasakthi: life and times of a DMK film.' *Economic and Political Weekly,* annual number, March: 759–70. (Reprinted in Ravi Vasudevan (2000) *Making meaning in Indian cinema.* Delhi: Oxford University Press: 65–96.)

Pandian, M.S.S. (1992) *The image trap.* Delhi: Sage Publications.

Parekh, Bhikhu (1997) *Gandhi.* Past masters. Oxford: Oxford University Press.

Phalke, D.G. (1987) 'Dossier: Swadeshi moving pictures (Dhundiraj Phalke).' Special Issue: Asian cinema.' Ed. by Brian Shoesmith & Tom O'Regan. *Continuum: The Australian Journal of Media & Culture,* 2(1): 51–73.

Phillips, Adam (1993) *On kissing, tickling and being bored.* London: Faber and Faber.

Phillips, Adam (1996) *Monogamy.* London: Faber and Faber.

Phillips, Adam (1999) *Darwin's worms.* London: Faber and Faber.

Pinault, David (2001) *Horse of Karbala: Muslim devotional life in India.* New York: Palgrave MacMillan.

Pinney, Christopher (1997) *Camera indica: the social life of Indian photographs.* London: Reaktion Books.

Pinney, Christopher (2000) 'Public, popular and other cultures.' In Rachel Dwyer and Christopher Pinney (eds) *Pleasure and the nation: the history, consumption and politics of public culture in India*. Delhi: Oxford University Press: 1–34.

Pinney, Christopher (2002) 'The Indian work of art in the age of mechanical reproduction: or, what happens when peasants "get hold" of images.' In Faye D. Ginsburg, Lila Abu-Lughod and Brian Larkin (eds) *Media worlds: anthropology on new terrain*. Berkeley: University of California Press: 355–69.

Pinney, Christopher (2004) *'Photos of the gods': the printed image and political struggle in India*. London: Reaktion Books.

Pinto, Jerry (2006) *Helen, the H-bomb*. New Delhi: Penguin.

Plate, S. Brent (ed.) (2003) *Representing religion in world cinema: filmmaking, mythmaking, culturemaking*. New York: Palgrave Macmillan.

Prasad, M. Madhava (1998) *Ideology of the Hindi film: a historical construction*. Delhi: Oxford University Press.

Pritchett, Frances (1994) *Nets of awareness: Urdu poetry and its critics*. Berkeley: University of California Press.

Rai, Alok (2001) *Hindi nationalism*. Hyderabad: Orient Longman.

Rai, Alok (2005) 'The persistence of Hindustani.' *Annual of Urdu Studies*, 20. http://www.urdustudies.com/Issue20/index.html. Viewed 10 August 2005.

Rajadhyaksha, Ashish (1987) 'Neo-traditionalism: film as popular art in India. *Framework*, 32/33: 20–67.

Rajadhyakhsa, Ashish (1993) 'The epic melodrama: themes of nationality in Indian cinema.' *Journal of Arts and Ideas*, 35–6: 55–70.

Rajadhyaksha, Ashish (1993) 'The Phalke era: conflict of traditional form and modern technology.' In Tejaswini Niranjana, P. Sudhir and Vivek Dhareshwar (eds). *Interrogating modernity: culture and colonialism in India*. Calcutta: Seagull Books: 47–82.

Rajadhyaksha, Ashish (1994) 'India's silent cinema: a viewer's view.' In Suresh Chabria and Paolo Cherchi Usai (eds) *Light of Asia: Indian silent cinema, 1912–1935*. New Delhi: Wiley Eastern: 25–40.

Rajadhyaksha, Ashish and Paul Willemen (1999, 2nd ed.) *An encyclopaedia of Indian cinema*. London: British Film Institute.

Rajagopal, Arvind (2001) *Politics after television: Hindu nationalism and the reshaping of the public in India*. Cambridge: Cambridge University Press.

Ramachandran, T.M. (ed.) (1985) *70 years of Indian cinema (1913–1983)*. Bombay: Cinema India International.

Ramanujan, A.K. (1973) *Speaking of Shiva*. London: Penguin.

Ramanujan, A.K. (1981) *Hymns for the drowning: poems for Visnu*. Princeton: Princeton University Press.

Ramanujan, A.K. (1985) *Poems of love and war: from the eight anthologies and the ten long poems of classical Tamil*. Ed. and trans. by A.K. Ramanujan. New York: Columbia University Press.

Ramanujan, A.K. (1999) *Collected essays of A.K. Ramanujan*. Ed. Vinay Dharwadker. Delhi: Oxford University Press.

Rangoonwalla, Firoze (ed.) (1970) *Phalke centenary souvenir*. Bombay: Phalke Centenary Celebration Committee.

Rangoonwalla, Firoze (1975) *Seventy-five years of Indian cinema*. New Delhi: Indian Book Company.

Reuben, Bunny (1994) *Mehboob . . . India's DeMille: the first biography*. New Delhi: HarperCollins.

Richman, Paula (1991) *Many Ramayanas: the diversity of a narrative tradition in South Asia*. Berkeley: University of California Press.

Rigopoulos, Antonio (1993) *The life and teachings of Sai Baba of Shirdi*. New York: State University of New York Press.

Roy, Asim (2005) 'Introduction.' In Mushirul Hasan and Asim Roy (eds) *Living together separately: cultural India in history and politics*. New Delhi: Oxford University Press: 1–28.

Roy, Olivier (2004) *Globalised Islam*. London: C. Hurst & Co.

Russell, Ralph and Khurshidul Islam (1994) *Ghalib: life and letters*. Delhi: Oxford University Press.

'Ruswa', Muhammad Hadi (Mirza Mohammad Hadi Ruswa) (1996) *Umrao Jan Ada*. Trans. by David Matthews. New Delhi: Rupa. [1899]

Sadiq, Muhammad (1995) *A history of Urdu literature*. Delhi: Oxford University Press. [1964]

Said, E. (1978) *Orientalism*. London: Routledge and Kegan Paul.

Sangari, Kumkum (1990) 'Mirabai and the spiritual economy of bhakti.' Parts 1 and 2. *Economic and Political Weekly*, XXV, no. 27 (7 July): 1,464–75; no. 28 (14 July): 1,537–52.

Sarkar, Kobita (1982) *You can't please everyone: film censorship: the inside story*. Bombay: IBH Publishing House.

Sathe, V.P. (1984) 'Les cinémas gujarati et marathi.' In Aruna Vasudeva and Philippe Lenglet (eds) *Les cinémas indiens*. CinémAction 30. Paris: Editions du Cerf: 106–13.

Savarkar, Vinayak Damodar (1989) *Hindutva: who is a Hindu?* New Delhi: Bharti Sahitya Sadan.

Schrader, Paul (1972) *Transcendental style in film*. Berkeley: University of California Press.

Sen, Amartya (1998) 'Secularism and its discontents.' In Rajeev Bhargava (ed.) *Secularism and its critics*. Delhi: Oxford University Press: 454–85.

Shackle, Christopher (1986, 2nd ed.) *The Sikhs* [Minority Rights Group no.65], London.

Shackle, Christopher (1988) 'Sikhism.' In S. Sutherland (ed.) *The world's religions*. London: Routledge: 14–25.

Shackle, Christopher and Rupert Snell (1990) *Hindi and Urdu since 1800: a common reader*. London: School of Oriental and African Studies: 1–20.

Shah, Panna (1950) *The Indian film*. Bombay: Motion Picture Society of India.

Shahani, Kumar (1985) 'The saint poets of Prabhat.' In T.M. Ramachandran (ed.) *70 years of Indian cinema (1913–1983)*. Bombay: Cinema India International: 197–202.

Shoesmith, Brian (1987) 'Swadeshi cinema: cinema, politics and culture: the writings of D.G. Phalke.' Special Issue: Asian cinema. Ed. Brian Shoesmith & Tom O'Regan. *Continuum: The Australian Journal of Media & Culture*, 2(1): 44–50.

Smith, Jonathan Z. (1998) 'Religion, religions, religious.' In Mark C. Taylor (ed.) *Critical terms for religious studies*. Chicago: University of Chicago Press: 269–84.

Srinivas, S.V. (2001) 'Telugu folklore films: The case of Patala Bhairavi.' *Deep Focus: A Film Quarterly*, IX(1): 45–50. Also at www.sephis.org/pdf/srinivas2.pdf. Viewed 22 October 2004.

Stacey, Jackie (1993) *Star gazing: Hollywood cinema and female spectatorship.* London: Routledge.

Stewart, Tony K. (2002) 'Alternate structures of authority: Saya Pir on the frontiers of Bengal.' In David Gilmartin and Bruce B. Lawrence (eds) *Beyond Turk and Hindu: rethinking religious identities in Islamicate South Asia.* New Delhi: India Research Press: 21–54.

Suri, Manil (2001) *The death of Vishnu.* London: Bloomsbury.

Swallow, D.A. (1982) 'Ashes and powers: Myth, rite and miracle in an Indian god-man's cult.' *Modern Asian Studies,* 16(1): 123–58.

Taylor, Charles (2002) *Varieties of religion today: William James revisited.* Cambridge, Mass.: Harvard University Press.

Taylor, Mark C. (1998) *Critical terms for religious studies.* Chicago: University of Chicago Press.

Thomas, Rosie (1985) 'Indian cinema: pleasures and popularity: an introduction.' *Screen,* 26(3–4): 61–131.

Thomas, Rosie (1989) 'Sanctity and scandal: the mythologization of Mother India.' *Quarterly Review of Film and Video,* 11: 11–30.

Thomas, Rosie (1995) 'Melodrama and the negotiation of morality in mainstream Hindi film.' In C. Breckenridge (ed.) *Consuming modernity: public culture in a South Asian world.* Minneapolis and London: University of Minnesota Press: 157–82.

Thoraval, Yves (1998) *Les cinémas de l'Inde.* Paris: L'harmattan.

Todorov, Tzvetan (1984) *Mikhail Bakhtin: the dialogical principle.* Trans. W. Godzich. Minneapolis: University of Minnesota Press.

Tripathi, Bakul (1985) 'Gujarati cinema.' In T.M. Ramachandran (ed.) *70 years of Indian cinema (1913–1983).* Bombay: Cinema India International: 340–8.

Trivedi, Harish (2006) 'All kinds of Hindi: the evolving language of Hindi cinema.' In Vinay Lal and Ashis Nandy (eds) *Fingerprinting popular culture: the mythic and the iconic in Indian cinema.* Delhi: Oxford University Press: 51–86.

Tukaram (1991) *Says Tuka.* Trans. from the Marathi with an introduction by Dilip Chitre. New Delhi: Penguin.

Uberoi, Patricia (1997) 'Dharma and desire, freedom and destiny.' In Meenakshi Thapan (ed.) *Embodiment: essays on gender and identity.* Delhi: Oxford University Press: 145–71.

Uberoi, Patricia (1998) 'The diaspora comes home: disciplining desire in DDLJ.' *Contributions to Indian sociology* (n.s.), 32(2): 305–36.

Uberoi, Patricia (2000) 'Imagining the family: an ethnography of viewing "Hum aapke hain koun . . .!".' In Rachel Dwyer and Christopher Pinney (eds) *Pleasure and the nation: the history, consumption and politics of public culture in India.* Delhi: Oxford University Press: 309–51.

Upperstall (n.d.) http://upperstall.com/people/naushad.html. Viewed 28 May 2005.

van der Veer, Peter (1994) *Religious nationalism: Hindus and Muslims in India.* Berkeley: University of California Press.

Vasudev, Aruna (1978) *Liberty and licence in Indian cinema.* New Delhi: Vikas.

Vasudeva, Aruna and Philippe Lenglet (eds) (1984) *Les cinémas indiens.* Ciném-Action 30. Paris: Editions du Cerf.

Vasudevan, Ravi (1993) 'Shifting codes, dissolving identities: the Hindi social film of the 1950s as popular culture.' *Journal of Arts and Ideas,* 23–4: 51–79 (plus appendix).

Vasudevan, Ravi (1994) 'Other voices: Roja against the grain.' *Seminar*, 423: 43–7.

Vasudevan, Ravi (1995) 'Addressing the spectator of a "third world" national cinema: the Bombay "social" film of the 1940s and 1950s.' *Screen*, 36(4), Winter: 305–24.

Vasudevan, Ravi (1999) 'Review of Prasad 1998.' *Journal of Jadavpur Film Studies*, 1. (Full details unavailable.)

Vasudevan, Ravi (2000a) 'Bombay and its public.' In Rachel Dwyer and Christopher Pinney (eds) *Pleasure and the nation: the history, consumption and politics of public culture in India*. Delhi: Oxford University Press: 186–211.

Vasudevan, Ravi (2000b) 'The politics of cultural address in a "transitional" cinema: a case study of popular Indian cinema.' In Christine Gledhill and Linda Williams (eds) *Reinventing Film Studies*. London: Arnold: 130–64.

Vasudevan, Ravi (ed.) (2000c) *Making meaning in Indian cinema*. Delhi: Oxford University Press.

Vasudevan, Ravi (2003) 'Another history rises to the surface: melodrama in the age of digital simulation. Hey! Ram, Kamalahasan, 1999.' http://www.sarai.net/mediacity/filmcity/essays/heyram.htm. Viewed 28 July 2005.

Vasvani, Kishor (1998) *Cinemai bhasha aur Hindi samvadon ka vishleshan*. New Delhi: Hindi Book Centre.

Vaudeville, Charlotte (1974) *Kabir*. Oxford: Clarendon.

Vidal, Denis (2005) 'Darshan.' In Rachel Dwyer and Subir Sinha (eds) *Keywords*. http://www.soas.ac.uk/centres/centreinfo.cfm?navid=912. Viewed 15 December 2005.

Vries, Hent de and Samuel Weber (eds) (2001) *Religion and media*. In series Cultural memory in the present. Stanford: Stanford University Press.

Wadia, J.B.H. (1977) *Those were the days, Part I: Being a romanticized account of my early years and career as a silent film maker – between 1928 and 1933*. Bombay: J.B.H. Wadia.

Wadia, J.B.H. (n.d.) 'Vaman Avtar – a case of frivolous objection.' (Loose paper, no further details.)

Wartenberg, Thomas E. (1999) *Unlikely couples: movie romance as social criticism*. Thinking through cinema. Boulder, Colo.: Westview Press.

Watve, Bapu (1985) *V. Damle and S. Fattelal: a monograph*. Pune: National Film Archive of India.

Wenner, Dorothee (2005) *Fearless Nadia: the true story of Bollywood's original stunt queen*. New Delhi: Penguin.

White, Charles S. (1972) 'The Sai Baba movement: approaches to the study of Indian saints.' *Journal of Asian Studies*, 31(4) (August): 863–78.

Willemen, Paul (1994) 'Cinematic discourse: the problem of inner speech.' In *Looks and frictions: essays in cultural studies and film theory*. London: British Film Institute.

Index